# ICTACS 2006

The First International Conference on Theories
and Applications of Computer Science 2006

# ICTACS 2006

Ho Chi Minh City, Vietnam     3 – 5 August 2006

*Editors*

## Bao T Ho
*Japan Advanced Institute of Science & Technology, Japan*

## Thuy T B Dong • Duc A Duong • Thuc D Nguyen
*Vietnam National University, Vietnam*

**World Scientific**

NEW JERSEY · LONDON · SINGAPORE · BEIJING · SHANGHAI · HONG KONG · TAIPEI · CHENNAI

*Published by*

World Scientific Publishing Co. Pte. Ltd.

5 Toh Tuck Link, Singapore 596224

*USA office:* 27 Warren Street, Suite 401-402, Hackensack, NJ 07601

*UK office:* 57 Shelton Street, Covent Garden, London WC2H 9HE

**British Library Cataloguing-in-Publication Data**
A catalogue record for this book is available from the British Library.

**THEORIES AND APPLICATIONS OF COMPUTER SCIENCE**
**The First International Conference (ICTACS 2006)**

ISBN-13 978-981-270-063-6
ISBN-10 981-270-063-3

Printed in Singapore.

# PREFACE

On behalf of the Organizing Committee, it is a great pleasure for me to welcome you to The First International Conference on Theories and Applications of Computer Science (ICTACS'06).

The First International Conference on Theories and Applications of Computer Science (ICTACS'06) was co-organized by the Faculty of Information Technology, University of Science, VNU-HCM and Department of Science and Technology of Hochiminh City. ICTACS'06 aims to strengthen the collaboration between research scientists, engineers and practitioners in the area of computer science, and to offer computer scientists the opportunity to meet with international scientists and PhD students to share common interests, to exchange research results, and to present problems encountered during their research.

This year, we have received 63 paper submissions from numerous countries, such as the United States, France, Austrália, Switzerland, Ireland, India, Taiwan..., and Vietnam. Each paper has undergone a rigorous review process by the Program Committee and experts from prestigious universities and institutes world-wide. Finally, only 26 were selected for plenary presentation at the conference yielding the overall acceptance rate of 41.27%. Among them, 15 papers are the long papers and 11 are the short papers.

I would like to thank our sponsors, Mekong University, Computer Science Center of University of Science, VNU-HCM, University of Technological Education, HCMC Banking University, Minh Khai Pub Group, Khai Tri Company, and Nhat Nghe Computer Science Center, Da lat University.

Many individuals have contributed to the success of this conference. My sincere thanks go to all the authors and whose scientific contributions add a great deal to the quality of this gathering. Special thanks go to our invited speakers, Prof. Jay Bagga (BUS, USA), Prof. J. Schwenk (Ruhr-Univ. Bochum, Germany), Prof. Phong Q. Nguyen (ENS, France), and Prof. Y. C. Tay (NUS, Singapore). Furthermore, we would like to sincerely thank the Program Committee members and additional reviewers for their professional, efficient input to the review process. Last but not the least, the Organizing Committee is much appreciated for their enormous efforts and marvelous work.

Conference Chair,
Duong Anh Duc

# CONTENTS

*Local Organization:*

Thuc D. Nguyen, HCMUNS, VN

Du L.H. Tran, HCMUNS, VN

Vu Q. Lam, HCMUNS, VN

Tuan M. Pham, HCMUNS, VN

Triet M. Tran, HCMUNS, VN

# CHAPTER 1

# SOFTWARE SYSTEMS FOR IMPLEMENTING GRAPH ALGORITHMS FOR LEARNING AND RESEARCH

JAY BAGGA

*Department of Computer Science, Ball State University*
*Muncie, Indiana 47306, USA*

ADRIAN HEINZ

*Department of Computer Science, Ball State University*
*Muncie, Indiana 47306, USA*

Graph algorithms have several important applications in fields such as computer science, software engineering, mathematics, engineering, business, and bioinformatics. Researchers and practitioners in these disciplines often need to experiment with empirical data about graphs to gain deeper insights into their properties, which may lead to general proofs. Students also need to learn and be able to implement graph algorithms for their applications. However, these individuals often have varying backgrounds and training, and they may not have a working knowledge of programming tools to implement graph algorithms. The goal of our research is to create a software system which allows users to easily create and implement graph algorithms through a simple graphical user interface, without any coding. Towards this goal, we have developed several systems that can be used to draw and manipulate graphs as well as to execute graph algorithms. The development of the general system raises a number of interesting research questions that we will discuss. To illustrate the need for experimentation with different graph algorithms, we describe some examples of our research in different areas of graph theory and computational geometry. We also describe some features of our systems that we have found useful in teaching graph theory.

## 1. Introduction

In the last few decades the fields of graph theory and graph algorithms have experienced a very rapid growth. Much of this can be attributed to applications of graph theory and graph algorithms to a large of number of areas such as computer science, computer engineering, mathematics, business, sciences, bioinformatics, global information systems and several others. Applications of graphs are especially pervasive in almost all areas of computer science and information technology. This has fueled an explosive growth in research in this area. A large number of books, research journals, web sites and other online resources are now available.

Graph theory, graph algorithms and their applications are routinely included in courses in undergraduate and graduate programs in computer science, mathematics, engineering, business and several others. Students in these courses, researchers in pure and applied graph theory, and professionals who need to experiment with graph algorithms often have varying backgrounds. In particular, such persons need to work with graphs and implement graph algorithms, but they may not have the necessary programming skills to do so.

The goal of our project is to create software systems for easy manipulation and experimentation with graphs and graph algorithms. Such software systems can be used for learning and teaching, for implementing graph algorithms, for applications, and for conducting research where experimentation with graphs and empirical evidence are needed. Our objective is to develop general systems which allow students and practitioners to experiment with graphs and construct and implement graph algorithms without programming. Such development raises a number of important research questions. We discuss these below.

In this paper we describe our recent work and progress of our project. In Section 2, we describe some of these research topics and describe how our software systems have been used in this research. The research topics discussed in Section 2 are samples that are intended to illustrate the use of software systems that we are developing. In Section 3, we describe a number of systems that we have developed and used in teaching and research. In Section 4 we present a summary and discuss plans for our future work.

## 2. Some Research Topics in Graph Theory

In this section we describe how our software systems are helping us in teaching and research in graph theory graph algorithms and their applications. We developed these systems to help us investigate questions that arise in our research, and to give our students tools which help them gain a better understanding and experience with the complexity of the concepts and algorithms. While some of our tools are specialized to areas of our research interest, others are more general and extensible. Our goal is to develop a general tool which is extensible in the sense that new graph operations and graph algorithms can be easily added without any significant programming. Users from a variety of different background should be able to fully utilize the system with little preparation.

In the following subsections, we introduce three areas of active research. We give only a brief introduction and some definitions for each area and provide references where more details can be found. Our purpose is to describe how the use of our software tools is an integral and indispensable part of our research and teaching.

## 2.1. *Computational Geometry – Visibility Graphs*

The study of visibility graphs is an active area of research in computational geometry. Visibility graphs have applications in art gallery guard placement problems, robot path planning in the presence of obstacles, and computer graphics, among others [1]. We have been interested in the study of polygon and segment endpoint visibility graphs.

**Definition 1** Let $P$ be a polygon on $n$ vertices $v_1, v_2, ..., v_n$. The *polygon visibility graph G (P)* of $P$ has vertices $v_1, v_2, ..., v_n$, and two of these are adjacent if the line segment joining them is either an edge of $P$ or an internal diagonal of $P$.

**Definition 2** Let $S$ be a set of $n$ disjoint line segments $x_1 y_1, x_2 y_2, ..., x_n y_n$ in the plane, in general position. The *segment endpoint visibility graph G(S)* has $2n$ vertices $x_1, y_1, x_2, y_2, ..., x_n, y_n$ and two of these are adjacent if the line segment connecting them is either in $S$ or does not (internally) intersect any of the segments in $S$.

Visibility graphs have been extensively studied [2, 3, 4, 5, 6, 7, 8, 9, 10]. The breadth and depth of the results demonstrates that this is a rich field of study. According to O'Rourke [2], there are four goals of research in visibility graphs:

- **Characterization.** Characterize the class of graphs realizable by certain classes of geometric objects.
- **Recognition.** Find algorithms to recognize a graph as a visibility graph.
- **Reconstruction.** Find algorithms to output a geometric realization of visibility graphs.
- **Enumeration.** Find the number of visibility graphs under various restrictions.

Our research is in the area of the characterization of visibility graphs. In general, most of the problems in these four areas of research are hard. Visibility graphs of even small sizes are difficult to draw by hand. One of our software systems has helped us visualize such graphs and determine some properties. This system, Colossus is described in Section 3.2.

4

## 2.2. *Graph Drawing*

Graph drawing is an active area of research. Here we are concerned with efficient and aesthetic presentations of graphs (usually in the plane). See [11] for an excellent introduction to graph drawing. An annual conference on graph drawing has been held since 1992. See www.graphdrawing.org.

A graph is called *planar* if it can be drawn in the plane without any edges crossing. There are several well-known efficient algorithms to check a graph for planarity. We have implemented one such algorithm in our system JGraph. We describe JGraph in detail in Section 3.1. A well known theorem of Fáry [12] states that a planar graph can be drawn in the plane such that all edges are straight lines. In applications such as integrated circuit design, more specialized drawings of planar graphs might be required. An algorithm of de Fraysseix et al [13] draws a planar graph with straight line edges such that the vertices are points on a grid. We have implemented this algorithm in JGraph. See Section 3.1 for details.

## 2.3. *Graceful Labeling of a Graph*

Given a graph $G$ with $q$ edges a labeling of the nodes with distinct integers from the set $\{0, 1, 2, ..., q\}$ induces an edge labeling where the label of an edge is the absolute difference of the labels of the two nodes incident to that edge. Such a labeling is *graceful* if the edge labels are distinct. This concept was introduced in 1967 by Rosa [14]. See Gallian [15] for an excellent survey of graceful labelings. Graceful labelings have applications in coding theory, x-ray crystallography, radar, astronomy, circuit design and communication networks, addressing and data base management [15].

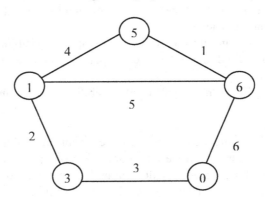

Figure 1. A graceful labeling of a graph.

We are interested in particular in graceful labelings of trees. Figure 1 shows a graceful labeling of a small graph.

The Ringel-Kotzig-Rosa conjecture [14] states that every tree has a graceful labeling. This almost forty year old conjecture is still open. Certain special classes of graphs such as paths, caterpillars, symmetrical trees and some others have shown be graceful. A computer search by Aldred and McKay [16] was used to show that all trees with up to 27 vertices are graceful. We have investigated different types of graceful labelings of paths. It was proved in [17] that the number of graceful labelings of the path of length n grows asymptotically at least as fast as $(5/3)^n$. We have used our system *Manohar* to investigate graceful labelings of caterpillars and lobsters, and also to investigate different patterns of graceful labelings of paths. See Section 3.3 for details.

### 2.4. *Teaching of Graph Theory and Graph Algorithms*

The first author has been involved in research and teaching of graph theory for more that twenty-five years. Over the last several years, we have used our software system JGraph in our graph algorithms classes. The majority of students in this class are computer science students, but some others such as those from mathematics and physics also enroll. Thus they come with a variety of backgrounds. JGraph can be used as a graph editor where users can draw, manipulate and experiment with different graphs. The extensive graphical user interface allows for graph manipulations with mouse clicks. Students can also execute and visualize (with animation) many well known graph algorithms. Students have found the animation feature especially useful since it helps them understand the workings of complex algorithms. New algorithms can be easily added to the system and algorithms in the system can be removed from the menu of available algorithms. Students have also used the system for classroom and term assignments and projects. JGraph is described in more detail in Section 3.1. The reader is invited to visit www.cs.bsu.edu/homepages/gnet for a demonstration version (JEdit 4.2) of this system. See [18] for a detailed discussion of an earlier version of JGraph.

### 3. Software Systems

In this section we describe in some detail our software systems. While we have found these systems useful in our research and teaching, it must be mentioned that these systems are themselves research projects in varying stages of development.

## 3.1. *JGraph*

JGraph is a system for creating graphs and running graph algorithms. The system has been used for research and teaching of graph theory in undergraduate and graduate level courses.

The system provides an easy-to-use graphical user interface in which the user can create graphs by adding vertices and connecting them by edges. It is possible to move individual vertices and edges around the window or to move multiple elements by selecting a component of the graph. The graph can also be manipulated by changing the colors of its elements. Rotation features are also available by selecting the rotation pivot point and the rotation angle.

Another feature of JGraph is that it contains drawings of certain special graphs. These are graphs that have been the focus of attention of the research community. These special graphs include: complete graphs $K_n$, complete bipartite graph $K_{m,n}$, hypercube graphs, platonic graphs, cycle, wheel, the Petersen graph and the Headwood graph. Graphs can be saved in a special format .GPH files for later retrieval.

One of the most important features of JGraph is its ability to execute graph algorithms. These algorithms can be applied to the currently displayed graph. Algorithms can be executed in an optional animation mode. This allows the user to clearly see each step of the execution of an algorithm. Algorithms are classified by the input required from the user. *Automatic algorithms* are those that can be directly applied to the current graph. For instance, the *blocks finding algorithm* finds all the blocks of a graph and uses different colors to display each block as well as cut-vertices. The second group of algorithms is referred to as *one-click* algorithms. In this group, the user is required to click on a vertex of the graph which becomes the input of the algorithm. *Prim's minimum spanning tree algorithm* falls into this category. Once the user has drawn a graph and selected a vertex, the algorithm will find the minimum spanning tree for the given graph and color its vertices and edges. The next category refers to algorithms which require a graph and two vertices as input. This category is called *two-click*. The *Floyd-Warshall shortest path algorithm* executes on the current graph and two vertices selected by the user. It then proceeds to calculate the shortest path between the two selected vertices and colors the vertices and edges on that path.

Some of the most complex algorithms implemented are the automatic algorithms *planarity testing* and *planarity drawing*. Planar graphs were defined in Section 2.2. The planarity testing algorithm receives a graph as input and determines whether or not it is planar. It also displays a message to the user with the result. The planarity drawing algorithm also receives a graph as input. If the input graph is non-planar, the algorithm displays a message informing the user than the graph cannot be drawn on a plane without edges crossing. On the other hand, if the graph is planar, the algorithm proceeds to arrange the vertices on a grid creating a planar drawing of the graph with non-crossing straight line edges.

Figure 2 displays a drawing of a graph with several edges crossing, and the result of running the planarity testing algorithm.

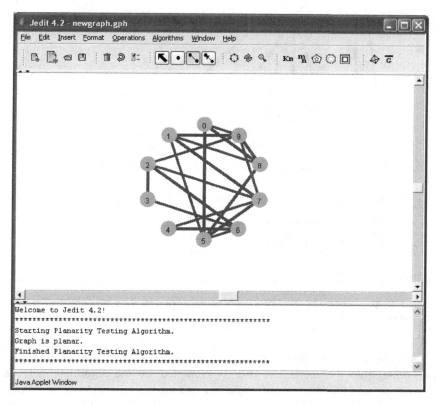

Figure 2. A graph drawn with several edge crossings and the result of running the planarity testing algorithm.

Figure 3 displays a planar drawing (of the graph of Figure 2) generated by the planarity drawing algorithm.

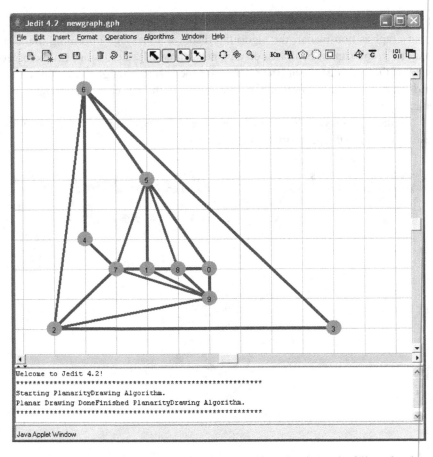

Figure 3. Output generated by the planarity drawing algorithm using the graph of Figure 2 as input, A planar embedding on a grid is displayed.

JGraph allows the user to easily add new algorithms. When selecting *new algorithm* from the menu, the user is prompted for the algorithm name, a description and the category of algorithm (automatic, one-click or two-click). After the input is completed, the system generates a template file in which the user can edit and add the new algorithm source code. Once the source code is completed and the file is saved, the next time JGraph runs, the new file will be compiled with the rest of the system and the new algorithm automatically added to the JGraph menu.

JGraph has been developed entirely under Java and therefore it can be run on any platform.

## 3.2. *Colossus*

A visibility graph is a graph of intervisible locations. Each node or vertex in the graph represents a point location, and each edge represents a visible connection between them (that is, if two locations can see each other, an edge is drawn between them. Colossus is a system for determining visibility graphs. The system includes a graphical user interface in which the user can draw a simple polygon. Colossus displays its visibility graph of the polygon and colors the ears and mouths. See [19] for definitions. The system performs the computation in real-time. Any changes to the configuration of the original graph are immediately reflected in its visibility graph. A screenshot of Colossus is shown in Figure 4.

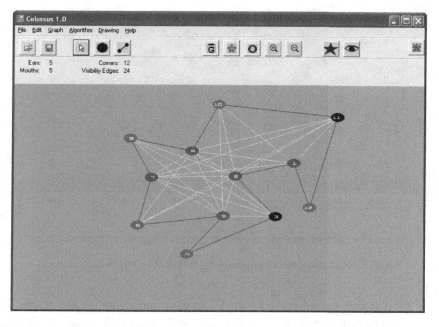

Figure 4. Screenshot of a visibility graph generated by Colossus. Ears and mouths correspond to vertices 4, 6, 8, 10, 12 and 1, 2, 5, 7, 9 respectively.

Another feature of Colossus is the ability to work with orthogonal graphs. When working in orthogonal mode, Colossus only allows horizontal or vertical edges among orthogonally aligned vertices.

### 3.3. *Manohar*

Manohar is a system for computing graceful labeling of graphs. See Section 2.3 for definitions. The system consists of a graphical user interface in which the user can draw a graph. When the input graph is completed, the system computes a graceful labeling of the graph and if it exists, it displays the graceful labeling on the screen. A screenshot of Manohar is illustrated in Figure 5.

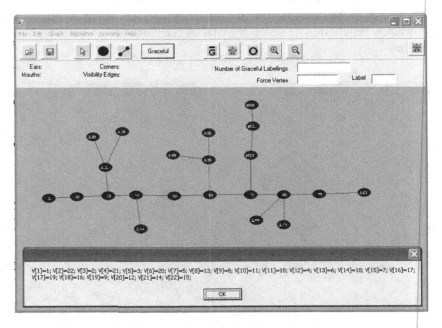

Figure 5. Screenshot of the output generated by Manohar for a tree with 22 vertices.

Even though Manohar can be used with many simple undirected graphs, it has been primarily used as a research tool for studying graceful labeling of trees. In particular, we have used Manohar as a research tool to investigate graceful labeling of certain special trees such as caterpillars and lobsters. See [15] for definitions.

## 3.4. *Graph Algorithm Constructor*

Graph Algorithm Constructor is our system for creating and running graph algorithms. The main feature of this system is that algorithms are created by drawing *flow diagrams* instead of writing source code and therefore no knowledge of programming is necessary to use the application. The system also incorporates a graph editor for drawing and manipulating graphs.

A flow diagram is a directed graph in which every vertex is an *entity*. Users can create a flow diagram by adding entities and connecting them. Entities consist of *elements, operations, control structures* and *algorithms*. An element is an atomic structure than can be randomly generated or input by the user. Examples of elements include graphs, trees and vertices. An operation is an action on an element or a group of elements. Operations require input and output. Examples of operations include *mark vertex, color vertex* and *find neighbor*. A control structure determines the execution flow. Examples of control structures include *loops, counters* and *conditionals*. An algorithm is defined by the flow diagram. Algorithms can be saved and later embedded in flow diagrams of other algorithms. A screenshot of Graph Algorithm Constructor is illustrated in Figure 6.

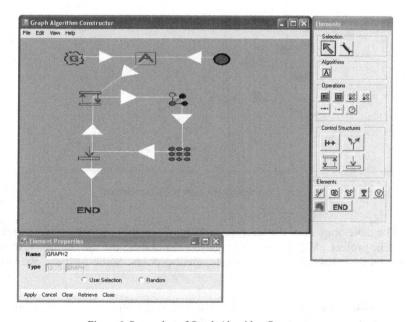

Figure 6. Screenshot of Graph Algorithm Constructor.

The flow diagram of an algorithm can be saved in a file for later use. The file format used is XML.

An algorithm created by the Graph Algorithm Constructor can be loaded and executed by the *Graph Algorithm Runner*. This is a part of the system which executes algorithms. It interprets the XML file created by the constructor and executes step by step showing the progress on the screen. The Graph Algorithm Runner has a graph editor where input graphs for an algorithm can be drawn or loaded from a directory of existing graphs. It also handles the display of the output graph and or other textual output as appropriate. A screenshot of the graph algorithm runner is shown in Figure 7. It shows an output graph on the left side and the XML tree in the panel on the right. The XML tree is obtained by parsing the XML file of the flow diagram. It allows the user to quickly see the structure of the file before running the algorithm.

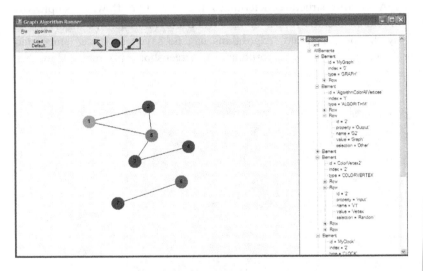

Figure 7. Screenshot of Graph Algorithm Runner.

The development of the Graph Algorithm Constructor system is an ongoing research project. We have investigated a number of interesting research questions that arose during this development process. Some of these questions are:

- **Classification of entities.** We are interested in using a minimal but complete set of entities as defined above. The classification of entities into four distinct types – elements, operations, control structures and algorithms – serves this purpose.

- **List of elements.** The elements are the building blocks of graphs such as vertices, and edges. These can also be special graphs such as trees and cycles.
- **List of operations.** We seek a sufficient set of independent graph operations that are needed for the most common tasks in graph algorithms.
- **List of control structures.** This list includes most of the control structures of a high-level programming language. The goal is to find a set of primitive operations to create a flow diagram.

## 4. Summary and Future Work

In this paper we have described several software systems that we have developed for use in research and teaching of graph theory, graph algorithms, and their applications. We described some areas of our research where our systems have been particularly helpful. Students in our graph algorithms classes have used these systems to experiment with graphs and execute graph algorithms. A general graph algorithm construction system is currently under development. This system allows the user to create and implement graph algorithms without much coding. We have investigated a number of research questions that arise during the process of such a system.

Our immediate goal is to complete the development of the algorithm constructor system. We will also continue to upgrade the software systems described in this paper. New features will be added as needed in research and teaching of graph algorithms and their applications.

## References

1. O'Rourke. Art Gallery Theorems and Algorithms. Oxford University Press, 1987.
2. J. O'Rourke. Visibility. In Handbook of Discrete and Computational Geometry, CRC Press, 1997.
3. X. Shen and H. Edelsbrunner. A tight lower bound on the size of visibility graphs. *Inform. Process. Lett.* **26**, pages 61-64, 1987/88.
4. J. Bagga, J. Emert, M. McGrew, and W. Toll. On the Sizes of Some Visibility Graphs. In *Congressus Numerantium*, **104**, pages 25-32, 1994.
5. J. Bagga, L.Gewali, and S.Ntafos. Visibility Edges, Mixed Edges, and Unique Triangulation. In *Proceedings of the 13th European Conf. on Comput. Geom.* page 11, 1997.

14

6. J. Bagga, S. Dey, L. Gewali, J. Emert, and M. McGrew. Contracted Visibility Graphs of Line Segments. In     Proc. 9th Canadian Conf. Comput.Geom., pages 76-81, 1997.

7. J. Bagga, J. Emert, and M. McGrew. Directed Polygon Visibility Graphs. In *Congressus Numerantium*, **132**, pages 61-67, 1998.

8. J. Bagga, J. Emert, and M. McGrew. Directed Polygons as Boundaries of Visibility Graphs. In *Congressus Numerantium*, **142**, pages 57-63, 2000.

9. J. Bagga, J. Emert, and M. McGrew. Directed Polygons as Boundaries of Visibility Graphs. In *Congressus Numerantium*, **142**, pages 57-63, 2000.

10. J. Bagga, J. Emert, and M. McGrew. Connectivity Properties of Visibility Graphs. In *Congressus Numerantium*, **165**, pages 189-194, 2003.

11. Graph Drawing, Algorithms for the Visualization of Graphs. Giuseppe Di Battista, Peter Eades , Roberto Tamassia, Ioannis G. Tollis. Prentice Hall, 1999. ISBN 0-13-301615-3

12. I. Fáry, On straight line representations of planar graphs, Acta Sci. Math. **11**(1948) 229-233.

13. H. de Fraysseix, J. Pach, and R. Pollack. How to draw a planar graph on a grid". Combinatorica, **10**(41-51), 1990.

14. A. Rosa, On Certain Valuations of the Vertices of a Graph", *Theory of Graphs (Proc. Internat. Symposium, Rome, 1966*, Gordon and Breach, N. Y. and Dunod Paris, 349-355, 1967.

15. Joseph A. Gallian, A Dynamic Survey of Graph Labeling, The Electronic Journal of Combinatorics, **5** (2005), #DS6.

16. R. E. Aldred and B. D. McKay, Graceful and harmonious labellings of trees, Bull. Inst. Combin. *Appl.* **23**, 69-72, 1998.

17. R. E. Aldred, J. Siran and M. Siran, A note on the graceful labelings of path. Discrete Math, **261** 27-30, 2003.

18. J. Bagga and A. Heinz. JGraph - A Java based system for drawing graphs and running graph algorithms, Lecture Notes in Computer Science, **2265** (2002), Springer Verlag.

19. G. H. Meisters. Polygons have ears. Amer. Math. Monthly **82** pages 648-651, 1975.

# CHAPTER 2

# A PROPOSED STATISTICAL MODEL FOR SPAM EMAIL DETECTION

DAT TRAN, WANLI MA AND DHARMENDRA SHARMA

*School of Information Sciences and Engineering, University of Canberra, Canberra, ACT 2601, Australia*

The keyword list-based spam email detection system uses keywords in a blacklist to detect spam emails. To avoid detection, keywords are written as misspellings, for example "virrus", "vi-rus" and "viruus" instead of "virus". The system needs to update the blacklist from time to time to detect spam emails containing such misspellings. However it is impossible to predict all possible misspellings for a given keyword to add those to the blacklist. This paper proposes a statistical framework to solve this problem. A keyword is represented as a Markov chain where letters are states. A Markov model is then built for the keyword. In order to decide an unknown word as a misspelling of a given keyword, a statistical hypothesis test is used. Experiments showed that the proposed statistical models could achieve the detection error rate of 0.1%.

## 1. Introduction

The use of electronic media nowadays encourage speedy and inexpensive data transmission, a large numbers of recipients are flooded with unsolicited commercial emails or unsolicited bulk emails, commonly known as spam emails. Several methods have been proposed to detect spam emails, but the volume of those mails still continues to grow [14].

A spam email detection system can be a server-based or client-based one. For organizations, a server-based spam email detection system seems to be a good solution. It has more advantages and gives administrators more control to eliminate unsolicited emails sent in bulk [13]. However, this system should not eliminate emails based on their contents. A client-based solution allows the user to control the information to which they wish to be exposed and to determine which emails are spams. This solution can reduce the number of spam messages received.

Several methods for detecting spam emails have been proposed in the literature. They are based on address lists, headers, keyword lists and content statistical analysis known as Bayesian filter [7]. The address list-based method can be implemented at both client and server level. The address blacklist contains addresses from which all emails are blocked. The normal address list contains addresses of people the user knows and wishes to communicate with. When the user receives a new spam email, he or she will add the address of the sender to the blacklist. The header-based system gets the information from the email header that is not shown by most email readers since the information is not normally important for the user but it is useful to know if the received email is a spam, for example an IP address which does not match the domain name. Similar to the address list-based system, the keyword list-based system has a blacklist of keywords which are the words used to detect spam emails. Keywords are collected from the subject, header or body of spam emails. The keyword list-based system is effective if it is made specifically for each user, therefore it is only appropriate for client-based systems or server-based systems for organizations who wish to control the information to which their staff members have access [13]. It takes time and effort to create a good keyword list and this list needs to be regularly updated in order to make them as effective as possible. Although there are not many keywords found in spam emails, but the problem for detection is that these keywords are written as misspelling words and change their misspellings from time to time. Users can understand the content of the email containing such misspellings but the keyword list-based system is unable to update the blacklist with those misspellings. For example, an email is regarded as a spam email because it contains the keyword "virus". After updating the blacklist with this keyword, the system is still unable to detect spam emails containing "viirus", "vi_rus", "virrus", or "virruus". Since there are numerous ways to produce misspellings for a given word, the email detection system becomes ineffective.

We propose a novel method to overcome the problem of misspelling words in spam emails. We consider the occurrences of letters in a keyword as a stochastic process and hence the keyword can be represented as a Markov chain where letters are states. The occurrence of the first letter in the keyword is characterized by the initial probability of the Markov chain and the occurrence of the other letter given the occurrence of its previous letter is characterized by the transition probability. Given the blacklist as a training set, the initial and transition probabilities for all Markov chains representing all keywords in the blacklist are calculated and the set of those probabilities is regarded as a Markov model for that blacklist. In order to detect a keyword and its misspellings, we build a Markov model for the keyword $W$ and use a statistical hypothesis test as follows. For an unknown word $X$ and a claimed keyword $W$, the task is to determine if $X$ is a misspelling of $W$. This task can be regarded as a basic hypothesis test between the null hypothesis $H_0$: $X$ is a misspelling of the claimed keyword $W$ against the alternative hypothesis H: $X$ is *not* a misspelling of the claimed keyword $W$. According to Neyman-Pearson Lemma, a likelihood ratio test is used as a score to measure the similarity between the unknown word and the keyword $W$. Our experiments showed that the scores obtained from misspellings we could produce for the keyword $W$ were not very different and hence with a preset threshold, we could detect those misspellings. As an extension, we believe that other misspellings of the keyword $W$ that we have not tested will also be detected using the same preset threshold. In our experiments, a blacklist of 50 keywords collected from spam emails is used. We also produced up to 10 misspellings for each keyword in the blacklist and test them against with 10000 normal words. Experiments showed that the proposed method can detect those keywords and their misspellings in spam emails with an equal error rate of 0.1%.

## 2. Markov Keyword Models

Let $X = \{X^{(1)}, X^{(2)}, ..., X^{(K)}\}$ be a set of $K$ random variable sequences, where $X^{(k)} = \{X_1^{(k)}, X_2^{(k)}, ..., X_{T_k}^{(k)}\}$ is a sequence of $T_k$ random variables, $k = 1, 2, ...,$ $K$ and $T_k > 0$. Let $\mathbf{V} = \{V_1, V_2, ..., V_M\}$ be the set of $M$ states in a Markov chain. Consider the conditional probabilities

$$P(X_t^{(k)} = x_t^{(k)} \mid X_{t-1}^{(k)} = x_{t-1}^{(k)}, ..., X_1^{(k)} = x_1^{(k)}) \tag{1}$$

where $x_t^{(k)}$, $k = 1, 2, ..., K$ and $t = 1, 2, ..., T_k$ are values taken by the corresponding variables $X_t^{(k)}$. These probabilities are very complicated for calculation, so the Markov assumption is applied to reduce the complexity

$$P(X_t^{(k)} = x_t^{(k)} \mid X_{t-1}^{(k)} = x_{t-1}^{(k)}, ..., X_1^{(k)} = x_1^{(k)}) = P(X_t^{(k)} = x_t^{(k)} \mid X_{t-1}^{(k)} = x_{t-1}^{(k)}) \tag{2}$$

where $k = 1, 2, ..., K$ and $t = 1, 2, ..., T_k$. This means that the event at time $t$ depends only on the immediately preceding event at time $t - 1$. The stochastic process based on the Markov assumption is called the *Markov process*. In order to restrict the variables $X_t^{(k)}$ taking values $x_t^{(k)}$ in the finite set $\mathbf{V}$, the *time-invariant assumption* is applied

$$P(X_1^{(k)} = x_1^{(k)}) = P(X_1^{(k)} = V_i) \tag{3}$$

$$P(X_t^{(k)} = x_t^{(k)} \mid X_{t-1}^{(k)} = x_{t-1}^{(k)}) = P(X_t^{(k)} = V_j \mid X_{t-1}^{(k)} = V_i) \tag{4}$$

where $k = 1, \ldots, K$, $t = 1, \ldots, T_k$, $i = 1, \ldots, M$ and $j = 1, \ldots, M$. Such the Markov process is called *Markov chain*.

Define the following parameters

$$\mathbf{q} = [q(i)], \quad q(i) = P(X_1^{(k)} = V_i) \tag{5}$$

$$\mathbf{p} = [p(i,j)] \quad p(i,j) = P(X_t^{(k)} = V_j \mid X_{t-1}^{(k)} = V_i) \tag{6}$$

where $k = 1, \ldots, K$, $K$ is the number of words in the training document, $t = 1, \ldots, T_k$, $T_k$ is the word length, $i = 1, \ldots, M$ and $j = 1, \ldots, M$, $M$ is the number of alphabetical letters. The set $\lambda = (\mathbf{q}, \mathbf{p})$ is called a Markov language model that represents the words in the training document as the Markov chains. A method to calculate the model set $\lambda = (\mathbf{q}, \mathbf{p})$ is presented as follows [18].

The Markov model $\lambda$ is built to represent the sequence of states $\mathbf{x}$, therefore we should find $\lambda$ such that the probability $P(\mathbf{X} = \mathbf{x} \mid \lambda)$ is maximised. In order to maximise the probability $P(\mathbf{X} = \mathbf{x} \mid \lambda)$, we first express it as a function of the model $\lambda = (\mathbf{q}, \mathbf{p})$, then equate its derivative to 0 to find the model set $\lambda$.

Let $p(x_{t-1}, x_t) = P(X_t = x_t \mid X_{t-1} = x_{t-1}, \lambda)$ and $q(x_1) = P(X_1 = x_1 \mid \lambda)$ we have

$$P(\mathbf{X} = \mathbf{x} \mid \lambda) = \prod_{k=1}^{K} q(x_1^{(k)}) \prod_{t=2}^{t=T_k} p(x_{t-1}^{(k)}, x_t^{(k)}). \tag{7}$$

Applying the time-invariant assumption in (3) and (4), and using (5) and (6), we can rewrite (7) as follows

$$P(\mathbf{X} = \mathbf{x} \mid \lambda) = \prod_{i=1}^{M} [q(i)]^{n_i} \prod_{j=1}^{M} [p(i,j)]^{n_{ij}} \tag{8}$$

where $n_i$ denotes the number of values $x_1^{(k)} = V_i$ and $n_{ij}$ denotes the number of pairs $(x_{t-1}^{(k)} = V_i, x_t^{(k)} = V_j)$ observed in the sequence $X^{(k)}$. It can be seen that

$$\sum_{i=1}^{M} n_i = K. \tag{9}$$

The probability in (8) can be rewritten as follows

$$\log[P(\mathbf{X} = \mathbf{x} \mid \lambda)] = \sum_{i=1}^{M} n_i \log q(i) + \sum_{i=1}^{M} \sum_{j=1}^{M} n_{ij} \log p(i,j) . \tag{10}$$

Since $\sum_{i=1}^{M} q(i) = 1$ and $\sum_{j=1}^{M} p(i,j) = 1$, the Lagrangian method is applied to maximise the probability in (10) over $\lambda$. Using the following Lagrangian

$$F(q(i), p(i,j), a, b_i)$$

$$= \sum_{i=1}^{M} n_i \log q(i) + a \left[ 1 - \sum_{i=1}^{M} q(i) \right] \tag{11}$$

$$+ \sum_{i=1}^{M} \sum_{j=1}^{M} n_{ij} \log p(i,j) + \sum_{i=1}^{M} b_i \left[ 1 - \sum_{j=1}^{M} p(i,j) \right]$$

where $a$ and $b_j$ are Lagrangian multipliers. Setting the derivative of $F$ to zero and solving the equation give

$$q(i) = \frac{n_i}{\sum_{s=1}^{M} n_s} \qquad p(i,j) = \frac{n_{ij}}{\sum_{s=1}^{M} n_{is}} . \tag{12}$$

The equations in (12) are used to determine the Markov keyword model for each keyword and the Markov keyword list model for the entire keyword list.

## 3. Misspelling Word Detection

In our statistical approach, the misspelling word detection problem is formulated as a problem of statistical hypothesis testing. For an unknown word $X$ and a claimed keyword $W$, the task is to determine if $X$ is a misspelling of $W$. This task can be regarded as a basic hypothesis test between the null hypothesis $H_0$: $X$ is a misspelling of the claimed keyword $W$ against the alternative hypothesis H: $X$ is *not* a misspelling of the claimed keyword $W$. According to Neyman-Pearson Lemma, if the probabilities of both the hypotheses are known exactly, the optimum test to decide between these two hypotheses is a likelihood ratio test given by

$$S(X) = \frac{P(X \mid H_0)}{P(X \mid H)} \begin{cases} > \theta & accept \;\; H_0 \\ \leq \theta & reject \;\; H_0 \end{cases} \tag{13}$$

where $\theta$ is a predefined decision threshold and $S(X)$ is referred to as the similarity score of the unknown word $X$. This approach provides a good theoretical formulation to the misspelling word detection problem.

However, in practical detection problems, it is impossible to obtain the exact probability density functions for either the null hypothesis or the alternative hypothesis. A parametric form of the distribution under each hypothesis is assumed to estimate these probability density functions. Let $\lambda_c$ be the claimed keyword model and $\lambda$ be a model representing all other words, i.e. impostors. Let $P(X \mid \lambda_c)$ and $P(X \mid \lambda)$ be the likelihood functions of the claimed keyword and impostors, respectively. The similarity score is calculated as follows

$$S(X) = \frac{P(X \mid \lambda_c)}{P(X \mid \lambda)} \begin{cases} > \theta & accept \;\; H_0 \\ \leq \theta & reject \;\; H_0 \end{cases} . \tag{14}$$

The denominator $P(X \mid \lambda)$ is called the normalization term and requires calculation of all impostors' likelihood functions. However it is impossible to do the calculation for all words in dictionary, hence a subset of $B$ "background" words is used to represent the population close to the claimed keyword [17]. We propose to use the keyword list as the background subset in our approach. Therefore Markov models we need to build for the system are the claimed keyword Markov model and the keyword list Markov model as shown in Figure 1.

The training and detection procedures of the proposed misspelling word detection tool are summarized as follows.

**Training:**

1. Given $K$ keywords in the blacklist
2. Train $K$ Markov keyword models using (12) where $X$ is the sequence of letters in the keyword used to calculate $n_i$ and $n_{ij}$
3. Train a Markov keyword list model using (12) where $X$ is the sequence of letters of all keywords in the keyword list used to calculate $n_i$ and $n_{ij}$

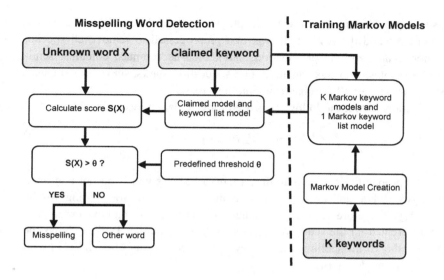

Figure 1. A proposed misspelling word detection tool for the spam email detection system.

**Detection:**

1. Given an unknown word regarded as a sequence of letters
   $X = (x_1, x_2, ..., x_T)$ , a claimed keyword and a predefined threshold $\theta$
2. Calculate the probabilities $P(X \mid \lambda_c)$ and $P(X \mid \lambda)$ using (7) where $\lambda_c$ is the claimed keyword model and $\lambda$ is the keyword list model
3. Calculate the similarity score $S(X)$ and compare it with the threshold $\theta$ using (14)
4. If the score is greater than the threshold, the unknown word is referred to as a misspelling of the claimed keyword

An email is regarded as a spam email if it contains a predefined number of keywords and/or their misspellings.

## 4. Experimental Results

We collected a set of 50 keywords from our emails classified as spam emails in the banking, pornography and advertisement categories. This set was used to build the keyword list model. Each word in this set was also built a keyword model, so the number of models in this experiment was 51. For each keyword, we produced 10 misspellings for testing. The test set therefore contained 500 misspellings. The minimum word length was set to 3 for all words in the keyword list and the test set. It was first preprocessed to remove all special, common characters and punctuation marks such as commas, columns, semi-columns, quotes, stops, exclamation marks, question marks, signs, etc. The next step was to convert all the characters into lowercases.

We found that if the following is used for calculation instead of (7)

$$P(X \mid \lambda) = q(x_1) + \sum_{t=2}^{T} p(x_{t-1}, x_t).$$ (15)

This probability calculation allows pairs of letters which do not appear in the keyword but appear in its misspellings will contribute nothing to the probability. Therefore the scores obtained for misspellings of a keyword are not very different from the score for the keyword. For example, Table 1 shows the score for the 10 misspellings of the keyword "virus" using (14) and (15) with the keyword model "virus".

Table 1. Scores of the keyword "virus" and its misspellings using (14) and (15) for calculation. The claimed model is the keyword "virus" model.

| virus | virrus | virruss | vvirus | viirus | vi-r-us | viruses | v!rus | viruus | vi_rus |
|-------|--------|---------|--------|--------|---------|---------|-------|--------|--------|
| 3.84 | 3.77 | 3.62 | 3.84 | 3.84 | 3.84 | 3.41 | 2.62 | 3.84 | 3.84 |

Based on this result, we can assume that other misspellings of the keyword "virus" that we have not tested also have similar scores. Therefore it is able to set a threshold to detect possible misspellings of a given keyword with a minimum false acceptance of other words.

We test the proposed system using the test set containing the 50 keywords, their 500 misspellings as mentioned above and 10000 normal words. Experiments showed that the proposed system could detect keywords and their misspellings in the test set with the equal error rate (false rejection error = false acceptance error) of 0.1% as shown in Figure 2.

## 5. Conclusion

We have presented a statistical modeling method to detect spam emails based on detecting keywords in emails. We are enhancing the research project to use the optical character recognition technology to extract the embedded text from the images as a pre-processing tool. We are also investigating the trigram method which can provide alternative models for spam email detection.

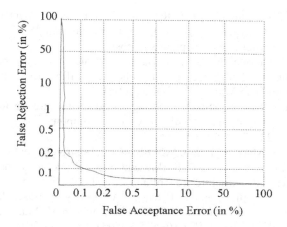

Figure 2. False acceptance error versus false rejection error for the test of 50 keywords, their 500 misspellings and 10000 normal words.

## Acknowledgements

The authors would like to acknowledge the support of the University of Canberra Divisional Research Grant

## References

1. M.D. Castillo and J.I. Serrano, "An Interactive Hybrid System for Identifying and Filtering Unsolicited Email", in Proceedings of the 2005 IEEE/WIC/ACM Int. Conference on Web Intelligence, 814-815 (2005)
2. H. Chim, "To Build a Blocklist Based on the Cost of Spam", in Lecture Notes in Computer Science, 3828, 510-519 (2005)
3. Z. Chuan, L. Xianliang and X. Qian, "A Novel Anti-spam Email Approach Based on LVQ", Lecture Notes in Computer Science, 3320, 180-183 (2004)
4. Z. Fu and I. Sarac, "A Computational Study of Naïve Bayesian Learning in Anti-spam Management", Lecture Notes in Computer Science, 3138, 824-830 (2004)
5. F.D. Garcia, J.-H. Hoepman and J. van Nieuwenhuizen, J., "Spam Filter Analysis", in Lecture Notes in Computer Science, 147, 395-410 (2004)
6. S. Ghose, J.-G. Jung and G.-S Jo, "Collaborative Detection of Spam in Peer-to-Peer Paradigm Based on Multi-agent Systems", in Lecture Notes in Computer Science, 3251, 971-974 (2004)
7. P. Graham, "Better Bayesian Filtering", http://paulgraham.com/better.html (2003)

8. G. Hulten, J. Goodman and R. Rounthwaite, "Filtering spam e-mail on a global scale", in Proceedings of the 13th international World Wide Web conference on Alternate track papers & posters, 366-367, (2004)

9. N. Kang, C. Domeniconi and D. Barbara, "Categorization and Keyword Identification of Unlabeled Documents", in Fifth IEEE International Conference on Data Mining, 677-680 (2005).

10. M. Lan and W. Zhou, "Spam Filtering based on Preference Ranking", in The Fifth International Conference on Computer and Information Technology 223-227 (2005)

11. L. Lazzari, M. Mari, A. Poggi, "CAFE - Collaborative Agents for Filtering E-mails", in the 14th IEEE International Workshops on Enabling Technologies: Infrastructure for Collaborative Enterprise, 356-361 (2005)

12. J. Metzger, M. Schillo and K. Fischer, "A Multiagent-Based Peer-to-Peer Network in Java for Distributed Spam Filtering", in V. Marik et al. (Eds): CEEMAS 2003, LNAI 2691, 616–625, (2003)

13. L. Pelletier, J. Almhana and V. Choulakian, "Adaptive Filtering of SPAM", in Proceedings of the Second Annual Conference on Communication Networks and Services Research, (2004)

14. S. L. Pfleeger and G. Bloom, "Canning Spam: Proposed Solutions to Unwanted Email", in IEEE Security & Privacy, 40-47 (2005).

15. M. Sasaki and H. Shinnou, "Spam Detection Using Text Clustering", in the International Conference on Cyberworlds, 316-319 (2005)

16. D. Tran and M. Wagner, "A Proposed Fuzzy Pattern Verification System", in Proceedings of the FUZZ-IEEE 2001 Conference, 2, 932-935 (2001)

17. D. Tran, "New Background Modeling for Speaker Verification", Proc. of the INTERSPEECH, ICSLP Conference, Korea, 4, 2605-2608 (2004).

18. D. Tran and D. Sharma, "Markov Models for Written Language Identification", in Proceedings of the 12th International Conference on Neural Information Processing, 67-70 (2005)

# CHAPTER 3

# COOPERATION IN THE PREY-PREDATOR PROBLEM WITH LEARNING CLASSIFIER SYSTEM

TRUNG HAU TRAN*, CÉDRIC SANZA, YVES DUTHEN

*1 Paul Sabatier University – Toulouse III, 118 route de Narbonne, 31062 Toulouse Cedex 4, France*
**hau@irit.fr*

DINH THUC NGUYEN

*University of Natural Sciences, 227 Nguyen Van Cu Street, District 5, HoChiMinh City, Vietnam*

This paper deals with learning cooperation in a group of predators chasing a prey. A learning predator has no knowledge about the environmental information. It only knows that it should adapt its actions to other predators' expectations. The learning classifier system is a very interesting tool for the machine learning technique. Indeed, it helps a learning agent to evaluate its actions and to take right actions corresponding to situations in order to have a better cooperation with other agents. The results show how the learning is constructed in such collective task.

## 1. Introduction

One of the advantages of the artificial life approaches is to generate autonomous virtual entities adapting to an environment. They learn how to take decisions accorded to situations during training time, while rewards reinforce their decisions and help them to adapt their behaviors to the environment. Moreover, thanks to the adaptive capacity they could perform a given task in an unknown environment with minimum error. Thus, the generation of autonomous adaptive agents simplifies the design of behaviors.

The learning classifier system (LCS), an artificial life approach introduced by Holland [7], is an adaptive system. It is a rule-based system, where each rule uses the form "IF condition THEN action". This system interacts with the environment through a sensor system (detectors) and a base of predefined behaviors (effectors). A credit assignment algorithm reinforces rules or relations between the detectors and the effectors by using rewards or penalties received from the environment. Besides, an evolutionary algorithm is used as a research motor for the evolution of the population of rules. Indeed, it searches the space of rules, assures the diversity of rules and generates new and potential rules for adapting to any situations in the environment. The continuous learning in LCS produces an efficient set of rules which will be exploited at the suitable moment.

In the following section, we present the various frameworks of LCS: Holland's LCS [7], Wilson's ZCS [15] and Bull's YCS [3]. Section 3 describes the application of classifier systems in our predator-prey problem. A discussion concludes this paper.

## 2. Learning Classifier System

### 2.1. *Holland's LCS*

LCS consists of three components:
- A set of rules $P$, called classifiers, is used for interacting with the environment.
- An evolutionary algorithm creates rules to adapt to any situation. GAs are commonly used in this component.
- A credit assignment updates the usefulness of selected classifiers through rewards or penalties received from the environment.

Each rule or classifier has condition part, action part, and a fitness (or strength) in the form: <condition>::<action> [strength]. The interpretation of a rule is as "IF condition THEN action" and a strength which indicates how well this rule has done in the past and evaluates its performance. The classifier condition of fixed length $L$ is initially generated with random values from the ternary alphabet {0, 1, #}, where # denotes a "don't care" symbol and acts as 0 or 1. For example, the classifier condition 010# matches the encoded messages 0100 and 0101, but does not match the one 0110. The classifier action must have the same length $L$ as the classifier condition and is coded as a binary string from {0, 1}. # is not admitted in the classifier action. A population of rules is evolved in LCS.

The schematic of Holland's LCS is shown in Figure 1. The following steps are looped each generation:

**Step 1:** The system receives a binary encoded message of fixed length $L$ describing the environment via the detectors and put this message on the message list.

**Step 2:** This message is scanned with the condition part of each classifier in the population $P$ in order to determine appropriate classifiers which are classed in the current match set $M$.

**Step 3:** The match set $M$ normally contains many classifiers corresponding to the input message. Thus which classifier will be selected during learning to activate its action? Choosing the one with the highest fitness or letting a chance to other ones (low fitness) exploring their actions relates to the dilemma between exploration and exploitation. The solution proposed by Holland is a bidding technique by finding the exploration-exploitation balance. Indeed, each classifier gives its bid to compete. The bid of a classifier $r_i$ depends on its fitness. The higher the fitness of a classifier is, the stronger its bid is and the more it has a chance to winning the competition in order to activate its action. A winner classifier is selected through stochastic bidding in proportion to its bid. This bidding is the opposite of the deterministic bidding where a winner classifier is the one having the highest bid. Then, its fitness is deducted an amount equal to its bid in order to decrease its chance of always winning the competition. Moreover, some classifiers in $P$ never or seldom bid because they almost mismatch input messages, so they have to pay a tax in proportion to their fitness in order to be eliminated rapidly. If the action part of the winner classifier is not eligible, it is treated as a message coming from the environment and the processes of inference will do activate other classifiers. On the contrary, the action part of the winner classifier is eligible, the system passes to step 4. When LCS finishes its learning, it has enough of knowledge to reason actions. In other words, it activates the classifier having the highest fitness without using the bidding technique.

$$bid\,(r_i) = k_0 * \text{fitness}\,(r_i),\, k_0 : \text{constant} \quad 0 < k_0 \leq 1 \qquad (1)$$

$$tax\,(r_i) = k_1 * \text{fitness}\,(r_i),\, k_1 : \text{constant} \quad 0 \leq k_1 < 1. \qquad (2)$$

**Step 4:** The eligible action is sent to the effectors which perform an indicated behavior in the base of behaviors.

**Step 5:** Reinforcement learning in LCS takes the information gotten from the environment to modify the fitness of classifiers in order to optimize the performance of the system. This information is a scalar value called reward telling the system about the quality of executed actions. Indeed, when the system gets a reward from the environment, it updates the fitness of the winner classifiers participated in the activation which are noted $r_{i,-k}, r_{i,-k+1}, \ldots, r_{i,-2}, r_{i,-1}, r_i$. The "Bucket Brigade" (BB) algorithm proposed by Holland [7] is used to

28

distribute bids between them. $r_i$ is the winner classifier advocating the eligible action sent to the effectors and the reward is paid to it. And then it contributes its bid to $r_{i,-1}$ as a reward, $r_{i,-1}$ contributes its bids to $r_{i,-2}$ as a reward and so on. Thus, the fitness of a classifier is updated as in (3). The weakness of the BB algorithm is to maintain long classifier chains, and then take a long time to reinforce.

$$fitness\,(r_i) \leftarrow fitness\,(r_i) - bid\,(r_i) + reward_i - tax(r_i)\,. \qquad (3)$$

**Step 6:** The system increases its performances by periodically applying a GA to $P$ with genetic operators during the learning time. The classifiers are considered as individuals and their strength as fitness in the GA. They share knowledge by mixing their condition and action parts through the crossover operator to produce new adaptive classifiers potentially. The mutation generates new classifiers to explore any possible situations. And the selection chooses classifiers used in two operators above and also eliminates the weakest ones. The role of the GA in traditional optimization problems is to search for the most adaptive rule, but in LCS is to generate a set of different types of rule which might cooperatively solve a specific problem.

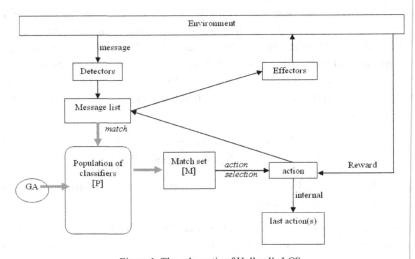

Figure 1. The schematic of Holland's LCS.

## 2.2. Wilson's ZCS: A Zeroth-level Classifier System

Wilson introduced ZCS [15] as a major evolution of Holland's LCS. The modifications were presented to remake a system more understandable but the performance of ZCS is still guaranteed with the one of the original LCS. In ZCS (Figure 2), the first change is that the message list is removed. Indeed, by precisely choosing the structure of messages sent by the detectors so that they represent a complete vision of situations of the environment it is not necessary to use the processes of inference. So, the condition part of a classifier is not forced to have the identical form with its action. The next change is that the action set $A$ was added. All classifiers in $A$ participate in the action selection and reinforcement learning.

$M$ is formed as in Holland's LCS. Roulette wheel selection [6] is applied to a list of actions from $M$ based on their probability in order to determine the winner action. The probability of an action from $M$ is in proportion to the sum of fitness of classifiers having this action. The members of $M$ each who have the same action as the winner action are classed in the current action set $A$, and this action is executed. In other words, the classifier fitness is used in the action selection. Starting with the initial random population or the empty one is little effect on performance.

Wilson proposed an implicit bucket brigade (IBB) algorithm relying on the BB algorithm to redistribute payoff between the action sets $A$ at the instant $t$ and $A_{-1}$ at the instant $t-1$. The IBB algorithm includes three steps. At first, a fraction $\beta$ of the fitness $f_i$ of each classifier in $A$ is retired from the fitness $f_i$ and this value is put on a common bucket B. Then if a reward $R$ is received by the system, each classifier shares a fraction $\beta$ of this reward with the other in $A$. Finally, a fraction $\gamma$ of the contents of the bucket B is divided equally between classifiers in $A_{-1}$ if the last is not empty. The bucket B is then emptied. Thus, the fitness $f_i$ of each classifier $i$ in $A$ at the instant $t$ is updated as follows ($A_{+1}$ representing $A$ at the instant $t+1$).

$$f_i(t) \leftarrow f_i(t) - \beta f_i(t) + \beta \frac{R}{\|[A]\|} + \gamma \frac{\sum_{j \in [A]_{+1}} \beta f_j(t+1)}{\|[A]\|} \qquad (4)$$

A GA is applied to the population of classifiers (probability $g$) in the exploration. When the GA is activated, two parent classifiers in $A$ are chosen using roulette wheel selection based on their fitness and their offspring are produced through two genetic operators: mutation (probability $\mu$) and crossover (single point with probability $\chi$). The offspring attributes are the average of the parent ones. A classifier in the population is selected to delete using roulette wheel selection based on the reciprocal of fitness. When the system mismatches an input message or the average of the match set fitness less than $\phi$ times the one of the population fitness, the cover operator is used to create a new classifier. Its action is randomly chosen, and its condition has the same bit as the message but some bits in its condition are replaced by "don't care" symbols (probability $\rho_{\#}$). The GA is not used in the exploitation.

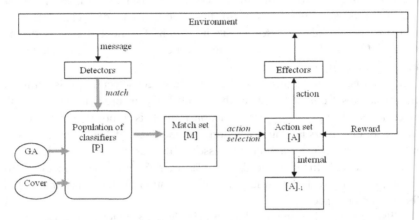

Figure 2. Wilson's ZCS.

## 2.3. YCS: A Simple Accuracy-based LCS

Bull in [3] presented YCS with the aim of make clear understand the accuracy-based fitness in general which was at first introduced in XCS [16]. Indeed, YCS bases on XCS but with a simple model. It consists of a set of classifiers in which its condition and action are coded as in ZCS. Each classifier is endowed with four principal attributes: a prediction $p_j$ evaluating its strength, a prediction error $\varepsilon_j$ indicating an estimate of the error in each classifier prediction, a fitness $f_j$ (the inverse of the prediction error $\varepsilon_j$) used in a GA's selection, and a niche size $a_j$ estimating the average size of the niches (action sets) in which that classifier participates. These attributes are initialized to a predefined value in the initial random population of classifiers. In the opposite of ZCS, the classifier prediction is used in the action selection and the classifier fitness in the reproduction in YCS. The match set $M$ is obtained in the normal way when the system receives an input message. The following action selection scheme is used here to form the action set $A$. The action $a_j$ corresponding to the highest prediction $p_j$ is selected deterministically in exploit periods. In explore periods the system decides with probability 0.5 to choose from a list of possible actions in $M$ an action randomly or an action corresponding to the highest average prediction.

When the system receives a reward $P$ from the environment, the attributes of each classifier in the action set $A$ are updated with learning rate $\beta$ ($0 < \beta \leq 1$) as follows:

$$\varepsilon_j \leftarrow \varepsilon_j + \beta(\underbrace{\|P - p_j\|}_{Error} - \varepsilon_j) \tag{5}$$

$$\alpha_j \leftarrow \alpha_j + \beta(\|A\| - \alpha_j) \tag{6}$$

$$p_j \leftarrow p_j + \beta(P - p_j) \tag{7}$$

$$f_j = \frac{1}{1 + \varepsilon_j} \tag{8}$$

A GA is used in YCS as in ZCS except in a case where a classifier in the population is selected to delete using roulette wheel selection based on its niche size.

## 3. Application of Classifier Systems

In this section, we present the application of classifier systems presented above to simulate the prey-predator problem.

### 3.1 Predator-Prey Simulation Settings

Our algorithm for the prey in [14] is summarized in Algorithm 1. The prey moving is programmed as a deterministic function of food sources and predators, and there is not any randomness involved. The prey is captured if positions around it in a small radius $r$ are occupied by all predators.

```
Find a nearest food source;
Go to this food source;
Eat this food source;
IF detect predators THEN
    FOR EACH predator around the prey DO
        Calculate an opposite direction to out of danger;
    ENDFOR
    Combine these directions to form one final direction;
    Take this final direction;
ENDIF
ELSE
    Pursue last action (i.e. go to a nearest food source or
    continue to escape the predators during N simulation steps);
END
```

Algorithm 1. The prey algorithm.

There are two types of predator: the programmed and the learning predator. The programmed predators perform a circulating motion strategy around prey. A second type of predator learns and cooperates with the predators of the first type in order to guarantee the collective strategy against prey. Only the learning predator is equipped with YCS that memorizes situation-action pairs called rules, evaluates them, predicts errors of its actions and triggers appropriate actions to better cooperate with other predators. The predators can visually detect the prey from any distance. All entities can move in any direction on the plane of the 3D virtual environment (Figure 3).

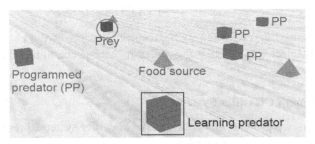

Figure 3. Prey-predator problem in the 3D virtual environment.

### 3.2. *Behavioral Programmed Predators*

The programmed predator perception is the environmental information about the angles between the predators relative to the prey direction (Figure 4). The prey direction is considered as the referential axis in the determination of these angles.

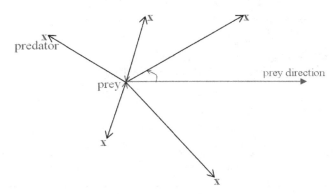

Figure 4. The predator perception is treated as input to the motor schemas.

The programmed predator calculates three motor schemas [1] (behaviors). The first one (*go-to-target*) allows it to approach its target, the second one (*spread-neighbors-out*) keeps it in the "middle" of its neighbors, and the last one (*wander*) makes a random move. The outputs of the *go-to-target*, *spread-neighbors-out*, *wander* schemas are the vectors ($\in \Re^3$) $\vec{v}_a$, $\vec{v}_r$, $\vec{v}_w$, respectively. The last schema subsumes the first two ones (see [2] for details of the subsumption architecture) and its output controls the predator direction moving $\vec{v}$ when it is activated in situations where all predators are localized in the negative prey direction. On the contrary, the weighted combination of the vectors of the first two schemas determines the predator direction moving $\vec{v}$ (Figure 6 without the "Classifier System" block). The second schema differs from the one in [14] in the formula. It's more meaningful than the old formula because the new formula assures entirely the description of the second schema. The schema parameters $\delta_a$, $\delta_r$ ($\in \Re$) (weights) correspond to the *go-to-target*, *spread-neighbors-out* schemas, respectively. Their values are fixed to the programmed predators.

The advantage of the motor schema approach is that it generates high level behaviors from a set of primitive behaviors (schemas) by determining the weight of each schema in final behaviors. So, a system based on this approach could improve its performance by adjusting these gains corresponding to each situation. A LCS will be a good candidate in this case. We go into detail how to integrate YCS of the learning predator into the motor schema approach in the following part.

### 3.3. *Behavioral Learning Predator*

The learning predator perceives the environment as the programmed predator one. In particular, it must encode the environmental information so that its YCS can interpret it. This information is transformed into an encoded message of angles between predators relative to the prey direction considered as the referential axis in the determination of which sector we begin numbering. In Figure 5, we divide the circle into 8 sectors, the center of the circle is the prey position, the symbol 'x' in a sector represents a predator in the perception, with sensor code 1; blank sectors have sensor code 0. An encoded message is in the form: $(i_0 i_1 i_2)(x_0 x_1 x_2 x_3 x_4 x_5 x_6 x_7)$. We use 3 bits $i_0 i_1 i_2$ to index what sector the learning predator is in (dot patterned sector in Figure 5). The left-hand bit $x_0$ is always sensor code of the first sector (grey sector in Figure 5), with the remainder ($x_1 \rightarrow x_7$) corresponding to sensor codes of the sectors proceeding counterclockwise. Hence, an encoded message of this situation for the learning agent is (110)(01110101).

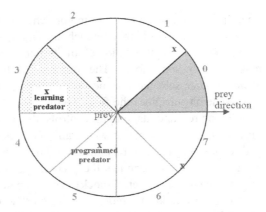

Figure 5. The learning predator treats the encoded perception as input to YCS.

The learning predator only knows two motor schemas: *go-to-target* and *spread-neighbors-out*. It is not equipped with the *wander* schema (Figure 6 without the *wander* schema). Its schema parameters $\delta_a$, $\delta_r$ are adjusted by its YCS. Thus, it differs from the programmed predators in these points.

Each action of the learning predator adjusts values of its parameters $\delta_a$, $\delta_r$. We define five possible actions for the classifier action as follows:

*#0*   Come to a target ($\delta_a=3$, $\delta_r=2$)
*#1*   Repel from a target ($\delta_a=-5$, $\delta_r=2$)
*#2*   Keep distance with neighbors ($\delta_a=0$, $\delta_r=1$)
*#3*   Stand up ($\delta_a=0$, $\delta_r=0$)
*#4\**   Random wandering ($\delta_a=-5$, $\delta_r=1$)

The local reward (LR) is particularly applied to the learning predator while the global reward (GR) is applied to a group of learning predators in some cases to favor cooperation. The LR reinforces actions of the learning agent. An agent compares its reasoning decision ($\vec{v}_{system}$ in (9)) with expectations $\vec{v}_{signal}$ (called coordination signals [4][5]) received from its neighbors (programmed predators). We define a signal as a vector guiding the predator moving. The difference between those signals and the reasoning decision is interpreted as LR to update appropriate classifiers in the action set $A$ advocating the last action. The IBB algorithm is used to reinforce classifiers in $\kappa$ previous action

---

* This action produces a random wandering for the learning predator. For example, here the parameters $\delta_a$, $\delta_r$ are updated to -5 and 1, respectively.

sets $A_{-k}$, ..., $A_{-2}$, $A_{-1}$. We consider that the action executed from $A_{-k}$ contributes an impact on the action executed from $A_{-k+1}$, the action executed from $A_{-k+1}$ contributes an impact on the action executed from $A_{-k+2}$, and so on. Thus classifiers in the previous action sets share the same reward (LR or GR) with classifiers in $A$.

$$reward = \cos(\vec{v}_{signal}, \vec{v}_{system})  \qquad (9)$$

### 3.4. Results

We use four programmed predators and one learning predator in our simulation. Positions of the predators are randomly generated on the plane (x,y) ($x \in \Re$, $y \in \Re+$) while the position of the prey is on the plane (x,y) ($x \in \Re$, $y \in \Re-$) (i.e. the prey is not initially surrounded by the predators) to avoid training the learning predator with easy cases. We tested our system in 3 runs, each run includes 50 explore tests to train the learning predator, 50 exploit tests to record the capture rate (i.e. fraction of the exploit tests which ends in a capture) which measures the performance of our system, and 15000 generations per test. A test ends if the prey leaves the plane, the prey is captured, or 15000 generations pass. A test ends without the prey captured, it is considered as a difficult test and we repeat it 10 times or until the prey is captured, so the learning predator can improve its decisions. Its YCS has 11 detectors, 5 effectors, a population of 3000 classifiers, $\beta$=0.2, $\mu$=0.092, $\chi$=0.5, and $\kappa$=9. GA is called every 20 generations in explore tests.

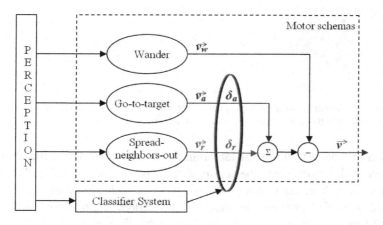

Figure 6. The behavioral predator.

The results show that the learning predator can trigger appropriate actions to cooperate with the programmed predators. As in Figure 7 the learning predator approaches the prey surrounded by the programmed predators. In Figure 8 the learning predator prevents the prey escaping from the direction *prey→learning_predator*. The average capture rate on 3 runs is about 98%.

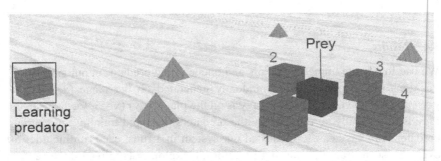

Figure 7. The learning predator (on the left) approaches the prey surrounded by four programmed predators noted 1, 2, 3, 4.

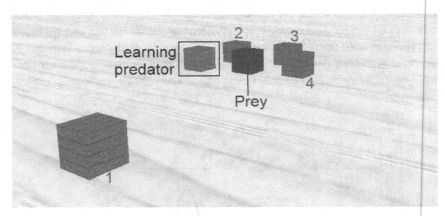

Figure 8. The learning predator (on the top left) is considered as wall in this situation to prevent the prey escaping from the direction *prey→learning_predator*.

During the last 30 tests of each run, the actions (*#0→ #4*) (defined in 3.3) are recorded. Among them, the *action #0* is the most executed action (Figure 9). Indeed, through it, the learning predator produces behaviors best satisfying to expectations of its partners. Besides, the other actions might also be selected up to situations during the simulation because of the diversity of actions generated by the system. In fact, our YCS has a set of different types of classifier which might cooperatively solve a specific problem. For example, in Figure 8, the *action #2* is selected by the system. Some classifiers recorded from the first run are listed in Table 1.

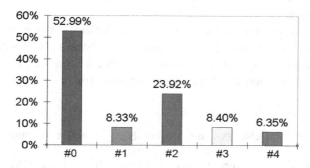

Figure 9. The percentage of each action (*#0*→ *#4*) executed during the last 30 tests of all runs.

Table 1. Some classifiers recorded from the first run.

| Condition | Action $a_j$ | Prediction $p_j$ | Error $\varepsilon_j$ | Fitness $f_j$ | Niche size $\alpha_j$ |
|---|---|---|---|---|---|
| 1#0 11 0# #0 01 | 0 | 997.10 | 1.75 | 36.41 | 5.00 |
| 101 0# #0 01 1# | 0 | 998.11 | 0.01 | 98.86 | 2.00 |
| 101 01 #1 1# 1# | 0 | 999.73 | 0.79 | 55.86 | 12.99 |
| 111 1# #1 00 0# | 0 | 999.90 | 0.01 | 99.23 | 19.99 |
| 1#0 #1 11 00 0# | 1 | 999.41 | 0.51 | 66.30 | 4.80 |
| 0#1 1# 00 1# 11 | 2 | 999.27 | 0.14 | 87.91 | 2.69 |
| 000 11 1# 10 0# | 2 | 999.39 | 0.05 | 95.68 | 4.00 |

## 4. Conclusion

This paper has given an introduction to the classifier systems. The role of a learning classifier system is to evolve a set of rules, called classifiers, in order to train an agent to perform an indicated task. This system was created for the first time by Holland. Wilson simplified the Holland's framework by introducing ZCS but still kept the performance of the original LCS. Then numerous models of the classifier systems arose such as XCS [16], Neural Classifier System [9]... and proved their efficiency in many domains such as in robotics [8], in the behavioral simulations (for example, in soccer simulations [11][12])...

Then we have presented one of the applications of the classifier systems in the prey-predator problem. The learning predator was equipped with a classifier system. This system learned expectations of other predators and helped the learning predator to trigger appropriate actions in order to accomplish its role in the cooperative strategy surrounding the prey. The results showed how learning was constructed and the learning predator took the advantage of the integration of YCS into the motor schema approach to produce the adaptive behaviors in the cooperation.

Further, we will accommodate the learning predator with the anticipation to look ahead and to act according to future states in order to obtain a desired state or avoid undesired one at present; for example anticipations of trajectories of its prey [13], of its partners to achieve a foraging task [10].

## References

[1] Arkin, R.C., Behavior-Based Robot Navigation for Extended Domains, *Adaptive Behavior*, 1(2):201–225, 1992.

[2] Brooks, R.A., A Robust Layered Control System for a Mobile Robot, *IEEE Journal of Robotics and Automation*, 2(1):14-23, 1986.

[3] Bull, L., A Simple Accuracy-based Learning Classifier System, *Technical Report* UWELCSG03-005, 2003.

[4] De Jong, E.D., Multi-Agent Coordination by Communication of Evaluations, MAAMAW'97 The Eighth European Workshop on Modelling Autonomous Agents in a Multi-Agent World, p63-78, 1997.

[5] De Jong, E.D., Coordination Developed by Learning from Evaluations, J.A. Padget (ed.) *Collaboration between Human and Artificial Societies*, p234-245, 1999.

[6] Goldberg, D.E., Genetic Algorithms in Search, Optimization, and Machine Learning, Addison-Wesley, Reading, Mass., 1989.

[7] Holland, J.H., Escaping Brittleness: The Possibilities of General-Purpose Learning Algorithms Applied to Parallel Rule-Based Systems, Mitchell, Michalski, and Carbonell, editors, *Machine Learning, an Artificial Intelligence Approach*, Volume II, chapter 20, p593-623, Morgan Kaufmann, 1986.

[8] Katagami, D., and Yamada, S., Real Robot Learning with Human Teaching, *The Fourth Japan-Australia Joint Workshop on Intelligent and Evolutionary Systems*, p263–270, Kanagawa, Japan, 2000.

[9] Nakano, R., Efficient Learning of Behavioral Rules, From Animals to Animats 6: SAB2000 Proceedings Supplement of the Sixth International Conference on Simulation of Adaptive Behavior, p178-184, Paris, France, 2000.

[10] Panatier, C., Sanza, C., and Duthen, Y., Adaptive Entity thanks to Behavioral Prediction, From Animals to Animats 6: SAB2000 Proceedings Supplement of the Sixth International Conference on Simulation of Adaptive Behavior, p295-303, Paris, France, 2000.

[11] Sanza, C., Panatier, C., and Duthen, Y., Communication and Interaction with Learning Agents in Virtual Soccer, *VW'2000 The Second International Conference on Virtual Worlds*, Jean-Claude Heudin Eds, p147-158, Paris, France, 2000.

[12] Sanza, C., Thesis Ph.D. « Evolution d'Entités Virtuelles Coopératives par Système de Classifieurs », Paul Sabatier University – Toulouse III, IRIT Laboratory (Institut de Recherche en Informatique de Toulouse), France, 2001.

[13] Tran, T.H., Sanza, C., and Duthen, Y., Study of the Anticipatory System in Simulation, *3IA'2004 The Seventh International Conference on Computer Graphics and Artificial Intelligence*, p129-136, Limoges, France, 2004.

[14] Tran, T.H., Sanza, C., and Duthen, Y., Learning Cooperation from Classifier Systems, *CIS'2005 International Conference on Computational Intelligence and Security*, Springer LNAI Vol.3801, p329-336, Xi'an, China, 2005.

[15] Wilson, S.W., ZCS: A Zeroth-level Classifier System, *Evolutionary Computation*, 2:1-18, 1994.

[16] Wilson, S.W., Classifier Fitness Based on Accuracy, *Evolutionary Computation*, 3(2):149-175, 1995.

# CHAPTER 4

# AUTOMATIC QUESTION EXTRACTION FROM MEETING AND DIALOG RECORDING

VU MINH QUANG, ERIC CASTELLI, PHAM NGOC YEN

*International research center MICA*
*IP Hanoi – CNRS/UMI-2954 – INP Grenoble*
*1,Dai Co Viet - Hanoi – Viet Nam*
*{minh-quang.vu,eric.castelli,ngoc-yen.pham}@mica.edu.vn*

Retrieving relevant parts of a meeting or a conversation recording can help the automatic summarization or indexing of the document. In this paper, we deal with an original task, almost never presented in the literature, which consists in automatically extracting questions utterances from a recording. In a first step, we have tried to develop and evaluate a question extraction system which uses only acoustic parameters and does not need any ASR output. The parameters used are extracted from the intonation curve and the classifier is a decision tree. Our first experiments on French meeting recordings lead to approximately 75% classification rate. An experiment in order to find the best set of acoustic parameters for this task is also presented in this paper. Finally, data analysis and experiments on another French dialog database show the need of using other cues like the lexical information from an ASR output, in order to improve question detection performance on spontaneous speech.

## 1. Introduction

With the purpose of wide use and access to multimedia documents, the design of efficient indexing algorithms that facilitate the retrieval of relevant information is an important issue. Concerning speech and audio documents, the transcription (ASR) of the audio channel is no longer the unique task that can be achieved, but it is now just an element among richer information. This concept of rich transcription (RT) is related to the recent evolution of the ASR domain. Research works used to be only concerned with dictation systems or transcription of telephonic data. Today, people in the domain deal with broadcast news data and even recordings taken from an ubiquitous environment, like a smart meeting room for instance. This evolution leads to new scientific problems, since the audio flow is no longer controlled but continuous and coming from multiple sources (speakers, microphones). Moreover, one may not only extract linguistic descriptors like ASR transcripts, but we want to produce a richly structured audio document from an initial raw data signal. Adding new linguistic descriptions like punctuation, sentence boundaries or disfluencies [1,2] but also non linguistic descriptors like speaker turns, other sounds (music, laugh, ...) and even emotions, is thus very challenging and useful. This evolution of the domain towards broadcast data and smart spaces also increases the need for indexation since the amount of data is much more important (for instance, the NIST smart room generates 1Go of data per minute of recording [3]). This also leads to new problems to be solved in term of scalability and complexity.

One possibility for indexing and/or accessing pertinent information in an audio document is the automatic extraction of "hot" moments in the audio flow. This is the purpose of this paper: we deal with an original task, almost never presented in the literature, which consists in automatically extracting question utterances from a recording. This task could permit to retrieve pertinent parts of a meeting or a conversation and help for automatic summarization for instance. The argument for this is that pertinent parts of a conversation or a meeting may be located around question (Q) utterances.

This work describes our first experiments in order to achieve this task. In a first step, we have tried to develop and evaluate a question extraction system which uses only acoustic parameters and does not need any ASR output (as done for disfluencies in [2] and [4]). As it is shown in this paper, we shall see that such an approach is only sub-optimal in terms of performance.

The paper is organized as follows: section 2 presents the resources used in our work (a telephone meeting corpus and a dialog corpus, both in French). The automatic question extraction system is described in section 3. In section 4, we present our first experiments and results on both databases, while section 5 concludes our work and gives some perspectives.

## 2. Required Resources

### 2.1. *Telephone Meeting Corpus (Deloc)*

Our telephone meeting corpus (called Deloc for "delocalized meetings") is made up of 13 meetings of 15 to 60 minutes, involving 3 to 5 speakers (spontaneous speech). The total duration is around 7 hours and the language is French.

Different types of meetings were collected which correspond to three categories: recruitment interviews; project discussions in a research team; and brainstorming-style talking.

From this corpus, we have manually extracted a subset composed of 852 sentences: 295 question (Q) sentences and 557 non-question (NQ) sentences.

## 2.2. *Client/Agent Dialog Corpus (Nespole)*

The NESPOLE[*] project was a common EU NSF funded project exploring future applications of automatic speech-to-speech translation in e-commerce and e-service sectors. The scenario of NESPOLE involves an Italian speaking agent, located in a tourism agency in Italy discussing with a client (English, German or French speaking) located anywhere via Internet and using audio-conferencing tools like *Netmeeting*. The client wants to organize a trip in the Trentino (Italia) area, and asks the agent for information concerning his trip. More information on this database can be found in [5]. We use in this experimentation a subset of the French-speaking part of this corpus; it consists in 440 Q- and 1936 NQ-sentences

## 3. Automatic Question Extraction System

### 3.1. *Feature Vector*

In French language, the interrogative form of a sentence is strongly related to its intonation curve. Therefore, we decided to use the evolution of the fundamental frequency (F0) to automatically detect questions in an audio input.

From this F0 curve, we derive a set of features which aim at describing the shape of the intonation curve. Some of these features may be found redundant or basic by the reader; however, our methodology is to first evaluate a set of parameters chosen without much preconception on the intonation curve for both Q and NQ classes. Then, a detailed discussion concerning the usefulness of each parameter will be provided in the experiments of section 4.2.2.

The parameters defined for our work are listed in Table 1. It is important to note here that, contrary to classical short term feature extraction procedures generally used in speech recognition, a unique long term feature vector is automatically extracted for each utterance of the database.

---

[*] *see : http://nespole.itc.it/*

Table 1. 12-dimensional feature vector derived from the F0-curve for each utterance.

| No | Parameter | Description |
|----|-----------|-------------|
| 1 | Min | Minimal value of F0 |
| 2 | Max | Maximal value of F0 |
| 3 | Range | Range of F0-values of the whole sentence (Max-Min) |
| 4 | Mean | Mean value of F0 |
| 5 | Median | Median value of F0 |
| 6 | HighGreater-ThanLow | Is sum of F0 values in first half-length smaller than sum of F0 values in last half-length of utterance? |
| 7 | RaisingSum | Sum of $F0_{i+1} - F0_i$ if $F0_{i+1} > F0_i$ |
| 8 | RaisingCount | How many $F0_{i+1} > F0_i$ |
| 9 | FallingSum | Sum of $F0_{i+1} - F0_i$ if $F0_{i+1} < F0_i$ |
| 10 | FallingCount | How many $F0_{i+1} < F0_i$ |
| 11 | IsRaising | Is F0 contour rising? *(yes/no)*. Test whether RaisingSum > FallingSum |
| 12 | NonZero-FrameCount | How many non-zero F0 values? |

These features can be divided into 2 main categories: the first 5 features are the statistics on F0 values, but the 7 next features describe the contour of F0 (raising or falling). The F0 contour was extracted using the Praat[†] software.

### 3.2. Decision Tree-Based Classifier

Traditionally, statistical-based methods such as Hidden Markov Model (HMM) or Gaussian Mixture Model (GMM) can be used to solve classification problems in speech processing. These statistical methods generally apply on short term features, extracted for instance at a 10ms frame rate. However, in our case, statistical methods are hard to use since we do not use short term feature vectors, as explained in the previous section: one feature vector only is extracted for the whole utterance to be classified, which excludes the use of conventional statistical classifiers.

Thus, decision trees, which correspond to another classical machine learning (ML) method [6,7] are a good alternative.

In that case, the process is classically divided into two separated stages: training and testing. The training stage is to build a tree-model to represent a set of known instances while the testing stage involves the use of this model to

---

[†] http://www.fon.hum.uva.nl/praat/

evaluate other unknown instances. Decision tree is a *divide-and-conquer* approach to the problem of learning from a set of independent examples (a concrete example is called *instance*). Nodes in a decision tree involve testing a particular condition, which usually compares an attribute value with a constant. Some other trees compare two attributes with each other, or utilize some functions of one or more attributes. Leaf nodes give a classification for all instances that satisfy all conditions leading to this leaf, or a set of classifications, or a probability distribution over all possible classifications. To classify an unknown instance, it is routed down the tree according to the values of attributes tested in successive nodes, until it reaches a leaf. The instance is classified according to the class assigned to this leaf.

For this work, we have used an implementation of decision-tree algorithms that is included in the open-source toolkit Weka[‡] which is a collection of algorithm implementations written in Java for data mining tasks such as classification, regression, clustering, and association rules.

## 4. Experiments and Results

### 4.1. *Train/Test Protocol*

For the meeting corpus (Deloc), we use 200 Q-utterances and 200 NQ-utterances for training and the remaining utterances for testing (95Q + 357NQ). For the client/agent conversations corpus (Nespole), we use 50 Q-utterances and 50 NQ-utterances for training, and the remaining utterances for testing (390Q + 1886NQ).

For the training data, a decision tree is constructed (the decision-tree algorithm used in our experiments is called "C4.5"[§]) and the obtained classifier is evaluated on the remaining test data.

The evaluation is either based on a confusion matrix between questions (Q) and non-question (NQ) classes, or on measures coming from the information retrieval domain such as recall (R), precision (P) and F-ratio, where :

$$R = \frac{N_{\text{correctly detected questions}}}{N_{\text{total questions in the test set}}} \qquad P = \frac{N_{\text{correctly detected questions}}}{N_{\text{total questions detected}}} \qquad FRatio = \frac{2P \cdot R}{P + R}$$

‡ http://www.cs.waikato.ac.nz/~ml/weka/

§ Ross Quinlan, 1993 C4.5: Programs for Machine Learning, Morgan Kaufmann Publishers, San Mateo, CA

46

## 4.2. *Experiments on Telephone Meeting Data (Deloc)*

In this experimentation, we have applied a classic *50-fold cross validation* protocol in order to increase the total number of tests made. We repeated 50 times the process of dividing randomly the whole corpus into 2 parts (200Q+200NQ for training; the rest 95Q+357NQ for test). We then obtained 50 decision trees, each with a different classification performance. From these results, we have calculated the average performance values. Note that the process of training and testing is very fast with decision trees.

Table 2 shows the confusion matrix for Q/NQ classification. The figures correspond to the average performance over all 50 cross-validation configurations. The average good classification rate is around 75%.

Table 2. Confusion matrix on test data: average values.

| Question | Non Question | ← classified as |
|---|---|---|
| 73(77%) | 22(23%) | Question |
| 93(26%) | 264(74%) | Non Question |

However, it is also interesting to evaluate our question extraction system in terms of precision/recall figures. This is shown in Table 3 where the figures correspond to the average performance over all 50 cross-validation configurations (we also give standard deviations). These results show that our system leads to an acceptable recall (77% of the Q-utterances were retrieved by the system) while the precision is lower, due to a relatively large part of NQ-utterances classified as questions. Looking at the standard deviation calculated over 50 cross-validation configurations, we can say that the system presents a correct stability.

Table 3. Average performance measures (precision, recall, F-ratio) on test data for the Q-detection task.

| | Precision | Recall | F-ratio |
|---|---|---|---|
| Average | 44% | 77% | 56% |
| Standard deviation | 4% | 7% | 3,5% |

This experiment gives us an idea of our first system performance but does not help us to know which acoustic feature is useful for question extraction and which is not. Moreover, since some of these features are correlated with each other, one could try to reduce the original feature set. This is the purpose of the experiment presented in the next section.

### 4.2.1. *Features ordered by importance*

In order to know how strongly a feature contributes to the classification process, we have performed a "leave-one-out" procedure (as done in [8]). Starting with all N=12 features listed in Table 1, the procedure begins by evaluating the performance of each of the N-1 features. The best subset (in terms of F-ratio performance on training data calculated by averaging 50 cross-validation configurations) is determined, and the feature not included in this subset is then considered as the worst feature. This feature is eliminated and the procedure restarts with N-1 remaining features. The whole process is repeated until all features are eliminated. The inverse sequence of suppressed features gives us the list of features ranked from the most effective to the less effective (or most important to less important) for the specific Q/NQ classification task.

This "leave-one-out" procedure lead to the following order of importance (from the most important to the least important feature : 1) *isRaising* 2) *Range* 3) *Min* 4) *fallingCount* 5) *highGreaterThanLow* 6) *raisingCount* 7) *raisingSum* 8) *Median* 9) *Max* 10) *nonZeroFramesCount* 11) *Mean* 12) *fallingSum*.

We observe that *isRaising* and *range* parameters are the two most important ones to classify an utterance between Q and NQ classes. The *isRaising* feature is logically important to detect questions in French since it corresponds to the case where the F0 contour of a sentence is raising. The second most important parameter is the range of the F0 values within the whole sentence. If the decision tree makes use of these two features *isRaising* and *range* only, the obtained F-ratio is already 54% (to be compared with the 56% obtained with the 12 parameters). Our decision tree can be thus simplified and use two rules only. It is however important to note that some features of the initial parameter set (*min, max, RaisingSum, FallingSum*) still need to be extracted to calculate these two remaining features.

### 4.2.2. *Comparison with a "baseline" system*

In order to really understand what is under the performance obtained in the first experiment, we have compared our system performance to a system that gives a classification output in a basic or random way. For this, we have distinguished three types of "basic" systems: (a) one system that always classifies sentences as Q; (b) one system that always classifies sentences as NQ; and (c) one system that classifies sentences as Q or NQ randomly with a 50% probability. With the data set given in this experimentation, we obtain the following table of F-ratio performance for these random systems in comparison with our reference system

48

using 12 parameters (these rates are calculated on test data). In any case, we see that our system is significantly better.

Table 4.  F-ratio for "basic" or "random" systems and for our system on meeting test data.

| Always Q (a) | Always NQ (b) | Random 50% Q/NQ (c) | Our system |
|---|---|---|---|
| 35% | 0% | 29% | **56%** |

## 4.3.  *Experimentation on Client/Agent Recordings (Nespole)*

### 4.3.1.  *Analysis of test data*

Contrarily to the meeting corpus which was manually annotated into Q/NQ classes, the Nespole corpus was originally transcribed without any label corresponding to Q or NQ. We then obtained the Q/NQ labels *a posteriori* by automatically searching question marks into the transcriptions of each speaker turn. Before starting our experiments, we first made a qualitative analysis of the test utterances by looking at the F0 profile (rising or flat curve) on each of them. The results of this qualitative analysis on Nespole test data are shown in Table 5.

Table 5.  Qualitative analysis of Nespole test data.

| Class | Q (390) | NQ (1886) |
|---|---|---|
| F0 curve profile | Rising (299) | Rising (1056) |
|  | Flat (91) | Flat (830) |

This analysis shows that for Q-utterances the F0 curve is mostly rising (in 77% of cases) but not always. It means that the intonation information given by the F0 curve is not the only information used by an annotator to label an utterance as Q. Moreover, we can remark that the number of rising profiles for NQ-utterances is surprisingly high (more than a half of the NQ-utterances!). In fact, this corpus contains a lot of short speaker turns such as *"allo?"*; *"oui*[**]*"*; *"d'accord*[††]*"*; *"mhm"*… All of them have the F0 contour rising but only the first one (allo?) is labeled as a question. For these short speaker turns, it is manifest that the person is waiting for the response of his interlocutor, or more generally,

---

[**] *yes*
[††] *Ok, agree*

is waiting for the rest of his interlocutor's discourse. This situation happens especially when the agent talks about something for a long time (may be several minutes) and the client wants to manifest that he is still on the line.

Thus, this qualitative analysis shows that using F0 curve profile only to detect questions can lead to a relatively good recall, but to an unsatisfactory precision, as preliminary observed in section 4.2.

### 4.3.2. *Experimental evaluation and discussion*

To evaluate at least the efficiency of our algorithm on this corpus for "well formed" utterances, we have tested it on a subset of the test data made up of the 299 Q-utterances with a rising F0 curve, and the 830 NQ-utterances with a flat F0 curve. The decision tree was constructed with 50-Q and 50-NQ utterances manually chosen.

In that favorable case, our system lead to 84% recall and 100% precision, but we are aware that some other parameters and methods should be used to be able to detect Q-utterances with a flat profile or to reject NQ-utterances with a rising one. We currently investigate the use of others parameters, for instance lexical information coming from an ASR output or parameters derived from the energy curve.

## 5. Conclusion

Retrieving pertinent parts of a meeting or a conversation recording can help for automatic summarization or indexing of the document. In this paper, we have dealt with an original task, almost never presented in the literature, which consists in automatically extracting questions utterances from a recording. In a first step, we have tried to develop and evaluate a question extraction system which uses only acoustic parameters and does not need any ASR output. The parameters used are extracted from the intonation curve and the classifier is a decision tree built using the C4.5 algorithm. Our first experiments on French meeting recordings lead to a good classification rate of approximately 75%. An experiment in order to find the best acoustic parameters for this task was also presented in this paper. Finally, data analysis and experiments on another database have shown the need of using other cues like the lexical information from an ASR output or energy, in order to improve question detection performance on spontaneous speech. Moreover, we plan to apply this question detection system to a tonal language like Vietnamese to see whether the same parameters can be used or not.

# References

1. FERRER L., SHRIBERG E., STOLCKE A., "A Prosody-Based Approach to End-of-Utterance Detection That Does Not Require Speech Recognition", IEEE Int. Conf. on Acoustics, Speech and Signal Processing (ICASSP), vol. I, Hong Kong, 2003, pp. 608-611.
2. SHRIBERG, E., BATES, R. & STOLCKE, A. "A prosody-only decision-tree model for disfluency detection". Eurospeech 1997. Rhodes, Greece.
3. STANDFORD V., GAROFOLO J., GALIBERT O., MICHEL M., LAPRUN C., "The NIST Smart Space and Meeting Room Projects: Signal, Acquisition, Annotation and Metrics", Proc of ICASSP 2003, Hong-Kong, China, Mai 2003.
4. WANG D., LU L., ZHANG H.J., "Speech Segmentation Without Speech Recognition", IEEE Int. Conf. on Acoustics, Speech and Signal Processing (ICASSP), vol I, april 2003, pp. 468-471.
5. MANA N., BURGER S., CATTONI R., BESACIER L., MACLAREN V., McDONOUGH J., METZE F., "The NESPOLE! VoIP Multilingual Corpora in Tourism and Medical Domains" Eurospeech 2003, Geneva, 1-4 Sept. 2003.
6. MARQUEZ L., "Machine learning and Natural Language processing", Technical Report LSI-00-45-R, Universitat Politechnica de Catalunya, 2000.
7. WITTEN I.H., FRANK E., Data mining: Pratical machine learning tools and techniques with Java implementations, Morgan Kaufmann, 1999.
8. L. BESACIER, J.F. BONASTRE, C. FREDOUILLE, "Localization and selection of speaker-specific information with statistical modeling". Speech Communication, n°31 (2000), pp 89-106

# CHAPTER 5

# IMAGE FILTERING USING VISUAL INFORMATION CONSISTENCY

VAN B. DANG

*Faculty of Information Technology, University of Natural Sciences,*
*Ho Chi Minh City, Vietnam*


DUY-DINH LE

*Faculty of Information Technology, University of Natural Sciences,*
*Ho Chi Minh City, Vietnam.*
*National Institute of Informatics, Tokyo, Japan*


DUC A. DUONG

*Faculty of Information Technology, University of Natural Sciences,*
*Ho Chi Minh City, Vietnam*

We propose a simple but reliable method to filter a collection of images of some object category that might contain many outlier images. Such collections are straightforward to obtain, for example, by using Google Image Search. To retrieve most of objects relevant to the category, visual information consistency is used. We use SIFT (Scale Invariant Feature Transform), a state of the art method for representing images with descriptors which are invariant to scale and orientation, to compute the similarity between two images and form a graph of which nodes are images and edges connected by two nodes are weighted by the similarity between two associated images to describe the consistency degree. Then, a subgraph is extracted by a greedy densest component algorithm to return the result images. The proposed approach has been tested on different categories and shown promising results.

## 1. Introduction

There are more and more data available on the Internet these days. The need of searching images over the large scale of data becomes important. However, content based image retrieval is still a challenging problem because of restricted results that semantic gaps are difficult to fill up [17]. Techniques used in current Internet image search system, Google image search [18], for example, is mainly based on words – the filename of the image and the text near the image on the webpage [6]. This approach is good enough to quickly find out related ones from millions of images on the web, but along with them are hundreds of unrelated images which make the total outcome is not as good as the approach itself. In order to get better retrieval effectiveness, visual information of images should be incorporated. Figure 1 describes such a system.

Searching images with highly visual consistency is challenging but important since it has vast applications, such as to improve retrieval results which are helpful to another application such as automatic training sample collection for object detection and recognition. It can help to save significant time of intensive labor annotation.

Recently, lots of viewpoint invariant descriptors have been developed for image matching [9, 10, 11], object recognition [2, 3, 4] and image retrieval [7, 8]. SIFT (Scale Invariant Feature Transform) appears to be outstanding among them for its successful application in many problems such as object recognition [1, 5] and face recognition [12]. Thus, SIFT is eligible for similarity measuring.

Fergus et al. [14] proposed a method to re-rank the output of an image search engine with prosperous conclusion. Their approach extended the method of Fergus et al. [15] to allow parts to be heterogeneous. However, the entire model of which aim is to re-rank images rather than reject irrelevant ones is rather complex to implement. Meanwhile, Ozkan and Duygulu have recently proposed a graph-based method to select interested faces from news photographs [13], which brings impressive results. Nevertheless, original approach in [13] just aims to select images containing faces of a particular person, not for objects in general.

In this paper, we propose a method to effectively reject outlier images out of any given large collection using their visual consistency degree depicted in Figure 1. Similarity between images is measured by SIFT descriptors [1]. Interest points are first calculated. Initial matches between two images are defined as pairs of interest points having the minimum distance. True matches are then decided by applying a constraint named unique match [13]. For any given collection, the dominant objects are the most likely to be the subjects or the meaning of the entire collection. Therefore, we form a graph of which nodes represent images and edges represent the similarity between them. The densest component of the graph which stands for the sub collection of related images is then found using a greedy densest component algorithm [16]. Our approach has been tested on filtering outlier images in collections taken from Google image search showing prosperous results.

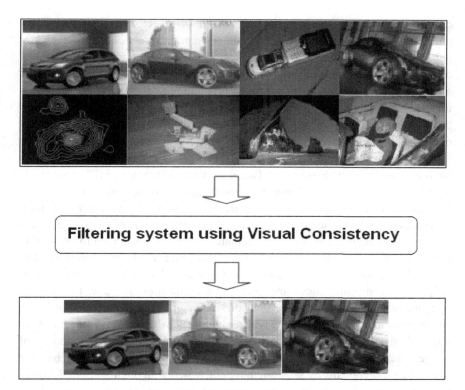

Figure 1. Images returned by Google image search for the query "car" contain several outlier images. Visual consistency should be examined in order to achieve a better retrieval quality.

In the following sections, we first introduce how SIFT descriptors are used for measuring similarity. Then, we describe our method to construct similarity graph from the extracted similarity information of images. After that, the process of finding the densest component from the graph is explained. Finally, we show the results of our experiments on collections of several categories taken from the returns of Google image search.

## 2. Representing the Similarity of Images

SIFT descriptors have been applied successfully in many applications such as object recognition [1, 5] and face recognition [12] since it has been proved to be invariant to changes in orientation and scale [1]. SIFT operator consists of four major stages. Firstly, interest points are found by scanning the image over location and scale to assure that keypoints will be invariant to scale. Secondly,

54

candidate keypoints are accurately localized or rejected if they are found unstable. Thirdly, one ore more dominant orientations are assigned to each key point based on its local image properties. Finally, a local image descriptor is created for each key point based on its local image patch. The local descriptor of a keypoint is represented relatively to its orientation assigned above so that it is invariant to rotation. Thus, the descriptor is highly distinctive yet invariant to transformation, which makes it eligible for measuring the similarity between objects, hence for measuring the similarity between images.

Images of the same object under different conditions are more likely to be similar to each other than others. Based on that assumption, SIFT operator is used to extract keypoints along as their local descriptors of images. Each pair of keypoints which has the minimum value of Euclidean distance between their descriptors is selected as an initial match between the pair of images to which the keypoints belong. However, initial matches are not guaranteed to be reliable as you can see in Figure 2, where matches are rather confusing. Consequently, we apply a constraint named unique match constraint which is introduced in [13]. This constraint states that many false matches are due to multiple assignments, which exists more than one point in image A are assigned to a single point in image B, or to one way assignments, which exists one point $A_1$ in image A matches one point $B_1$ in image B, but $B_1$ matches another point $A_2$ of image A or does not have any matches at all. They eliminate false matches due to multiple assignments by selecting only one match with the minimum distance. False matches due to one way assignment are eliminated by removing the links which do not have any corresponding assignment from the other side. An example of applying this constraint is shown in Figure 2.

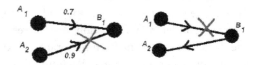

Figure 2. Multiple assignments is shown on the left and one way assignment is on the right. False matches due to multiple assignments are elimimated by selecting only one match with minimum distance. False matches due to one way assignment are eliminated by removing the links which do not have any corresponding assignment from the other side.

## 3. Constructing the Similarity Graph

After all matches are guaranteed to be correct, a similarity graph is constructed. Each node of the graph represents an image in the collection which is represented by the whole graph. Any matches between any pairs of images will create an edge connecting the corresponding nodes of which weight is also the number of matches between them. Such graph can be represented by a matrix M of which value at M[i][j] denotes the weight between $i^{th}$ and $j^{th}$ nodes. As proposed in [13], an edge is weighted by the average distance of all matches between the two connected nodes:

$$dist(A, B) = \frac{\sum_{i=1}^{N} D(i)}{N}$$

where N is the number of matches and D(i) is the Euclidean distance between the SIFT descriptors of the two points in the $i^{th}$ match. However, our experiments have shown that the value of the average distance is not reliable enough. There are some exactly true matches may have a very low value of average distance while they come from completely different objects, of which proof may be found in the Experiments section. Therefore, the number of matches has been selected as weights instead. The left picture of Figure 4 demonstrates such a similarity graph of which each node represents an image. The number on the edge represents the number of matches between two connected nodes.

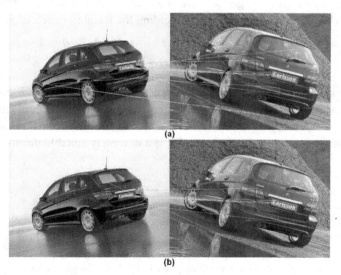

Figure 3. (a) shows the initial matches between SIFT descriptors. (b) shows the remain ones after applying unique match constraint.

## 4. Finding the Densest Component Using a Greedy Graph Algorithm

In this section, we briefly describe the algorithm proposed in [16]. Once the similarity graph has been formed, our aim is to find the densest component because nodes of images containing similar object which is also the dominant in the collection will be closed to each other while distant from others. In the algorithm proposed in [4], the density of a subset S of V in graph G(V, E) is defined as:

$$f(S) = \frac{|E(S)|}{|S|}$$

where V is the set of all vertices and E is the set of all edges in G, then E(S) is the set of all edges induced by subset S. The subset S that maximizes f(S) will be the densest component of the graph G.

The algorithm in [4] starts with S = G, and f(S) = f(G). In each round of iteration, vertex with minimum degree will be removed from S. The iteration progresses until S is empty. Ultimately, subset S that has maximum value of f(S) will be the densest component of the graph G.

Nevertheless, the algorithm above only works well for a binary graph [13]. Therefore, before applying such algorithm, we first need to convert the current weighted graph into the binary form which means weights are now 0 or 1 representing there is no edges or there is an edge between two connected nodes respectively. The work is done by thresholding the weight of each edge:

$$M[i][j] = \begin{cases} 1 & if \quad M[i][j] > = \theta \\ 0 & otherwise \end{cases}$$

where $\theta$ is the threshold value. Since we are thresholding on the number of matches which will decide if those two corresponding images are similar, the value of 3 which is the minimum number of matches that can form a reliable recognition proposed by David Lowe [1] is a definitely suitable threshold value.

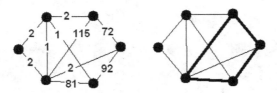

Figure 4. Example of converting a weighted graph into a binary graph. Nodes, edges and their weights are given in the left image. Thresholding weight of edges with a value of 3 constructs the graph in the right image.

Figure 4 illustrates the process of converting a similarity graph into binary form by a threshold value of 3.

## 5. Experiments

Our approach is demonstrated on several collections taken from Google image search. They are collections of images of clocks, shoes, frontal face of George Bush, Tony Blair and Ariel Sharons which are also keywords for the Google search engine. Most of these categories have been selected for demonstrating by Fergus et al. [15].

Firstly, all collections which consist of top 100 images returned by Google with an average value of outlier rate of 40% are downloaded and resize to assure that the major axis of any images is no larger than 400 pixels for better performance. Images are converted to grayscale since color information is not needed. Processing from this moment on is exactly the same for all collections. SIFT descriptors are calculated for all images in the collection. Initial matches are then produced for each pair of images by finding all pairs of points which have the minimum distance of their descriptors. These matches are then filtered by the unique match constraint to return the true matches list. The reject rate of the constraint given by our experiments is similar to the value clearly stated in [13].

Secondly, a similarity graph is constructed for the collection and thresholded to form binary graph. Our observation has shown that number of matches is a better value to be thresholded than the average distance as proposed in [13] since there are many matches which are exactly true matches with a pretty small dissimilarity value – no smaller than that of correct matches – though the two connected points come from two totally different images as in Figure 5. Fortunately, the number of matches of this type between any pair of images is extremely small – the maximum value we have observed so far is 2 which can be effectively rejected by the value of 3 proposed by Lowe [1].

The precision of our system is rather stable while the recall value varies from collection to collection. A collection of frontal face of Tony Blair returned by Google when queried "Tony Blair" consists of top 100 images, 13 of which are good images. Our system returns 8 from those 13 good images with 62% value of recall and 100% value of precision, see Figure 7 for illustration. On the collection of shoes with 70 good images, however, recall falls to 34% with 24 good images returned while precision is also 100%. Table 1 shows details of the results which are visualized in Figure 6. Example of shoes filtering is illustrated in Figure 8. It is worth noting that there is a variety of shoes which look rather different from others together with lots of outlier images in the collection yet they are correctly selected as final outcome. The system developed by Duygulu et al [13] can only find images containing face of a single person corresponding to the query, whereas our system is able to find all images containing dominant objects – in plural, such as different kind of shoes – using their visual information. Our proposed system is exactly what we have claimed: a system effectively rejecting outlier images from a large collections using visual consistency degree.

The problem we are solving is more general than one stated in [13]. However, retrieving images containing face of a particular person from news photographs may be considered as filtering out non-face images. Therefore, the two problems are similar in some aspects and thus, the results can be compared. They achieve 68% of recall and 71% of precision on average and the best results they reach is up to 83.93% of recall and 100% of precision on the collection of Gray Davis. Meanwhile, the best result we achieve is also up to 100% of precision and 61% of recall (as of Tony Blair) while on average 45% of recall

Figure 5. A true match which is not exactly true. It is a match between two points from completely different objects. However, it has such a low value of dissimilarity that may be result in the binary graph. Only by thresholding on the number of matches can it be eliminated.

Table 1. System precision and recall on several particular collections.

|  | Precision | Recall |
|---|---|---|
| **Tony Blair** | 100% | 61% |
| **Ariel Sharons** | 100% | 50% |
| **George Bush** | 63% | 50% |
| **Shoes** | 100% | 34% |
| **Clock** | 100% | 30% |

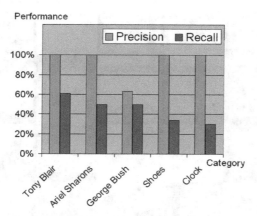

Figure 6. Performance chart of the proposed system. The system is tested on 5 collections. The left bar of each pair represents precision while the other represents recall.

Figure 7. (a) A subset of collection containing faces of Tony Blair. (b) All the images returned by our System. The system achieve 100% of Precision since it completely filter our outlier images.

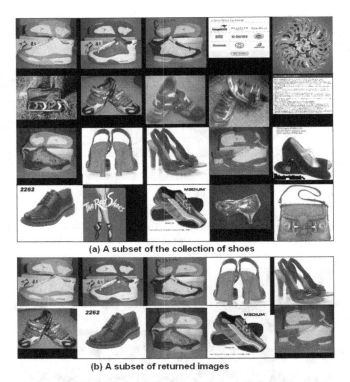

**(a) A subset of the collection of shoes**

**(b) A subset of returned images**

Figure 8. (a) A subset of the shoes collection. (b) A subset of selected images returned by our system. Note that though the collection consists of a variety of shoes (which looks very different from others) as well as outlier images, the result is very promising.

and 92% of precision. It is clear that our system is no worse than theirs on precision though our recall is not very good. Nevertheless, their approach is designed to work on faces. Consequently, they apply a constraint named Geometrical Constraints [13] which assures matched points to be at similar position, for example, the left eyes usually resides around the middle-left of a face. Needless to say, designed to work on object in general, our system cannot apply the so-called Geometrical Constraints, which helps to eliminate false matches due to geometrical problems. Moreover, as mentioned above, they create the binary graph by thresholding the average distance, which will let many false matches past leading to a raise in recall and of course, a fall in precision.

As we may know, recall can be boosted up by a sacrifice on precision. Our experiments also show that reducing the threshold value to 2 when converting

Table 2. Precision and recall at the threshold value of 2. A raise in recall brings a fall in precision.

|  | Precision | Recall |
|---|---|---|
| Tony Blair | 56% | 70% |
| Shoes | 62% | 43% |
| Clock | 49% | 45% |

the similarity graph into binary form, which will also reduce the reject rate to false matches, results in a small raise in recall along as a fall in precision. Table 2 below provides all the details.

Since designed to effectively reject unrelated images and a low value of recall can be overcome by increasing the size of the collection, we decide to choose 3 as our system threshold for the number of matches. For example, such a system with a recall of 50% may find 40 images for a collection of 100 images, then by giving a larger collection, such as 1000, the number of good images found will raise relatively. The process of enlarging the size of collections can easily be implemented by accepting more images from the returns by Google. Moreover, a high precision value also proves the returns of our system are highly consistent with no or very few outlier images left.

## 6. Conclusion and Future Work

We propose a simple but reliable method to filter outlier images from any give collections using visual consistency degree. Similarity between images is calculated by SIFT descriptors [1] which have been proved to be invariant to image scale and orientation. A graph is formed with nodes representing images and edges representing similarity degree between the two connected nodes. With the assumption that relevant images are similar to each other than with others, corresponding nodes will have more edges connecting to each others. Therefore, the process of finding the largest group of related images can be migrated to that of finding the densest component of the graph, which is implemented by a greedy graph algorithm [16]. Since the algorithm only works well for binary graphs, similarity graph is thresholded on the number of matches between nodes to form a binary graph prior to the finding process.

Our system achieves a high average precision of 92% which means the returned images are highly consistent while a low value of recall can be overcome by increasing the size of the collection. The results make it a reliable system to filter large collection of images using their visual information and to be used to collect samples for any training process in combination with Google image search engine. The problem and the approach in the whole is novel.

In order to take advantage of the greedy graph algorithm [16], we need to convert the similarity graph into binary form. It is this process that looses some information. Algorithms which are not limited on binary graph may be good substitutions. Furthermore, our experiments have shown that SIFT descriptors do not work well with objects of classes which have high within- class variation, so the incorporation of other viewpoint invariant descriptors may be helpful.

## References

[1] D. G. Lowe. Distinctive image features from scale invariant keypoints. *International Journal of Computer Vision*, 60(2), 2004.

[2] D. Lowe. Object recognition from local scale-invariant features. In *Proc. ICCV*, pages 1150–1157, 1999.

[3] S. Obdrzalek and J. Matas. Object recognition using local affine frames on distinguished regions. In *Proc. BMVC.*, pages 113–122, 2002.

[4] F. Rothganger, S. Lazebnik, C. Schmid, and J. Ponce. 3d object modeling and recognition using affine-invariant patches and multiview spatial constraints. In *Proc. CVPR*, 2003.

[5] S. Helmer and D. Lowe. Object recognition with many local features. In *Workshop on Generative Model Based Vision 2004(GMBV)*, Washington D.C.

[6] S. Brin and L. Page. The anatomy of a large-scale hypertextual web search engine. In *7th Int. WWW Conference*, 1998.

[7] C. Schmid and R. Mohr. Local greyvalue invariants for image retrieval. *IEEE PAMI*, 19(5):530–534, 1997.

[8] J. Sivic and A. Zisserman. Video google: A text retrieval approach to object matching in videos. In *Proc. ICCV*, 2003.

[9] F. Schaffalitzky and A. Zisserman. Multi-view matching for unordered image sets, or "How do I organize my holiday snaps?". In *Proc. ECCV*, volume 1, pages 414–431. Springer-Verlag, 2002.

[10] D. Tell and S. Carlsson. Combining appearance and topology for wide baseline matching. In *Proc. ECCV*, LNCS 2350, pages 68–81. Springer-Verlag, 2002.

[11] T. Tuytelaars and L. Van Gool. Wide baseline stereo matching based on local, affinely invariant regions. In *Proc. BMVC.*, pages 412–425, 2000.

[12] J. Sivic, M. Everingham, and A. Zisserman. Person spotting: video shot retrieval for face sets. In *International Conference on Image and Video Retrieval (CIVR 2005), Singapore*, 2005.

[13] Derya Ozkan and Pinar Duygulu. A Graph Based Approach for Naming Faces in News Photos. *In Proceedings of IEEE Conference on Computer Vision and Pattern Recognition*, New York, NY, June 17-22, 2006.

[14] Fergus, R., Perona, P. and Zisserman, A. A Visual Category Filter for Google Images. *Proc. of the 8th European Conf. on Computer Vision, ECCV 2004*.

[15] R. Fergus, P. Perona, and A. Zisserman. Object class recognition by unsupervised scaleinvariant learning. In *Proc. CVPR*, 2003.

[16] M. Charikar. Greedy approximation algorithms for finding dense components in a graph. In *APPROX '00: Proc. of the 3rd International Workshop on Approximation Algorithms for Combinatorial Optimization*, London, UK, 2000.

[17] A. Smeulders, M. Worring, S. Santini, and A. Gupta. Content based image retrieval at the end of the early years. IEEE *Transactions on Pattern Analysis and Machine Intelligence, 22(12):1349-1380, 2000.*

[18] http://www.google.com/imghp

# CHAPTER 6

# GRAPH-BASED MODEL FOR OBJECT RECOGNITION

PHAM TRONG TON

*Institut National Polytechnique de Grenoble (INPG), France*

AUGUSTIN LUX
TRAN THI THANH HAI

*INRIA Rhône-Alpes, 655 av. de l'Europe, Montbonnot, France*

This paper presents a method for modeling objects at multiple scales using a graph-based model and a strategy for matching of two structure hierarchies. The visual features such as ridge and peak detected at certain scales correspond to a node in an *Attributed Relational Graph* (ARG). Edges are inserted between nodes on two consecutive scales based on how the region associated to the feature at one scale is covered by the region associated to the other feature at the next scale. Using this representation, the process of object recognition is expressed as a matching problem of two graphs, known as the problem of searching for the maximal sub-graph isomorphism in graph theory. However graph matching is a highly complex and time-consuming. For matching two attributed relational graphs, the dissimilarity measure between two nodes is computed. In order to reduce the search space of the algorithm, symbolic constraints based on feature types are proposed. This technique is simple and well-adapted to our object model. We demonstrate our approach on an image database with some variations of object in images such as rotation, translation and small resolution change.

## 1. Introduction

Object recognition is a fundamental problem in computer vision. Its application is very large and concerns many domains such as: artificial vision systems, object tracking, classification, stereo vision ...etc. Given a new image, matching is simply defined as the process of associating the new element with the labeled element.

### 1.1. *Building Object Model at Multiple Scale*

For object recognition, we may need an appearance model for the presentation of object. The presentation must be robust to some transformations and noise in image. There are two usual types of perturbation in image, namely,

(i) geometrical transformations (e.g. translation, rotation and scale changes) and (ii) photometrical transformations (e.g. illumination change, texture and color change.). We present here a symbolic representation of objects in images which can be used for modeling some general type of objects. Feature extraction is based on detecting ridges and peaks at multiple scales developed by H. Tran [3]. Ridges and peaks are visual features that provide compact and informative structural shape description of an image. This representation of image features at multiple scales has long been a powerful paradigm in computer vision [1, 6], offering several attractive properties. In the coarse scale, the abstract structure of an object is presented by long ridges lines. On other hand, the details of an object are represented by short ridge lines and peaks at finer scale. This representation supports the processing of information at multiple levels of resolution. Moreover, the computational complexity of many tasks can be reduced by using the result of processing at coarse scales to constrain processing at finer scale.

Given two such hierarchical features, we consider two main problems in the construction of a graph-based model: (i) what features make up the nodes and its attributes? (ii) how can we link two nodes in graph? We represent our object model by an attributed relational graph. Each node is labeled with attributes such as geometrical properties and its topological signature vector. Furthermore, we can label edges with the relational inter-scale of two nodes correspondences. The ARG representation is effectively more informative than the representation by using a classic graph.

## 1.2. *Matching Algorithm*

Given two graphs, we seek a method to reduce the computational complexity of traditional matching algorithms [4, 5, 11]. We propose a method for efficiently matching based on node-by-node basis. The matching algorithm takes into account the information of the geometrical properties (i.e., scale, length and direction) of the feature and the topology of nodes in the graph to compute the similarity between two nodes. In order to reduce the search space of the algorithm, symbolic constraints based on types of features are proposed. This method profits from recent research in graph spectral domain in using the topology signature vector [10] for fast searching of the sub-graph isomorphism of two graphs.

### 1.3. *Organisation*

In section 2, we present our method for building the graph-based model from the extracted features. We also give some definitions about the multiple scale features in this section. The matching algorithm will be explained in section 3. Section 4 presents experimental results of our method with a small image dataset. Finally, we conclude and give some perspectives in section 5.

## 2. Multiple Scale Features and Hierarchical Object Model

Ridges and peaks provide a compact and informative description about object shape and the details of an object. However, to represent the model of an object we need to combine these features in a coherent structure. We choose to represent this knowledge with an attributed relational graph.

### 2.1. *Ridge and Peak Definitions*

In this section, we briefly present the definition of ridges and peaks and how do we detect them in images. More details about this aspect have been given in a previous paper [3].

Let $I(x, y)$ be a 2D image and $\sigma$ be a detecting scale, the local surface at one point in image is defined as the convolution of the image with the kernel of Gaussian filter $L(x, y, \sigma) = I(x, y) \otimes G(x, y, \sigma)$. Let $\lambda_1, \lambda_2$ two eigenvalues of the Hessian matrix be two main curvatures of the local surface associated to the point $P(x, y)$. $P$ is considered as a ridge point if it verifies two following conditions:

(i)    The Laplacian of Gaussian (LOG) verifies a local extremum in the direction corresponding with the largest curvature of the associated surface.

(ii)   Two principal curvatures (respectively the eigenvalues $\lambda_1, \lambda_2$ of the Hessian matrix) have the same sign and their values are considerably different.

On the contrary, if the LOG at P admits a local extremum in all direction, we have a peak in this surface.

The Figure 1 show the local surface associated with a ridge point and a peak. The two orthogonal directions correspond with the two main curvature of the local surface. Intuitively, in the case of the ridge point, these two values are very different. Nevertheless, in the case of peak, these two principal curvatures have the same value.

Ridge point detected in the previously are isolated points. We need an algorithm for linking these connected ridge points to build ridge lines which gives a better representation of object shape (see Figure 2). We assign two ridge points to the same ridge line if two following conditions are satisfied: (i) two points are located in an 8 nearest neighbor (connectedness criterion) and (ii) two points must have the same direction (direction criterion)

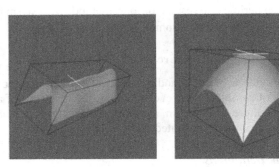

Figure 1. The local surface and two principal curvatures associated with a ridge point (left) and a peak (right).

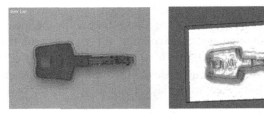

Figure 2. Ridges and peaks detected at $\sigma_4 = 4\sqrt{2}$ : image overlap (left), visualization in 3D of local surface (right).

Our goal is constructing an object model at multiple scales. To obtain this we need to detect features at multiple scales. We have adopted the notion DOLP[*] represented by J. Crowley *et al.* [1] to construct the Laplacian pyramid of the image scale space. More precisely, ridges and peaks are detected on surfaces defined by image $I$ convolved with the Gaussian kernel $G(\sigma)$ by varying the value of the scale:

$$L(x, y, \sigma) = G(\sigma) * I(x, y)$$

where $G(\sigma) = \dfrac{1}{2\pi\sigma^2} e^{-\frac{x^2+y^2}{2\sigma^2}}$ , $\sigma = (\sqrt{2})^i$ , $i = \{0, 1, \dots N\}$.

---

[*] Different Of Low Pass transform.

## 2.2. *Building Graph-Based Representation*

Following a philosophy similar to the one proposed in [1, 7, 10], we represent each object by an attributed relational graph. In this way, we have a hierarchical structural description of the object.

Let $G = (V, E, R)$ denote an ARG, each ARG consist of two sets: a set of nodes $V$ with various types of attributes $R$ assigned to them and a set of edges $E$. We are interested here in two principal problems in constructing the ARG:

(i)    **ARG nodes and associated attributes**: the features such as "ridge" and "peak" define a set of nodes in our ARG model. We attach to a node three properties of ridge and peak $R = \{geometrical\ properties,\ directional\ histogram,\ and\ topology\ signature\ vector\}$. According to these properties, it is presented by the following attributes (Figure 3):

- Feature type: Ridge (C), Peak (P)
- Scale $\sigma$: corresponds with the level in the graph
- Length $l$: the total number of ridge points linked to perform a ridge line. In case of peak, its length is only one pixel.
- Directional histogram $h = n_i$, $i = \{0,\ 1,\ 2,\ 3\}$, $n_i$ is the number of ridge points having the direction $i$.
- Topological signature vector ($tsv$): represents the topology of nodes encoding in the ARG.

(ii)   **ARG edge linking**: an edge defines the link of two nodes $V_i^k$ et $V_j^{k+1}$ at two consecutive levels. To set up the set of edges, we compute the ratio of the overlapping region associated with the feature of each node at two consecutive levels $V_i^{k+1}$ and $V_j^k$. If this ratio is higher than a defined threshold (set at 0.6), we construct an edge linking these two regions $V_j^{k+1} \rightarrow V_i^k$ ( Figure 4).

Obviously, an ARG is a well-suited structure to represent the structure of the hierarchical features extracted in our object model. Moreover, this structure permits encoding the node attributed with the relational information or the real value and yet more informative in the case of topological vector. We explain in

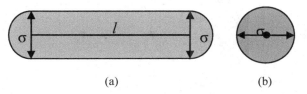

(a)                              (b)

Figure 3. Modeling of geometrical attributes of ridge node (a) and peak node (b).

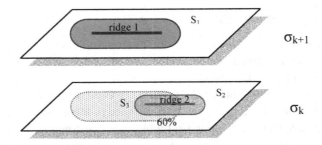

Figure 4. The overlapping region of two features defines the existence of the edge between two nodes.

more details in the following section on how we capture the structural information of nodes in an ARG with a low-dimensional vector.

### 2.3. *Encoding Graph Structure*

The notion of topological signature vector is introduced recently in the domain of computer vision by Shokoufandek et *al.* [10]. To describe the topology of an ARG, we turn to the domain of eigenspace of graphs. Firstly, we present our graph relation by a symmetric {0, 1} adjacency matrix, with 1 indicating an edge between adjacent nodes in the graph and 0 otherwise. The eigenvalues of a graph's adjacency matrix encode important structural properties of the graph.

Secondly, we determine the adjacency matrix of the sub-graph locating in each node. Then, we compute the eigenvector for each of these adjacency matrices and sort the eigenvalues in decreasing order by absolute value. Let $S_i = |\lambda_1| + |\lambda_2| + ... + |\lambda_k|$ be the sum of the $k$ largest absolute values. The sorted $S_i$'s become the components of the topological vector assigned to the ARG's parent node.

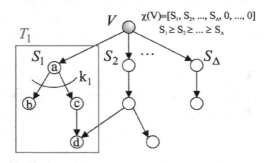

Figure 5. Constructing of the topological signature vector in an ARG.

Finally, the topological vector is normalized to k dimensional vector with 0's filled in case the dimension of vector is smaller than *k*. More specifically, k is called the factor normalization of the topological signature vector.

Using this presentation of the graph's topological structure is demonstrated that is well performed with some minor perturbation (addition/deletion of nodes) from the original graph. This could be improving the performance of recognition system with the presence of some additional noise and partial occlusion in the original images. Additionally, the presenting of the topological signature vector facilitate the process of searching the sub-graph isomorphism by comparing node by node based on the dissimilarity between topological vectors.

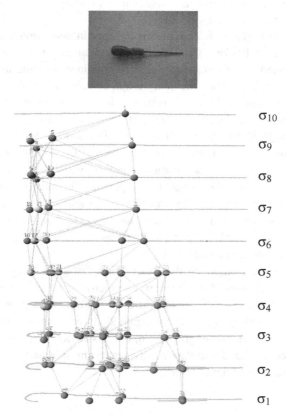

Figure 6. Representation of the multi-scale features of a screwdriver in an ARG. Ridge and peak detected at 10 consecutive scales ($\sigma_1 = \sqrt{2}$ and $\sigma_{10} = 10\sqrt{2}$ ). Ridge lines correspond with green nodes, positive peaks correspond with red nodes and negative peaks correspond with yellow nodes.

## 3. Hierarchical Matching Algorithm

Once all graph-based object models are constructed and labeled, we stock these graphs in a database. Afterward, to recognize the new object we need a matching algorithm to find the best correspondence between query ARG and the model ARGs. The matching algorithm of two ARGs could be considered as the particular case of graph matching.

Let $G_1$ and $G_2$ be two graphs, we faced often with three main graph matching problems in graph theory:

(i)  **Graph isomorphism** consists in verifying if two graphs $G_1$ and $G_2$ have the identical structure.

(ii)  **Sub-graph isomorphism** consists in searching for the isomorphism of $G_1$ with the sub-graphs of $G_2$.

(iii)  **Double sub-graph isomorphism** consists in searching all the possible isomorphism between the sub-graphs of $G_1$ and the sub-graphs of $G_2$.

As mentioned earlier, our major challenge is in computing an approximate sub-graph isomorphism when the query graph contains a minor perturbation due to noise and geometrical transformations. In working with the constructed graph-based model, we have also realized three simplifications with respect to the classical algorithms [4, 5, 11] in our ARG model. First, recognition in computer vision is sometimes a fuzzy problem (due to the imprecision and incompleteness of data in acquisition system) while the algorithm is only applicable for finding the exact isomorphism. Second, a graph matching algorithm uses only structural information on graph while the ARG contains parametrical information of the visual features that can help to discriminate different objects. Third, classical algorithms explore a large search space, which we have reduced considerably.

Our algorithm is based on the observation that if two objects are similar then their features must have similar parametric properties and topological structure. Consequently, the main process of our algorithm is searching sequentially for finding the best correspondence between the nodes in query graph and the nodes in model graphs. So, two nodes could be said to be in close correspondence if the dissimilarity between them is small and satisfies the symbolic constraints of feature type.

### 3.1. *Outline*

The details of our matching algorithm are presented in [12]. In this section, we introduce only the outline of this algorithm. Let $G_N(V_N, E_N, R_N)$ be the query

ARG, $G_M(V_M, E_M, R_M)$ be the model ARG. We starting at the highest level of graph model, then the proposed matching algorithm is as follow:

(i)    The first step consists in searching for the root node in the query graph to match with a root node of the model graph. Let us denote these root nodes respectively by $V_N$ and $V_M$. Finding of query root node is vivid step for the precision of our algorithm because the query object may be sustains some perturbation in changing scale.

(ii)    At each graph level, we verify firstly the symbolic constrains in order to fast reject nodes with incompatible type. Then the correspondence of two nodes is decided based on the dissimilarity measure between two nodes.

(iii)    Repeat the second step until we do not find any nodes for matching in the next level or the two graphs have reached its height.

The proposed algorithm is simply a greedy search and executes very fast. On the contrary, the result obtained is not always an optimal solution. In the case of the more complex graph, our algorithm gives an approximated correspondence of two graphs that can be satisfied regardless of the computational complexity of the optimal sub-graph isomorphism algorithm. In the next sections, we present in detail how we constrain the feature type of two nodes and how we measure the dissimilarity between two nodes.

## 3.2. Symbolic Constraints Formulation

We have defined for each node a symbol which is corresponding with type of features such as (C) for ridge line and (P) for peak. Two nodes are corresponding if its symbols are compatibles. Therefore, we have two type of this mutual relation: Ridge-Ridge (C-C) and Peak-Peak (P-P). These conditions help us reject efficiently the incompatible pair's nodes and yield the matching process faster than the classical matching algorithm.

## 3.3. Measuring of Dissimilarity

The dissimilarity between two graphs is defined as a function of geometrical and topological descriptor vectors associated to nodes and links in each graph. Given two graphs $G_N$ and $G_M$, let $u \in V_N$ and $v \in V_M$ be two nodes of the query graph $G_N$ and the model graph $G_M$. The dissimilarity between $u$ and $v$ is computed in the terms of the dissimilarity in geometry ($d_{geo}$) and the dissimilarity in topology ($d_{top}$):

(i)   **Geometrical dissimilarity** is measured by the difference of numerical properties (i.e. length $l$ and scale $\sigma$ ) $(d_R)$ and the Euclidian distance of their directional histograms $(d_h)$.

$$d_{geo}(u,v) = \sum_{x \in R} d_x(u,v) + d_h(h_1,h_2)$$

$$d_R(u,v) = \left| \frac{a-b}{a+b} \right| \text{ and } d_h(h_1,h_2) = \sqrt{\sum_{i=0}^{3}(h_{1_i} - h_{2_i})^2}$$

(ii)  **Topological dissimilarity** is computed by the Euclidian distance of two vectors. Note that the topological signature vector (*tsv*) is normalized so that its elements taken the value in range of [0, 1].

$$d_{top}(u,v) = \sqrt{\sum_{i=0}^{k}(tsv^1{}_i - tsv^2{}_i)^2}$$

$k$ is the normalized factor of two graph $G_N$ and $G_M$

## 4.   Experimental Result

At a first glance, we want to demonstrate the possibility of using our graph-based model for generic object recognition. Our second goal is testing for the robust of our model with some kind of perturbation in object query image (i.e. translation, orientation change, scale change and illumination change).

Figure 7 shows the images used in our experimental taken by a digital camera and size normalized to 300x300 pixels. The fist line contains of 8 model images which correspond with 6 object classes: 2 screwdrivers, 1 scissor, 1 stapler, 1 eraser, 2 keys and 1 razor. The second line shows 28 query images used for testing our graph model. For each of eight object models, we had about 3-4 different example queries, slightly varying in scale (about 15%-30% original size), orientation (from 30° to 180°) and illumination.

The Figure 8 shows the results in matching of two screwdrivers. The query screwdriver had rotated $45^0$ from the original model. Ridges and peaks are detected at 9 scales (i.e. from scale $\sigma_2 = 2\sqrt{2}$ to scale $\sigma_{10} = 10\sqrt{2}$ ). We visualize our graph in the 3D environment in which the violet nodes represent the matched nodes of two graphs by using our matching algorithm. We found that nodes corresponding to the main ridges are well matched with a very small dissimilarity. For other nodes we fixed a threshold value (i.e. 1.2 in our experimentation) on the dissimilarity to keep the best correspondence between two nodes.

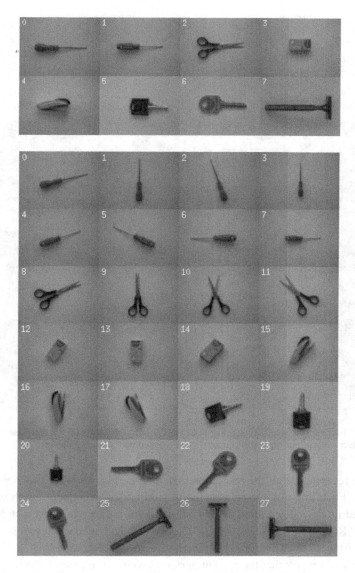

Figure 7. Image datasets used in our experimentation. First line: model object images, second line: query object images.

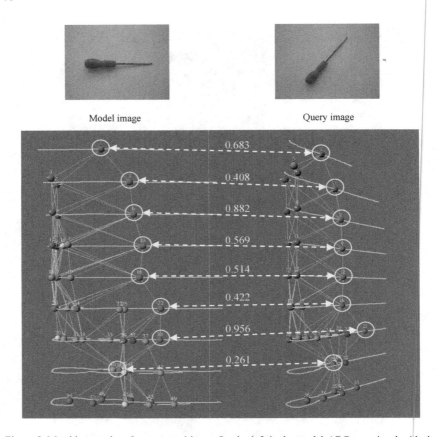

Model image                                  Query image

Figure 8. Matching results of two screwdrivers. On the left is the model ARG associated with the model object while on the right is the query ARG associated with the query object.

We recapitulate all the results on matching 28 queries with 8 models in the Table 1. Each line of table reflects the dissimilarity of the query graph with the 8 labeled models. The values on the column **Min** indicate the best match of the model ARGs with the query ARGs. Our system had successful recognized 26 object instances over 28 trials, yielding a 93% recognition rate.

We also remark that the system performs well in the case of changing intra-configuration of the object such as the scissor. This can be explained by the invariant properties of the configuration of the graph-based model. This yield an idea about using the graph-based model to represent deformable objects (such as human tracking). Rather, we are simply demonstrating that our ARG model is applicable to a variety of domains and under a variety of image conditions.

Table 1. Results of the matching the queries object **I** with the models object **M**. The values **Min** indicate the best match of the model with query.

| I \ M | 0 | 1 | 2 | 3 | 4 | 5 | 6 | 7 | Min |
|---|---|---|---|---|---|---|---|---|---|
| 0 | 0,552 | 2,691 | 1,277 | 17,308 | 1,52 | 2,95 | 1,694 | 2,948 | 0,552 |
| 1 | 0,901 | 3,54 | 1,28 | 14,177 | 1,255 | 8,093 | 2,623 | 2,817 | 0,901 |
| 2 | 0,635 | 1,88 | 0,943 | 13,269 | 1,838 | 6,788 | 1,398 | 2,586 | 0,635 |
| 3 | 1,888 | 1,192 | 34,981 | 2,885 | 2,042 | 29,551 | 39,093 | 44,117 | 1,192 |
| 4 | 10,668 | 0,906 | 61,802 | 5,493 | 2,292 | 2,875 | 69,968 | 78,001 | 0,906 |
| 5 | 64,464 | 0,633 | 2,989 | 1,289 | 2,52 | 2,122 | 66,779 | 77,36 | 0,633 |
| 6 | 8,998 | 0,548 | 3,671 | 1,908 | 2,12 | 2,983 | 59,457 | 70,815 | 0,548 |
| 7 | 76,49 | 0,792 | 4,76 | 1,604 | 68,102 | 2,824 | 58,65 | 71,904 | 0,792 |
| 8 | 8,073 | 7,127 | 1,544 | 7,747 | 1,779 | 4,422 | 2,308 | 5,31 | 1,544 |
| 9 | 2,641 | 4,943 | 1,031 | 5,935 | 2,975 | 3,572 | 1,685 | 3,492 | 1,031 |
| 10 | 7,652 | 7,965 | 2,941 | 38,464 | 3,992 | 32,707 | 4,11 | 33,161 | 2,941 |
| 11 | 25,351 | 32,856 | 2,595 | 37,96 | 10,245 | 34,126 | 4,487 | 27,687 | 2,595 |
| 12 | 115,16 | 3,341 | 6,307 | 2,214 | 103,48 | 3,436 | 92,27 | 116,83 | 2,214 |
| 13 | 92,129 | 1,886 | 71,194 | 0,524 | 84,016 | 2,51 | 6,294 | 96,597 | 0,524 |
| 14 | 11,019 | 8,384 | 4,029 | 3,91 | 6,682 | 1,779 | 2,305 | 39,045 | 1,779 |
| 15 | 12,943 | 32,663 | 13,372 | 39,381 | 3,624 | 34,919 | 22,249 | 29,211 | 3,624 |
| 16 | 1,08 | 18,925 | 1,697 | 23,988 | 0,674 | 20,353 | 2,142 | 6,479 | 0,674 |
| 17 | 8,805 | 1,631 | 1,252 | 24,841 | 1,161 | 2,809 | 1,792 | 3,629 | 1,161 |
| 18 | 81,546 | 2,331 | 6,559 | 1,916 | 73,316 | 1,065 | 4,355 | 87,085 | 1,065 |
| 19 | 89,787 | 2,884 | 13,071 | 2,323 | 81,778 | 0,546 | 5,237 | 98,765 | 0,546 |
| 20 | 120,47 | 26,751 | 96,885 | 1,534 | 112,36 | 1,498 | 91,832 | 126,70 | 1,498 |
| 21 | 4,25 | 40,702 | 2,321 | 11,533 | 4,019 | 3,81 | 0,865 | 4,128 | 0,865 |
| 22 | 5,208 | 4,752 | 1,918 | 6,483 | 2,778 | 9,72 | 0,863 | 4,349 | 0,863 |
| 23 | 3,836 | 3,245 | 1,165 | 6,696 | 2,203 | 4,881 | 0,396 | 4,479 | 0,396 |
| 24 | 3,332 | 3,007 | 1,261 | 8,425 | 3,229 | 3,968 | 0,742 | 6,191 | 0,742 |
| 25 | 3,979 | 26,98 | 2,641 | 31,573 | 2,298 | 27,597 | 1,627 | 1,56 | 1,56 |
| 26 | 3,682 | 19,996 | 1,917 | 20,651 | 4,558 | 18,232 | 2,569 | 1,583 | 1,583 |
| 27 | 5,978 | 23,658 | 4,045 | 25,995 | 5,66 | 23,963 | 3,052 | 0,581 | 0,581 |

▢ screwdriver n°1  ▇ screwdriver n°2  ▇ scissor  ▨ eraser  ▇ stapler  ▇ key n°1  ▢ key n°2  ▇ razor

## 5. Conclusion

We have presented in this paper our approach for modeling object model at multi-scale by using an attributed relational graph. The experimental result in a small image datasets has demonstrated that the model is robust to different transformations such as spatial translation, rotation and a slightly change of scale. This is also the strong point of the symbolic features such as ridge and peak which are invariant to such transformations.

Moreover, we have proposed a matching algorithm that adapted to the ARG model. To finding the best correspondence of the query graph with the model graphs, we computed the dissimilarity between two graphs based on the measuring of geometric distance and topologic distance. Thank to symbolic constraints on feature types the matching process executes more efficiently and faster. This framework can be extended to recognize more complex image datasets that demands also for some improvement of the current algorithm.

## References

1. J.L. Crowley and A.C. Parker. "A Representation for Shape Based on Peaks and Ridges in the Difference of Low-Pass Transform", *IEEE PAMI*, pp. 156-169, 1984.
2. Y. Dufournaud, C. Schmid and R. Horaud. "Matching Image with Different Resolutions". *In CVPR*, Vol. 1, 612-618, 2000.
3. H. Tran and A. Lux. "A method for ridge extraction", *Asian Conference on Computer Vision*, 2004.
4. J. Mc Gregor. "Backtrack Search Algorithms and the Maximal Common Subgraph Problem", *Software-Practice and Experience*, pp. 23-34, 1982.
5. J. R. Ullmann. "An algorithm for subgraph isomorphism", *Journal of the ACM*, 23(1), p. 31-42, 1976.
6. T. Lindeberg. *Scale-Space Theory in Computer Vision*, Kluwer Academic Publishers, Dordrecht, 1994.
7. S.Z. Li. "Matching: invariant to translations, rotations and scale changes", *Pattern Recognition*, 583-594, 1992.
8. D. G. Lowe. "Object recognition from local scale-invariant feature". *ICCV*, pp. 1150–1157, 1999.
9. B. Messmer, H. Bunke. "Subgraph isomorphism in polynomial time", *Technical Report IAM-95-003*, University of Bern, 1995.
10. Ali Shokoufandeh, Diego Macrini, Sven J. Dickinson, Kaleem Siddiqi, Steven W. Zucker. "Indexing Hierarchical Structures Using Graph Spectral", *IEEE PAMI*, 27(7), p. 1125-1140, Jul. 2005
11. L.P. Cordella, P. Foggia, C. Sansone, F. Tortorella, M. Vento. "Graph Matching: A Fast Algorithm and its Evaluation", *in ICPR*, pp. 1582-1584, 1998.
12. T.T. Pham, *Méthode de mise en correspondance hiérarchique en reconnaissance d'objets*, Master's Thesis, Institut National Polytechnique de Grenoble, 2005.

# CHAPTER 7

# IMAGE RETRIEVAL BASED ON VISUAL INFORMATION CONCEPTS AND AUTOMATIC IMAGE ANNOTATION

QUOC NGOC LY, ANH DUC DUONG
THACH THAO DUONG, DUC THANH NGO

*Vietnam National University-Ho Chi Minh City, 227 Nguyen Van Cu Street, 5 District*
*Ho Chi Minh City, Vietnam*

Nowadays, we are living in the content-based image retrieval (CBIR) age. The users would like to give the semantic queries, but the semantic understanding of images remains an important research challenge for the image and video retrieval community. We have approached the CBIR at semantics level by using visual information concepts (VIC) and automatic image annotation (AIA). We have linked the semantic concepts to the image at two levels, the common level and the private level. In the common level, we used the VIC and linking automatically VIC to image data based on the priori knowledge. In the private level, we performed the AIA based on the cross-media relevance model with some improvements. The content image retrieval process is based on the comparison of the intermediate descriptor values in VIC associated with both the semantic data and the image data. Irrelevant images are rejected and the remaining images are ranked by AIA. Our experiment results have shown that the performance of our system is better in the meanings of precision and recall than the traditional systems only based query images or only based on VIC or AIA.

## 1. Introduction

Visual perception is the power of the human in understanding a scene and describing it by language. While the human perform visual perception effortlessly and robustly, visual perception is still a major challenge for digital vision systems. Unfortunately, the human don't know the principle of their visual perception, so they only can invent the mechanisms to be close to the results and the performance of human vision. When using the content-based image retrieval system (CBIR system), human beings always wish for easily representing contents that they would like to retrieve.

Each image has two main kinds of information : visual information and semantic information, for example, an image of an apple has visual information as red color and semantic information as an apple. So our CBIR system based on the visual information concepts (VIC) and automatic image annotation (AIA) to retrieve images. Nowadays, an interesting advance to define knowledge in a computer vision is to use the visual information concepts. VIC are the set of the concepts of visual information as color, textures, shape, spatial relations, motion,... VIC are important because we can use them to describe the objects as retrieve the images, they are the shared conceptualizations.

VIC are widely used in the research field of CBIR with the name as Object Ontology [16] or Visual Concept Ontology [3]. We used VIC at the intermediate level : between the low level visual features and the semantic concepts the user queries for. We don't use the term Ontology because we only use the VIC, we don't use the relations between them.

Our approach involves the building VIC consisting of color concepts, texture concepts, and shape concepts. These VIC are application independent. These VIC are built based on some existing Object Ontology (OO) [16] or Visual Concept Ontology (VCO) [13] with some improvements . After that, we link automatically the VIC to the images data by images segmentation and regions clustering process. In this paper, our aim is to propose a shared knowledge representation of image contents at a higher level than low level image features and not dependent of an application domain.

The concept is inspired by the nature of information processing in the brain which is modular, from coarse to fine. So our strategy in retrieval is to see the forest before the tree. VIC are used in first to gather the candidate images close to the VIC of query, and after that they can be filtered by AIA to gather the resulting images close to the semantic concepts of query.

This paper is structured as following. In section 2, we review related works. In section 3, we represent image retrieval based on VIC. In section 4, we introduce automatic image annotation. In section 5, we combine VIC and AIA for image retrieval. In section 6, we show some results from our experiments. We conclude in section 7.

## 2. Related Works

In [9], querying is based on a logical composition of regions templates with the goal to reach a higher semantic level. The user doesn't have a whole image but can select some blobs appropriate to the mental image. This approach is at an intermediate semantic level.

In [16], the authors propose an Object Ontology which is a set of qualitative description of the semantic concepts the user queries for. Low level arithmetic descriptors extracted from images are automatically associated with these intermediate qualitative descriptors. The content image retrieval process is based on the comparison of the intermediate descriptor values associated with both the semantic concept and the image regions. Irrelevant regions are rejected and the remaining regions are ranked according a relevance feedback mechanism based on support vector machines.

In [3,10], the authors have represented the VCO consisting of color concepts, texture concepts and spatial concepts. The color concepts based on the ISCC-NBS color dictionary, the texture concepts are inspired from the results from two experiments led by the cognitive science community and two approaches to linking the VCO to image data : a machine learning approach and an a priori knowledge based approach.

In [12], deals with the problem to model the correspondence between global keywords and image regions using statistical machine translation but it does not explicitly treat semantics as image classes and, therefore, provides little guarantees that the semantic annotations are optimal in a recognition or retrieval sense.

In [7], the authors use the cross-media relevance model to automatic image annotation and retrieval; they assume that the image annotation problem can be viewed as analogous to the cross-lingual retrieval problem. The advantage of these semi-supervised approaches is that they require comparably few training examples for the annotation of large amounts of image data and the performance with respect to precision, recall and accuracy of these methods is higher than the former for effective use in image retrieval system.

In this paper, our aim is to propose a shared knowledge representation of image contents at a higher level than low level image features and not dependent of an application domain, and knowledge is extracted from the images at a higher details based on automatic image annotation. So we can retrieve the image at semantic level based on two phases, the first phase is used to retrieve the image having the VIC as the query at the coarse level, this phase has a function as pre-processing step. And the final phase, we filtered the results at the finer level by automatic image annotation.

## 3.  Image Retrieval based on Visual Information Concepts

### 3.1.  *Visual Information Concepts*

VIC, as a common vocabulary, enables the communication between the intermediate visual level and the semantic level. These VIC are used to visually describe semantic concepts. Linking VIC to image data problem consists in making the link between the visual concept and the low-level visual features. To build this link, we used an a priori knowledge based approach [3] and the techniques for automatically image segmentation and regions clustering as described in [13].

With VIC, we can link the intermediate qualitative description with the semantic concepts the user queries for and with Linking VIC to image data, we can link the intermediate qualitative descriptors with the low-level visual features. So we can fill in the semantic gap between the semantic level and the image level.

Our VIC consisted of three parts : color concepts, texture concepts and shape concepts because the color features, texture features and shape features are the standard features of images. These VIC are application independent.

Color concepts are based on experiments performed by the cognitive science community on the visual perception of color by humans. In [10], based on the ISCC-NBS lexicon, the authors uses English terms to describe colors in HSV color model with 28 hue's terms, 3 saturation's terms and 5 lightness's terms. And we use the color naming for retrieving images with 10 hue's terms, 3 saturation's terms and 5 lightness's terms as following :

$$Color \rightarrow \begin{cases} Hue \\ Saturation \\ Lightness \end{cases},$$

$$Hue \rightarrow \begin{cases} Red \\ Orange \\ Yellow \\ Green \\ Cyan \\ Blue \\ Violet \\ Brown \\ Pink \\ Grey \end{cases}, Saturation \rightarrow \begin{cases} Moderate \\ Strong \\ Vivid \end{cases}, Lightness \rightarrow \begin{cases} Verydark \\ Dark \\ Medium \\ Light \\ VeryLight \end{cases}$$

We can perceive the same meanings of one image represented in color mode or grayscale mode. And we can perceive the different meanings of the two regions with the same color. What is the feature that plays the important role in this situation. Shape is an important property and carries with it a great deal of information which is essential when we want to recognize objects, distinguish between objects, describing object and manipulate them. The shape of an object can be defined as the description of the properties of its boundary (boundary-based approaches) or its interior (region based approaches). A set of terms used to describe object shapes is:

$$Shape \rightarrow \begin{Bmatrix} ObjectShape \\ Objectsize \end{Bmatrix}, \ ObjectShape \rightarrow \begin{Bmatrix} GlobalShape \\ LocalShape \end{Bmatrix}$$

$$GlobalShape \rightarrow \begin{Bmatrix} Round \\ Ellipse \\ Square \\ Rectangular \\ Triangle \\ Curve \\ Line \\ Convex \\ Concave \\ Irregular \end{Bmatrix}$$

$$LocalShape \rightarrow \{TangentSpaceRepresentation\} \ [1]$$

$$Objectsize \rightarrow \begin{Bmatrix} Small & Wide \\ Medium & Narrow \\ Large & High \\ Long & Low \\ Short \end{Bmatrix} \ [3]$$

We can perceive the different meanings of the two regions having the same color and shape features, for example the sky and the beach. What is the feature that plays the important role in this situation. Texture is an important property and carries with it a great deal of information which is essential when we want to recognize objects, distinguish between objects, describing object and manipulate them. This part of the VIC is inspired from the results from the texture features of [15]. A set of terms used to describe texture are:

$$TextureConcept \rightarrow \begin{Bmatrix} Nature \\ Sensitivity \end{Bmatrix},$$

$$Nature \rightarrow \begin{Bmatrix} Coarseness \\ Contrast \\ Directionality \\ Linelikeness \\ Regularity \\ Roughness \end{Bmatrix} \quad [15]$$

$$Sensitivity \rightarrow \begin{Bmatrix} Small \\ Medium \\ Large \end{Bmatrix}$$

These VIC can be used as a guide for the description of the user queries with no query images and manual pre-annotation.

### 3.2. *Linking VIC to Image Data*

In this paper, the main goal of Linking VIC to image data is to perform linking between the VIC to the region cluster's representatives (RC's Rep). It is very difficult (or impossible) to linking the whole semantics concepts with the image data, but linking the VIC to the RC's Rep can be performed easier. In this paper, we used an a priori knowledge based approach [3], links between low level RC's Rep visual features and VIC are built explicitly.

We divided the image into the square grid, each square grid has color features and texture features, and we clustered them into the regions by Hierarchical Agglomerative Clustering [HAC] Algorithm [13]. After this step, we have an image $I_i$ consisted of a set of regions $R_i = \{r_{ij}, j = 1..NR_i\}$.

To reduce the features from the image region database, we clustered the regions. After image segmentation, each region $r_{ij}$ has been extracted color concepts, texture concept and shape concepts. We denoted them as:

Color concepts $CC_{ij} = \{cc_{ij}(k), k = 1..N_{CC_{ij}}\}$,

Texture concepts $TC_{ij} = \{tc_{ij}(l), l = 1..N_{TC_{ij}}\}$,

Shape concepts $SC_{ij} = \{sc_{ij}(m), m = 1..N_{SC_{ij}}\}$.

We used HAC algorithm [13] (or based on VIC) to cluster the set of regions $R = \{r_{ij}, i = 1..NI, j = 1..NR_i\}$ into M clusters. We denoted them as $CLUS = \{clus_k, k = 1..M\}$, each $clus_k$ has the representative denoted as $rep_{clus_k}$. At last, we have linked the VIC to the RC's Rep. This process is performed automatically.

## 3.3. *Query by VIC*

In this paper, our main purpose is to combine Visual Information Concepts and Automatic Image Annotation to retrieve image at semantic level. Query by VIC help us to represent easily our idea in retrieving images. There are so many objects, but fortunately, they have some common VIC. We cannot approach the retrieving problem by recognizing all objects because it is impossible, but we can retrieve them easily by VIC. One important thing in query by VIC is we need not a prior query image.

Each object can be described by VIC for query. It helps us to resolve the synonym problem (one object can be represented by other visual features). For example, with the query is the rose, we can described it easily by the color concepts as red, yellow, white. If we use query image, it's difficult to find the rose image with different colors.

The resulting images shall be the images having the regions belong the clusters with the representatives's VIC close to query's VIC.

The precision in this stage is not high, but the recall is rather well. This stage has the function as the pre-processing step. This stage help us to gather the images carrying the visual information as requests but the semantics are not guaranteed yet.

## 4. Automatic Image Annotation

It's very difficult (or it's impossible) to gather the semantics of images if we just only based on low level visual features. So it's necessary to intefere by human knowledge. But it takes long times and high costs to manually annotation the entire large image database, and because it grows with a high rate, this approach has a poor performance. But if we can just only manually annotate the small training images set and after that we can automatically annotate the entire image database, it's a promising approach. Automatic image annotation (AIA) is really a supervised learning progress. At this step we intend to attach the semantics to images based on the cross-media relevance model [7] with some improvements. In the off-line step, it has four main steps as image segmentation, regions clustering, manually linking images to words and automatic linking images to words.

## 4.1. Represent Image by the Representatives

Image segmentation and region clustering are performed as represented in section 3.2. Then, we represent each image by the representatives $rep_{clus_k}$ based on the nearest neighborhood of the regions with the representatives.

## 4.2. Manual Linking Images to Words

After segmentation the image training set, based on the results of segmentation and clustering, we manually annotate the region's clusters. The images will inherit the semantics from the region's clusters. After this step, we have two sets in each image, the first set is $REP_{I_i} = \{rep_{clus_k}, k = 1..N_{REP_{I_i}}\}$ or to abbreviate $REP_{I_i} = \{rep_k, k = 1..N_{REP_{I_i}}\}$ and the second set is $W_{I_i} = \{w_l, l = 1..N_{W_{I_i}}\}$.

## 4.3. Automatic Linking Images to Words

The purpose of AIA is, with an unannotated image, select automatically the keywords of the vocabulary to describe it. The annotation based on the training set, the pre-annotated images. Our approach is inspired from the cross-media relevance models [7]. The concept of object represents one of the main types of the semantic connections between image and text.

To annotate an image $I$, the authors in [7] estimate the probability $P(w|I)$ for every word $w$ in the vocabulary. $P(w|I)$ is approximated by the co occurrence of word $w$ and the image's representatives $\{rep_k, k = 1..M\}$ :

$$P(w \mid I) \approx P(w \mid rep_1 ... rep_M) \tag{1}$$

The training set $T$ of annotated images is used to estimate the joint probability of observing the word $w$ and the representatives $rep_1 ... rep_M$ in the same image. The joint distribution can be computed as the expectation over the images in the training set $T$ [7] :

$$P(w, rep_1, ..., rep_M) = \sum_{I \in T} P(J)P(w, rep_1, ..., rep_M \mid J) \tag{2}$$

Assumed that the events of observing $w$ and $rep_1, ..., rep_M$ are mutually independent, equation (2) can be rewritten as follows:

$$P(w, rep_1, ..., rep_M) = \sum_{J \in T} P(J)P(w \mid J) \prod_{i=1}^{M} P(rep_i \mid J) \tag{3}$$

Assume that the prior probabilities $P(J)$ are uniform over all images in $T$, $P(w|J)$ and $P(rep_i|J)$ can be estimated based on smoothed maximum likelihood [7]:

$$P(w|J) = (1-\alpha)\frac{N(w,J)}{|J_w|} + \alpha\frac{N(w,T)}{|T|} \tag{4}$$

$$P(rep_i|J) = (1-\beta)\frac{N(rep_i,J)}{|J_{rep_i}|} + \beta\frac{N(rep_i,T)}{|T|} \tag{5}$$

$N(w,J)$ denotes the number of times the word $w$ occurs in image $J$,

$N(w,T)$ denotes the number of times the word $w$ occurs in the training set $T$,

$N(rep_i,J)$ denotes the number of times the representatives $rep_i$ occurs in image $J$.

$N(rep_i,T)$ denotes the number of times the representatives $rep_i$ occurs in the training set $T$.

$|J_w|$ stands for the total number of all words occur in image $J$.

$|J_{rep_i}|$ stands for the total number of representatives occur in image $J$.

$|T|$ denotes the size of the training set $T$.

$\alpha, \beta$ determine the degree of interpolation between the maximum likelihood estimates and the background probability for the words and the representatives respectively.

This method involves a linear interpolation of the maximum likelihood model with the collection model, using a coefficient $\alpha, \beta$ to control the influence of each model.

Compared with the cross-media relevance model [7], we have two improvements, we have clustered the regions based on the hierarchical model of VIC and we manually annotated the whole image after segmentation and clustering stage, the best regions were the candidates to annotate for the whole image.

## 5. Image Retrieval based on VIC and AIA

An image has two main kinds of information : visual information and semantics. We used VIC to gather the images carrying the visual information as the query and used AIA to filter the irrelevant images, the resulting images having the visual information and semantics as the query. In our system, image retrieval based on semantic level. The user can query the semantic objects using the keywords. The retrieval progress is performed through two phases. In the first phase, the semantic objects are described using the intermediate-level descriptors based on VIC. For example, a beach is described by color concepts, texture concepts, and shape concepts as:

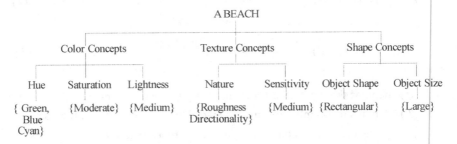

Denoted the set of candidate images having the color concepts, texture concepts and shape concepts as *CSet*, *TSet* and *SSet*. The relevance images should be:

$$RI = CSet \cap TSet \cap SSet$$

The purpose of the first phase is to exclude the images don't have the regions with relevant visual information. In this phase we don't need a query image or the annotation in the image. The candidate images can be filtered in the second phase.

In the second phase, we can use the vocabulary predefined to select more exactly the images that contain objects mentioned in the query.

Given the query $Q = w_1...w_k$, and the image $I = \{rep_1,..., rep_m\}$, the probability of drawing $Q$ from the model of $I$ is:

$$P(Q \mid I) = \prod_{j=1}^{k} p(w_j \mid I), I \in RI \quad [7].$$

It allows us to produce ranked lists of images for final results. We used this technique to replace relevance feedback technique.

The precison is low in retrieving images if it is just only based on VIC. It takes long time to retrieve images if it is just only based on AIA. Combining VIC and AIA in retrieving images, we can gather the images carrying the visual information and semantics as the query, the precision is higher, time-saving.

## 6.  Experiments

We have experimented on the image database consisted of 9560 different images in some categories as:

Natural scene: landscape, flower, fruit, animals.

Artificial scene: City, car, train, ship, plane, cloths, logo.

Man activities: Sports activities

In the off-line step, we have achieved some results as:

From 9560 images, we extracted 47820 regions and clustered them in 150 clusters for color based, 18 clusters for texture based on texture concepts, 30 clusters for shape based on shape concepts.

And manual annotated by the list of words are consisted of 395 words as :

Cloud, beach, mountain, grass ... (landscape);

Rose, sunflower, gladiolus ... (flower);

Apple, orange, durian, banana ... (fruit);

Bear, tiger, monkey... (Animals);

...

We used two values Precision and Recall to evaluate the performance of our system.

Precision = Number of relevance detected images / Total number of detected images.

Recall = Number of relevance detected images / Total number of relevance images

The average precision in query by images is about 63 percent, and the average recall is about 65 percent.

The average precision in the first phase (using VCO) is about 50 percent, and in the second phase (using AIA) is about 72 percent.

The average recall in the first phase (using VCO) is about 73 percent, and in the second phase (using AIA) is about 70 percent.

The experiments showed that this approach can narrow the gap between the low-level features and the semantics of images. With our retrieval system, we can query close to human thinking.

## 7.  Conclusions

We have approached the content-based image retrieval at semantics level by using the visual information concepts and automatic image annotation to fill in the gap between low-level features and semantics of images. In our system, the users can easily represent their ideas in retrieving. Their ideas can be represented by query text and some visual concepts of human. So we can retrieve the images at the semantic level based on two phases, the first phase is used to retrieve the image having the visual concept as the query at the coarse level, this phase has a function as pre-processing step, and the final phase we filtered the results at the finer level by automatic image annotation.

We have represented our efficient and user-friendly image retrieval system; this system is a part of our system named VIROS (Visual Information Retrieval of Saigon). In the future, we shall develop our system to the image retrieval system with the abstract query.

## References

1. Alberto Chavez-Aragon, Oleg Starostenko. *Image Retrieval by Ontological Description of Shapes (IRONS), Early Results.* Proceedings of the First Canadian Conference on Computer and Robot Vision (CRV'04)
2. Al Bovik, *Handbook of Image and Video Processing,* Academic Press, (2000).
3. C.Hudelot, N.Maillot, M.Thonnat. *Symbol Grounding for Semantic Image Interpretation : From Image Data to Semantics.* International Workshop on Semantic Knowledge in Computer Vision (in association with ICCV 2005), Beijing, 16 October 2005)
4. D.Bimbo, *Visual Information Retrieval,* Morgan Kaufmann, (1999).
5. G.Sheikholeslami, W.Chang, A.Zhang *"SemQuery : Semantic Clustering and Querying on Heterogeneous features for Visual data"* in IEEE Trans. Knowledge and Data Engineering vol. 14, no.5: IEEE, pp. 988-1002, (2002).
6. I. Kompatsiaris, E. Triantafillou, M.G. Strintzis, *"Region-based color image indexing and retrieval"* in IEEE International Conference on Image Processing (ICIC'01): IEEE, (2001).
7. Jeon, V.Lavrenko, R.Mammatha, *"Automatic Image Annotation and Retrieval using Cross-Media Relevance Models"* in SIGIR '03: ACM, (2003).
8. N.Bhushan,A.R.Rao,and G.L.Lohse. *The texture lexicon : Understanding the categorization of visual texture terms and their relationship to texture images. Cognitive Science,* 21(2):219-246, 1997
9. N. Boujemaa, J.Fauqueur, et V. Gouet, *"What's beyond query by example? to appear in Trends and Advances in Content-Based Image and Video Retrieval"* in LNCS, Springer Verlag, (2004).
10. N.Maillot, M. Thonnat, A. Boucher. *Towards Ontology Based Cognitive Vision (Long Version).* Machine Vision and Applications (MVA), Springer-VerlagHeidelberg, December 2004, 16(1), pp 33–40.

11. P.Salembier, F.Marques, *"Region-based representations of image and video : Segmentation tools for multimedia services"* in IEEE Trans. On Circuits and Systems for Video Technology, vol.9, no.8: IEEE, December (1999).

12. Pinar Duygulu,Kobus Barnard, Nando de Freitas, David Forsyth, *"Object Recognition as Machine Translation : Learning a lexicon for a fixed image vocabulary"* in Europe Conference on Computer Vision (ECCV) Copenhagen, (2002)

13. Quoc Ngoc Ly, Anh Duc Duong, *"Hierarchical Data Model in Content-based Image Retrieval"* in International Journal of Information Technology, International Conference on Intelligent Computing (ICIC2005), (2005).

14. Rafael C. Gonzalez, Richard E.Woods, *Digital Image Processing Second Edition,* Prentice-Hall Inc., (2002).

15. Tamura, H., Mori, S., Yamawaki, T.: *Textural features corresponding to visual perception.* IEEE Trans on Systems, Man and Cybernetics 8 (1978) 460-472.

16. Vasileios Mezaris, Ioannis Kompatsiaris, and Michael G. Strintzis, *"Region-based Image Retrieval using an Object Ontology and Relevance Feedback"* in Eurasip Journal on applied signal processing, vol. 2004, No. 6, pp. 886-901, June (2004).

## CHAPTER 8

## MULTIMODAL INTERACTIONS FOR MULTIMEDIA CONTENT ANALYSIS

T. MARTIN[1,2]*, A. BOUCHER[3,1] and J.-M. OGIER[2]

[1]*MICA Center*
*C10, Truong Dai Hoc Bach Khoa*
*1 Dai Co Viet*
*Hanoi, Vietnam*
*thomas.martin@mica.edu.vn*

[2]*L3i - Univ. of La Rochelle*
*17042 La Rochelle cedex 1*
*La Rochelle, France*
*alain.boucher@auf.org*

[3]*IFI*
*ngo 42 Ta Quan Buu*
*Hanoi, Vietnam*
*jean-marc.ogier@univ-lr.fr*

In this paper, we are presenting a model for multimodal content analysis. We are distinguishing between media and modality, which helps us to define and to characterize 3 inter-modal relations. Then we are applying this model for recorded course analysis for e-learning. Different useful relations between modalities are explained and detailed for this application. We are also describing on two other applications: telemonitoring and minute meetings. Then we compare the use of multimodality in these applications with existing inter-modal relations.

## 1. Introduction

Nowadays, as the available multimedia content grows every day, the need for automatic content analysis is becoming increasingly important. For example, information retrieval in broadcast news archives requires to index different medias available. Many projects currently focus on these research topics (content analysis, media enrichment...) but most of these works are

---

*Funded by French Ministry of Foreign Affairs.

focused on one sole media, and are unaware of other medias. Because information is not concentrated in one media but distributed among all the medias, such approaches are losing important parts of this information and ignore media interactions. Recently, many research works [1] have focused on the use of multiple modalities to increase the potentiality of analysis. However, to our knowledge, there is no existing framework for multimodal analysis, and there is only few serious analysis of the possibilities of interaction between modalities. In this paper, we propose a first attempt to develop such a framework.

In the next section, we will give some definitions, followed by a review of the existing literature in multimodal analysis. Then we will present our model. After that, we will analyze some applications, to enhance and describe the possible interactions that can exist between modalities in different situations. We will conclude with a discussion on inter-modal relations.

## 2. Multimodality

There is often a confusion in the literature between the concept of media and the concept of modality. In many papers, the authors use both words refering to the same concept. This does not seems to be exact as we can see the two different concepts in the context of content analysis. We propose to define a modality as a refinement of the media concept. A media is characterized mostly by its nature (for example audio, video, text), while a modality is characterized by both its nature and the physical structure of the provided information (for example video text *vs* motion). One media can then be divided in multiple modalities, following two criteria: the semantic structuration of the information and the algorithms involved in the analysis process. While the concept of media is independant from the application, the concept of modality is application dependant.

As proposed in [2] we will use generic modalities listed in three main families. First, the audio family includes different modalities in terms of structuration like speech, music or sound. Second, we distinguish between still image and motion (video) in visual family. While both being acquired from a camera, motion contains time structuration and is more rich in term of content than still image. Third, the text family includes printed text and handwritten text.

This split of media into modalities can surely be discussed and different organization can be proposed. We will use this scheme through this paper using several examples taken from some applications to illustrate our choice.

We insist on the fact that the information contained in each modality has a different structuration, regarding the algorithms that can be used, the difficulty for content extraction and for the semantic that can be given to it.

Once modality is defined, the next step is to define multimodality. In video indexing context, Snoek and Worring [1] have proposed to define multimodality from the author's point of view: it is "the capacity of an author of the video document to express a semantic idea, by combining a layout with a specific content, using at least two information channels". The inter-modal relation is then located at a high level using semantic. On the contrary, in the context of speech recognition, Zhi *et al.* [3] have implemented the multimodal integration just after the feature extraction phase and an alignment step. In this case, multimodal integration takes place at low level. Both these definitions are incomplete. Furthermore, several multimodal applications found in the literature use two modalities, audio and video, and the multimodal part of these application is often limited to a fusion step. Examples of such works include applications for video indexing such as [4] where a high level fusion step is processed after speaker segmentation in audio and shot detection in video. Shao *et al.* [5] process a multimodal summarizing of musical video using both audio and video contents. In the same domain, Zhu *et al.* [6] is performing video text extraction and lyrics structure analysis in karaoke contents using multimodal approaches. Song *et al.* [7] is recognizing emotions using a fusion step just after feature extraction in audio and video. Zhu and Zhou [8] are combining audio and video analysis for scene change detection. They have classified audio shots into semantic types and process shot detection in video They integrate then these results to have robust detection. Murai *et al.* [9] and Zhi *et al.* [3] are using facial analysis (video) to improve speech recognition (audio). [9] is detecting shots in video containing speech whereas [3] is combining lip movements and audio features to process speech recognition. Zotkin *et al.* [10] is proposing a tracking method based on multiple cameras and a microphone array. Bigün *et al.* [11] is proposing a scheme for multimodal biometric authentication using three modalities: fingerprint, face and speech. Fusion is processed after individual modality recognition.

We propose a more general definition for multimodality as an interaction process between two or more modalities. This process is based on an inter-modal relation. We have identified three different types of inter-modal relations [2]: trigger, integration and collaboration. The trigger relation (see *fig.* 1) is the most simple relation: an event detected in one modality activates an analysis process to start in another modality. The integration relation (see *fig.* 2) is already widely used and is mainly characterized by its interaction level. The analysis processes are done separately for each modality, but followed by a process of integration (fusion or others) of their results. Look at [1] for a review of existing works using widely the integration relation for the application of multimodal video indexing. The third relation is collaboration, and (see *fig.* 3). it is the strongest multimodal relation, consisting in a close interaction of two modalities during the anal-

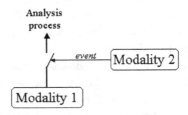

Figure 1. In the trigger relation, the analysis process for one modality is activated with an event detected in another modality.

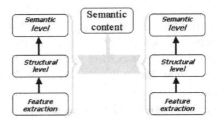

Figure 2. The integration relation provides higher level information combining two or more modalities. The integration can be done at different levels.

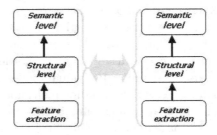

Figure 3. The collaboration relation improves the analysis process for one modality using the results another one. This relation can be bidirectionnal.

ysis process itself. The results of the analysis of one modality are used for analyzing a second one.

## 3. Video Analysis for E-Learning

Our main application for multimodality is e-learning through the MARVEL project. The goal of MARVEL (Multimodal Analysis of Recorded Video for E-Learning) is the production of tools and techniques for multimedia documents oriented for e-learning. The complete course of a professor is recorded in live. Furthermore, textual sources such as course slides may be available. The recorded material from live courses is analyzed and used to produce interactive e-courses. This can be seen as an application of video analysis to produce rich media content. The slides used by the professor in the class can be automatically replaced by an appropriate file in the e-course, being synchronized with the professor explanations. The course given by the professor is indexed using various markers, from speech, text or image analysis. The main aim of this project consists in providing semi-automatic tools to produce e-learning courses from recorded live normal courses.

In this project, three different medias are available: audio, video and lecture material (essentially the slides). Following the model proposed in section 2, we have identified five different modalities: *printed text* which contains the text of the slides and, if available, from other external textual sources. This modality is present in both video and lecture material media; *handwritten text* which represents the text written on the whiteboard; *graphics* which include all the graphics and images present in the slides. *motion* which contains the motion content of the video media; *speech* which contains the teacher's explanations. To simplify the explanations in this paper, we will not take into account the *graphic* modality and we consider only the textual parts of the slides. We are making a difference between *handwritten text* and *printed text* for two reasons. First, as presented in section 2, the nature of both modalities is different (handwritten text *vs* printed text). The second reason is specific to this application: the two modalities do not contain the same data. Even if the contents of both modalities are related to the course, one (*printed text* is more structured than the other. The *printed text* modality is avalaible in two different medias: video and text. It is a good example to illustrate our distinction between media and modality (section 2). Even if it is available into two different medias, the *printed text* still contains the same information, with the same structuration. Once detected and extracted from the video media, the analysis processes involved are similar whatever the media.

The application is divided into two distinct parts: scenario extraction and content indexing. The scenario is given mainly by the video. The teacher's behavior (see *fig.* 4) is analyzed to extract the course scenario (explaining the current slide, writing on whiteboard, talking to the class, ...). This will be used later as a layout during the e-course production. Other regions of interest such as the screen or the whiteboard are detected. Detection of slide changes or new writing on the whiteboard are events that will be used. The content indexing of available media has to be done using the speech given by the teacher, the printed text on the slides and the handwritten text on the whiteboard. These three sources are complementary to show all the content of the course. Different inter-modal interactions are identified here.

During the first part of the application (scenario extraction), 3 trigger relations (see *fig.* 5) are involved.

These relations are directly related to the actors who interact in a course: teacher, whiteboard and screen. The trigger source is the *motion* modality. First, the "slide transition" event triggers the *printed text* detection and recognition. Second, the "teacher points at screen" event triggers the

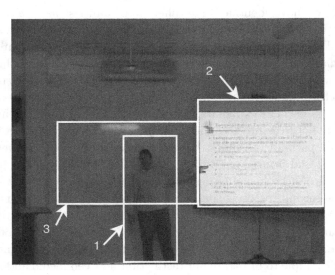

Figure 4.    Frame extracted from a recorded course. White shapes highlight identified actors of the application: the teacher (1), the screen (2) and the whiteboard (3).

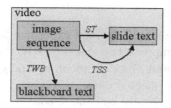

Figure 5. Scenario extraction. The event detection in the *image sequence* triggers differents analysis process in both *printed text* and *manuscript text*. Events involved are "Teacher Points at Screen" (TPS), "Teacher Writes on Whiteboard" (TWB) and "Slide Transition" (ST).

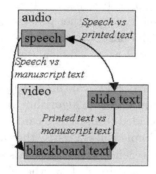

Figure 6. Content indexing. Three modalities are callaborating in the MARVEL application: *speech*, *printed text* and *manuscript text*.

point of interest search. Third, similar to the first, the "teacher writes on whiteboard" event triggers the *handwritten text* recognition process.

The second part of the application (content indexing) contains most of the inter-modal relations (see *fig.* 6). First, the *speech-printed text* interaction. This is a bimodal and bidirectional collaboration interaction, with its main direction from *speech* to *printed text*. This is particularly true if the *printed text* modality is only available in the video media. In case of noisy environment, cross-recognition of both *speech* and *printed text* is possible and useful. In this case, *motion-speech* interaction can be also useful [3,9]. Recognition of *handwritten text* is a difficult task, especially in video. We propose to help recognition of *handwritten text* using both *speech* and *printed text* modalities. Both relations, *speech-handwritten text* and *speech-printed text*, are bimodal and unidirectional.

## 4. Experiments

Our model has to be validated through experiments on real material. The experiment protocol comprises two steps. Firstly, the recording of a course according to a beforehand given protocol; secondly, the analysis through several experiments on collected data.

We have defined a protocol to control course recording. Two cameras are used in order to have both a large view on the scene and a close view on the screen (slides) and the whiteboard zones. The complete acquisition schema is presented in *fig.* 7. The first camera records a fixed large view of the lecture and give access to the general course of the lecture such as teacher behavior, while the second records a close view of both the screen (see *fig.* 8) and the whiteboard (see *fig.* 9) alternatively, providing lecture content with sufficient quality for further processing.

With regard to the audio part, we use a high-frequency microphone for recording the teacher as well as an ambient microphone for the students (see *fig.* 7).

As we just want to have video captures of the screen and the white-board, an efficient real time tracking algorithm is not necessary to control the camera. We rather decided to move the camera focus from one zone to the other following two simple rules. Firstly, the camera switches from the screen to the board if the teacher writes or points something on the white-board. Secondly, the camera switches from the whiteboard to the screen if

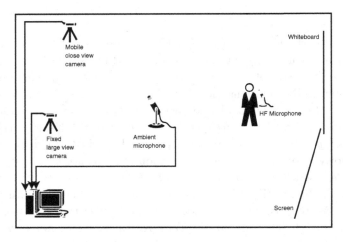

Figure 7. The teacher gives the lecture. Two cameras and two microphones record it.

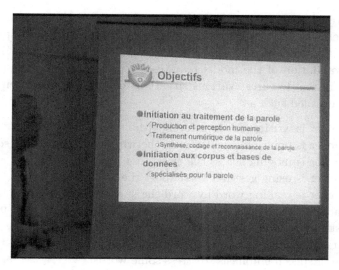

Figure 8. Screen view extracted from mobile camera record. A close view of the screen is needed to match it with lecture material and also try to identify parts of the slide the teacher is pointing.

Figure 9. Whiteboard view extracted from mobile camera record. A close view of the whiteboard is usefull for further handwritten text recognition.

a slide transition occurs or if the teacher points something at the screen. These events can be detected in the large view using relatively simple image processing techniques.

The validation of the model requires a representative set of situations occuring in real lectures. Various situations of interest have been defined and are recorded such as:

- the teacher is writing on the whiteboard;
- the teacher is pointing something at the whiteboard or on the screen;
- the teacher is moving across the classroom;
- the teacher is using gestures to support the speech;
- the teacher is reading word by word the shown slide;
- the teacher is explaining orally the content of the slide without using the same structure (word ordering);
- teacher-student interactions (such as question/answer session;
- the use of speech emphasis to stress some words;
- the use of demonstrative expressions to indicate a figure or a zone on the screen or the whiteboard;
- the use of the slide words in the oral speech;
- the use of synonymous words than the slide words in the oral speech.

From all the collected data, we are currently analysing different interactions in order to validate our model.

We are currently mainly focusing on the *printed text-speech* relation. After a recognition step, we are performing multiple experiments such as:

- temporally link the words in both modalities
- follow the speech on the slide text, like a karaoke.

This has to be done to measure the relation between *printed text* and *speech*. As second step, we will attempt to introduce the result of the *printed text* recognition in the speech recognition process and reciprocally. As both recognition processes make use of language models, we plan to achieve the collaboration between both modalities at this level.

The validation of the trigger relation will be done by implementing the tracking method presented above to switch between the screen and the whiteboard with the close camera. In a further step, other interactions will be studied, such as focusing on the words pointed by the teacher for the language model (for speech recognition).

## 5. Other Applications

We plan to apply our model to a few other applications. One application, like MARVEL, cannot contain all possible inter-modal interactions. Then we are interested at two other different applications. First, medical tele-monitoring aims, by transforming home in a smart environment, to allow elderly or ill people to keep autonomy in their life, thus to live at home. A fast detection of emergency situations allows a fast intervention of medical staff. Due to the variety of sensors – video cameras, microphones, local-ization sensors, specific medical equipments (such as electrocardiogram) in such application – used in a smart environment, the telemonitoring ap-plication is multimodal: *Motion* contains all the video information; *Sound* contains all the audio information; separation between speech and other audio information is useless in this application. *Sensors* modality gather the available signals (motion sensors, ECG,...). These three modalities are respectively parts of the video, the audio and the signal media. Due to the nature of this application, we are paying attention to only one person, the monitored person. This person is evolving in a smart environment, going from one room to another and doing tasks. Sometimes, the person can be in a crisis situation. To detect this situation, the telemonitoring system needs to detect abnormal behavior. However, detection is not sufficient: a behav-ior understanding process is necessary to identify real emergency situations through false alarms. Audio-video monitoring can be used for behavior un-derstanding, by scenario extraction. This scenario extraction is the result of an integration relation between both *sound* and *motion* modalities. This step is preceded by a bidirectionnal collaboration relation between these two modalities. In fact, video elements can help sound recognition and re-sults of this sound recognition can also help video recognition. The other available sensors can also be involved in audio-video scenario extraction. For example, localization sensors can provide usefull information for audio-video recognition. The second interesting application is for minute meetings, which consist in producing automatic multimedia minutes of meetings, us-ing audio-video records. This application is similar to MARVEL project (for e-learning, see section 3). The main difference relies in the number of people. In MARVEL, the focus in only on the teacher, while for minute meetings, every person appearing in the audio-video streams is important. Modality relations are the same than in the MARVEL application, except for one more relation added between *speech* and *motion*. As one person is speaking, we can detect lip movements on video. Then, lip movements can help speaker segmentation in the speech modality. Generally, a meeting schedule is available, more or less detailed. This program is directly related to the audio-video content recorded during the meeting, and represent a first draft of scenario. The course of the meeting follows this schedule more or less accurately.

## 6. Conclusion

In this paper, we have analyzed multimodality and identified three different types of relations between the modalities. The first relation is trigger. This relation needs synchronized modalities. The second relation is integration. This relation needs data with a same structuration level as input. In fact, this relation takes the analysis results of two or more modalities to provide higher level information. The third relation is collaboration. This relation cannot be used between all the modalities but is really useful in case of modalities with different structurations. For example, speech recognition can help text recognition in video but the opposite is not obvious, except maybe for noisy environment. In that case, where the speech recognition rates quickly decrease, the use of video can improve recognition. Another point regarding the relations between modalities is that they are not exclusive. There can be a collaboration relation between two modalities followed by an integration relation. Collaboration will improve content extraction from the separate modalities whereas integration will process a fusion of these results. For example, in the e-learning application, speech recognition results will be used to improve the text recognition process and, after that, results of both processes will be integrated for indexing purpose. We

| relation | application | | |
|---|---|---|---|
| | MARVEL | MT | MM |
| speech/printed text | ci | | ci |
| speech/handwritten text | ci | | |
| sound/motion | | ci | |
| speech/motion | | | c |
| printed text/motion | t | | ct |
| handwritten text/motion | t | | |
| sensors/sound | | c | |
| sensors/motion | | c | |

Figure 10.   This table summarizes the different inter-modal relations identified in each application. MT stands for "medical telemonitoring" and MM for "minute meeting"; 'c', 'i' and 't' stand respectively for collaboration, integration and trigger relations.

have applied this model to three different applications: e-learning, medical telemonitoring and minute meeting (see *fig.* 10). Relations are application dependant but some relations are common to several applications. We are currently experimenting these relations on real material to validate and improve our model. We particularly focus on collaboration relations to show the utility of this relation.

## References

1. C. G. M. Snoek and M. Worring, *Multimedia Tools and Applications* **25**, 5 (2005).
2. T. Martin, A. Boucher and J.-M. Ogier, Multimodal analysis of recorded video for e-learning, in *Proc. of the 13th ACM Multimedia Conference*, (ACM Press, 2005).
3. Q. Zhi, M. Kaynak, K. Sengupta, A. D. Cheok and C. C. Ko, Hmm modeling for audio-visual speech recognition, in *Proc. of ICME*, (IEEE Computer Society, 2001).
4. S. Tsekeridou and I. Pitas, Audio-visual content analysis for content-based video indexing, in *Proc. of ICMCS*, 1999.
5. X. Shao, C. Xu and M. S. Kankanhalli, Automatically generating summaries for musical video., in *Proc. of ICIP*, 2003.
6. Y. Zhu, K. Chen and Q. Sun, Multimodal content-based structure analysis of karaoke music., in *Proc. of the 13th ACM Multimedia Conference*, (ACM Press, 2005).
7. M. Song, J. Bu, C. Chen and N. Li, Audio-visual based emotion recognition - a new approach, in *Proc. of CVPR*, 2004.
8. Y. Zhu and D. Zhou, Scene change detection based on audio and video content analysis, in *Proc. of ICCIMA*, 2003.
9. K. Murai, K. Kumatani and S. Nakamura, Speech detection by facial image for multimodal speech recognition, in *Proc. of ICME*, (IEEE Computer Society, 2001).
10. D. Zotkin, R. Duraiswami and L. S. Davis, Multimodal 3-d tracking and event detection via the particle filter, in *Proc. of Event*, 2001.
11. J. Bigün, J. Fiérrez-Aguilar, J. Ortega-Garcia and J. Gonzalez-Rodriguez, Multimodal biometric authentication using quality signals in mobile communications, in *Proc. of ICIAP*, 2003.

# CHAPTER 9

# REPRESENT THE CURVED FEATURES OF AN IMAGE DATA BASED ON WAVELET PACKET AND PRIME RIDGELET TRANSFORM

NGO QUOC VIET, TRAN THI LE, NGUYEN DINH THUC

*Vietnam National University - Natural Science University of HCM City,*
*227 Nguyen Van Cu, D.5, HCMC.*

This paper presents the method of multi-resolution analysis used in 2D image data to extract the curved edge features. The method is based on the combination of multi-resolution decomposition through Wavelet Packet and Prime Ridgelet transform. We call this combination Prime Wavelet Packet Contourlet Transform-PWPC. At each leave of Packet Wavelet Packet Tree, the prime ridgelet transform is applied on the band pass image or packet, which contains the high frequency data. The experiment shows that the PWPC coefficients are good approximations to curved edges. The speed of PWPC is faster than that of the basic Curvelet transform. This transform is very suitable to represent the noisy curved features that often exist in medicine or nano/micro images.

*Keywords*: wavelet packet, directional filter, curvelet, ridgelet, contourlet, multi-scale.

## 1. Introduction

In image processing applications, detection of curved features is very important. Normally, nano or biomedicine images are in bad quality due to some problems such as very noise, unclear, etc, so the methods of classical image segmentation (Canny, Sobel, Robert, etc) cannot work well in these ones. Some articles have used multi-scale analysis methods based on wavelet transform to detect zero-crossing points [1]. Although, in 1-D data multi-scale decomposition with wavelet transform is very effective in many practice applications. However, the wavelet coefficients do not show the relationships of the singularities along the orientation edge, or the specific line equation. Therefore, it is difficult to use wavelet coefficients to represent curved features in an image. It is necessary to build up the anisotropic transform in multi-scale analysis. In this study, we suggest the image decomposition based on math transformations. This transform must satisfy some criteria: multi-scale, localization, anisotropic, perfect reconstruction.

Candes introduced ridgelet transform in 1999 [2] to represent the linear features in an image. However, problem of Ridgelet transform is only suitable for global linear features of the image. That means, the ridgelet coefficients only "see" the singularities on the line. Meanwhile, the curvelet-based transforms can represent the curved features with localization and anisotropic properties. These methods use few coefficients to represent curves. In wavelet transform, the decomposition only use squares at every direction or scale, while the local anisotropic transforms use rectangles with different sizes and directions. We suggest the method for image representation by combining multi-scale decomposition based on Wavelet Packet, and directional filter based Prime Ridgelet Transformation with the special property of building optimal covering grid at every analyzing scale. The following figure demonstrates the difference between wavelet transform and global directional multi-scale decomposition called ridgelet [2], or local directional multi-scale scale Curvelet-like [3].

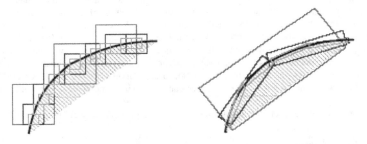

Figure 1. Wavelet transform uses squares, while the local anisotropic transforms use rectangles with different sizes and directions in image decomposition.

## 2. The Multi-scale Analysis by Wavelet Packet

The wavelet packet method is a generalization of wavelet decomposition that offers a richer range of possibilities for image analysis. In 2D wavelet decomposition, a data is split into an approximation and three details (vertical, horizontal, and diagonal), the approximation is then itself split into a second-level approximation and details, and the process is repeated.

Otherwise, in wavelet packet analysis, the details as well as the approximations can be split at every level.

We can use any function of wavelet transform for wavelet packet even complex function. We choose the functions Daubechies-x, Symlet, Coiflet, Biorthogonal for experiments.

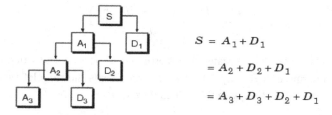

Figure 2. 1D wavelet decomposition.

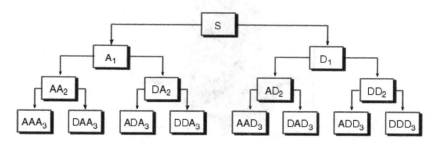

Figure 3. 1D Wavelet Packet decomposition.

## 3. Prime Ridgelet Transformation

Ridgelet transform was introduced in 1999 to represent multi-scale linear features. Thereafter, Donoho has introduced Curvelet transform based on partition of image into 'squares', and apply ridgelet transform in those squares. In the next part, we introduce continuous ridgelet transform and discrete version of this one.

### 3.1. *The Continuous Ridgelet Transform*

The continuous Ridgelet transform on 2-dimension data is defined as in [1]. Given $\psi$ be the function belong $L^2(R)$ and it obeys the condition

$$\int_R \frac{|\hat{\psi}(x)|^2}{|x|^2} dx < \infty \tag{1}$$

The function $\psi$ must obey the condition of vanishing. That is $\int \psi(x) dx = 0$. The ridgelet function is defined $\psi_{a,b,\theta} : R^2 \to R$

$$\psi_{a,b,\theta}(x,y) = \frac{1}{\sqrt{a}}\psi\left(\frac{(x\cos\theta + y\sin\theta - b)}{a}\right) \tag{2}$$

In that, $a$ is scale value greater than zero, $-\infty < b < \infty$ is the value of location, and $\theta$ is the angle in $[0, 2\pi]$. The figure 4 represents the ridgelet function based the Mexico hat function with the values $\theta=\pi/4$, $a=1$, and $b=0$.

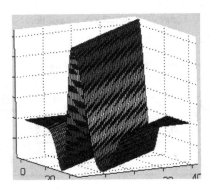

Figure 4. The ridgelet based on Mexico Hat.

Given a function $f : R^2 \rightarrow R$, ridgelet transform of function f is defined

$$RI_f(a,b,\theta) = \int_{R^2} f(x)\psi_{a,b,\theta}(x)dx. \tag{3}$$

The ridgelet transform is built on 1D wavelet transform in Radon domain. The general Radon transform of the function f is the set of integrals on the lines specified by $(\theta,t)$, where $\theta \in [0,2\pi), t \in R$:

$$Rf(\theta,t) = \int_{R^2} f(x_1,x_2)\delta(x_1\cos\theta + x_2\sin\theta - t)dx_1 dx_2, \tag{4}$$

where, $\delta$ is Dirac function. Therefore, ridgelet transform is 1D wavelet transform in projection slice of Radon transform. Each slice is determined by fixed value of angle $\theta$, and changing values of t parameter.

In comparison with 2D wavelet transform, we review the formula of 2D wavelet on function f.

$$WT_f(a_1,b_1,a_2,b_2) = \int_{R^2} \psi_{a_1,b_1,a_2,b_2}(x)f(x)dx, \text{ where}$$

$\psi_{a_1,b_1,a_2,b_2}(x) = \psi_{a_1,b_1}(x_1).\psi_{a_2,b_2}(x_2)$ is tensor product of 1D wavelets, and

$$\psi_{a,b}(t) = \frac{1}{\sqrt{a}}\psi\left(\frac{t-b}{a}\right).$$

It is easy to observe that wavelet transform with the location parameter $(b_1, b_2)$ is only effective to detect the point singularities in image. In there, the anisotropic features are not examined at any analysis scale. The ridgelet transform with the parameters $(b, \theta)$ representing intercept and slope is more effective to analyze the singularities along the line.

The inverse ridgelet transform formula is defined:

$$f(x) = \int_0^{2\pi} \int_{-\infty}^{\infty} \int_{-\infty}^{\infty} Rf(a,b,\theta)\psi_{a,b,\theta}(x)\frac{da}{a^3}\frac{d\theta}{4\pi}db \tag{5}$$

Ridgelet transform is 1D wavelet transform in Radon domain. It means that every projection slice in Radon domain, 1D Wavelet will be applied to get Ridgelet transform. Therefore, the optimal discrete Ridgelet transform is based on optimal discrete Radon transform.

## 3.2. *Prime Discrete Radon Transform*

The Prime Radon transform is defined as summations of image pixels over a certain set of lines. We based on the method was introduced in [4]. Given $Z_p = \{0,1,...,p-1\}$, where p is a prime number. We note $Z_p^* = Z_p + \{p\}$, $Z_p^2$ is finite grid with the values in $Z_p$. The Prime Radon transform of the function $f$ is defined as

$$r_k[l] = PRAT_f(k,l) = \frac{1}{\sqrt{p}}\sum_{(i,j)\in L_{k,l}} f(i,j) \tag{6}$$

where $L_k$, are the lines in $Z_p^2$.

$L_{k,l}$ is defined as $L_{k,l} = \{(i,j): j = ki+l, i \in Z_p\}, 0 < k < p$; $L_{p,l} = \{(l,j): j \in Z_p\}$.

Set of the lines in $L_{1,k}$ will cover $Z_p^2$ well. However, it is not the optimal grid to cover $Z_p^2$. Another discrete method was introduced to build the better grid of Radon transform in 2D data. The projection lines in $Z_p^2$ are defined

$$L_{a,b,t} = \{(i,j) \in Z_p^2 : ai + bj - t = 0; a,b,t \in Z_p, (a,b) \neq (0,0)\}. \tag{7}$$

It is easy to see that for a normal vector (a,b) , $\{L_{a,b,t} : t \in Z_p\}$ is a set of $p$ parallel lines in $Z_p^2$. The number of the lines with normal vector (a, b) is equal to the number of lines with normal vector (na, nb), for each n=0, 1, 2,.., p-1. Now, the discrete Radon in $Z_p^2$ is defined

$$r_{a,b}[t] = PRAT_f(a,b,t) = \frac{1}{\sqrt{p}} \sum_{(i,j)\in L_{a,b,t}} f(i,j) \qquad (8)$$

The projection lines in Radon transform for a fixed normal vector (a,b) is: $\left(r_{a,b}[0], r_{a,b}[1], .., r_{a,b}[p-1]\right)$. It is very important to select the normal vectors so that they can be an optimal grid on image. Normally, the lines in Radon transform are determined by normal vectors u:

$$u_k = \begin{cases} (-k,1) & k = 0,.., p-1 \\ (1,0) & k = p \end{cases} \qquad (9)$$

We can choose p+1 normal vectors as $(a_k, b_k) = nu_k$ $0 \leq n \leq p-1$, and $(a_p, b_p) = (1,0)$. We must choose the normal vectors to ensure each projection slice is smooth (or low frequency) so that it can be represented well by wavelet 1D. The normal vector should be chosen to be as "close" to the origin of the Fourier plane as possible. The set of normal vectors $\{(a_k^*, b_k^*) : k \in Z_p^*\}$ in (8) should be chosen such that they cover p+1 projections represented by set of $u_k$ as above. From the theorem of discrete Fourier projection slice, $r_{a,b}[t]$ is identical to the 2-D FFT of f[i,j] evaluated along a discrete slice through the origin at the direction (a,b). That is:

$$R_{a,b}[w] = F(aw, bw) \qquad (10)$$

Where, $R_{a,b}[w] = \frac{1}{\sqrt{p}} \sum_{t \in Z_p} r_{a,b}[t].W_p^{wt}$ , with $W_p = e^{-2i.\pi/p}$ .

The optimal normal vectors (a,b) for transformation in (8) should be chosen

$$(a_k^*, b_k^*) = \arg_{(a_k,b_k)\in\{nu_k : 1\leq n\leq p-1\}} \min \left\| \left(C_p(a_k), C_p(b_k)\right) \right\| , \qquad (11)$$

where, $C_p(x) = x - p.round(x/p)$. Hence $\left\| (C_p(a_k), C_p(b_k)) \right\|$ is the distance from the origin to the point ($a_k$, $b_k$) on the Fourier plane. Minimization is simply done for each k in Zp, by searching the smallest one in p-1 distances evaluated by (11). Now, we can get the optimal normal vectors in $Z_p^2$. The following figure demonstrates the difference between usual ordering lines and optimal lines with p = 17.

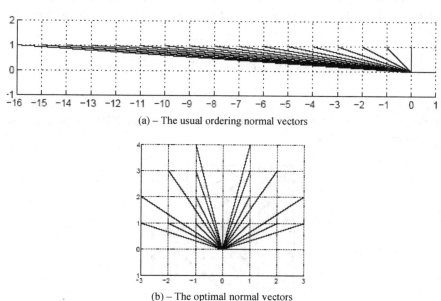

(a) – The usual ordering normal vectors

(b) – The optimal normal vectors

Figure 5. The normal vectors (extracted from [4]).

The Radon transform with the set of optimal lines determined in (11) can be evaluated by formula in (8). The Prime Radon transform is proof to be as tight frame. Beside that, Wavelet 1D transform in projection slices is also tight frame. Therefore, Prime Ridgelet Transform also has tight frame property.

## 4.    Prime Wavelet Packet Contourlet Transform

PWPC transform is combination of two transforms: multi-scale decomposition with WP and direction filters based on Prime Ridgelet transform-applied on packets (or leaves) of WP tree. At every level (j) of WP, we have approximation cA, and the band passes cV, cH, cD. PRID is applied on high band passes cH, cV, and cD. The number of directions of PRID at level (j) is chosen such that law of anisotropic *width ∝ length²* (rule of parabolic scaling) satisfied. We called level of WP j=1, 2... J, with j=1 for finest level, 1<j<J for coarser levels. We choose PRID with $(2^{(N_0-\lfloor j/2 \rfloor)}; N_0 \leq J)$ directions in band pass images of the level (j) in WP tree. This way we could achieve anisotropic scaling law.

It is easy to prove the comment above. The width of band pass $b_j$ (at level j) of WP tree is width=$2^j$, while the number of directions of Prime Ridgelet is $2^{(N_0-\lfloor j/2 \rfloor)}$. So:

$$width \approx 2^J, \ length \approx 2^j.2^{N_0-\lfloor j/2 \rfloor} = 2^{N_0}.2^{\lfloor j/2 \rfloor}$$
$$\Rightarrow width \propto length^2.$$

Figure 6 represents optimal WP tree at three levels, and PRID decomposition with directions in 3 levels is (8-4-4).

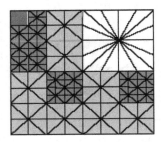

Figure 6. WP with three levels, and directions of PRID at these levels (8-4-4).

We use minimum of entropy measurement (Shannon, Log, P Norm) to build the optimal WP in $2^{4^{n-1}}$ packets [6]. In some cases, the optimal WP tree is also Wavelet decomposition tree. The Shannon entropy measurement is defined $E_1(s) = -\sum_i s_i^2 \log_2(s_i^2)$, LOG entropy by $E_2(s) = \sum_i \log_2(s_i^2)$, and norm p by

$$E_3(s) = \sum_i |s_i|^p = \|s\|_p^p.$$

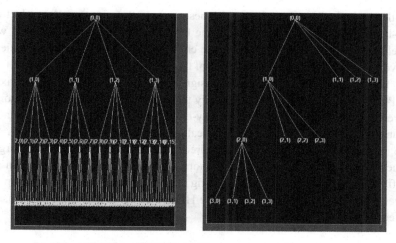

Figure 7. The normal WP tree and optimal WP tree with 03 levels.

Given $x = (x_1, x_2)$, $n = (n_1, n_2)$ be location variables, $\{j_i, p_i, q_i\}$ be indices of packet (leave node) of WP tree, $\psi$ be orthogonal function. The coefficients of WP are defined as

$$\psi_{j_{i,n}}^{p_i, q_i}(x) = 2^{-j_i/2} \psi(2^{-j_i}.x - n) \ . \tag{12}$$

The set $W_{j_i}^{p_i, q_i} = \left\{ \psi_{j_i}^{p_i, q_i}(x - 2^{j_i} n); n \in Z^2 \right\}$ represents the orthogonal base of $W_{ji}$, the packet at the level $(j_i)$. Now we apply PRID to $W_{j_i}^{p_i, q_i}$. The PRID filter at level l is called $S_k^l$

The set of $P_l$ sub bands is called $G_k^l$ corresponding to the filters $S_k^l$ applied to $W_{j_i}^{p_i, q_i}$. The set $G_k^l = \left\{ g_k^l(n - S_k^l.m); m, n \in Z^2, 0 \le k \le 2^l \right\}$ is orthogonal base of $W_{j_i}^{p_i, q_i}$. We will have

$$W_{j_i}^{p_i, q_i} = \oplus_{k=0}^{2^{l-1}} W_{j_i, k}^{p_i, q_i, l_i} \tag{13}$$

The value of each coefficient of PWPC is defined

$$\mu_{j_i, k, n}^{p_i, q_i, l_i} = \sum_{m \in Z^2} g_k^{l_i}(m - S_k^{l_i}.n).\psi_{j_i, m}^{p_i, q_i} \ . \tag{14}$$

Similar to WP, if we can choose the best packets then we can also select the non-linear features with minimum of the PWPC coefficients. The simplest way to select the significant coefficients is to choose the same number of coefficients in every wedge (after PRID transform) of the optimal WP tree.

There are some ways to keep the significant coefficients in each matrix of PWPC wedge. Logically, we can classify these matrices in two kinds: horizontal or vertical. We can scan the matrix row-by-row if its direction is horizontal or column-by-column if direction is vertical to keep the largest coefficients. We also can scan the coefficients via the direction of the wedge to keep the largest values. For example if wedge's direction is 45 degree, then we can scan the coefficients by the diagonal direction (fig 8a) of the wedge matrix and keep the largest values. Another way we can use Hilbert curve to scan the wedge matrix to keep the largest values (fig 8b).

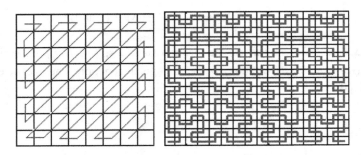

Figure 8. Scan the significant coefficients by: (a) angle of 45 degree. (b) Hilbert curve.

*It is easy to prove the following properties of PWPC transform*

- **Multi-Scale**: WP decomposition is multi-scale decomposition.
- **Directional**: directional PRID filters at each packet of WP tree.
- **Anisotropic**: the ratio between length and width of wedge in PRID transform satisfies parabolic scaling law.
- **Complete reconstruction and orthogonal base**: correct because of the decompositions (WP and PRID) are complete reconstruction and orthogonal if the wavelet functions used in transforms are orthogonal and complete reconstruction.

## 5. The Result of Experiments

We use the 256*256 images with curved edges for the experiment. Some images are nano ones with cells inside (figure 9), the others contain the curves (figure

10). We also use wavelet packet, ridgelet and curvelet transforms for these images. We keep the same number of the coefficients for those transforms, and then apply inverse transform with those coefficients. Sometimes, we use more coefficients in WP transform than those of the other transforms, but the result is worse than the local directional transforms. At the WP step of PWPC transform, the wavelet functions as Daubechies, Coif and Bior-7 are used. The result in the figure 9 shows that the quality of reconstruction image from the coefficients of WP is worst. With WPWC transform, we only keep from eight to sixteen coefficients for each wedge for reconstructing the image. We use 03 levels in WP. The number of packets of optimal WP tree is about 10. In each packet, there are at most 16 wedges for PRID transform. Therefore, we only keep 10*8*16=1080 coefficients to reconstruct the original image as in figure 9. With the artificial images as in figure 10 including curves in uniform background, we keep only from one to two coefficients for each wedge to reconstruct the image.

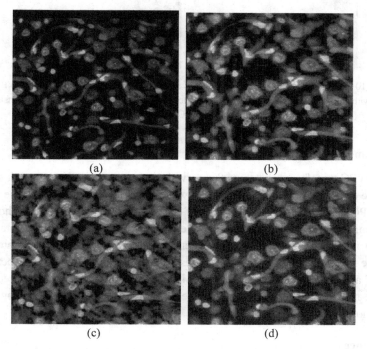

Figure 9. (a)-The original image containing cell nuclei (green), blood vessels (red), cytoplasm (blue). (b)-The reconstructed image from WP using Db3 with 32 coefficients for each packet. (c)-The reconstructed image from Curvelet transform. (d)-The reconstructed image from PWPC with sixteen coefficients for each wedge.

118

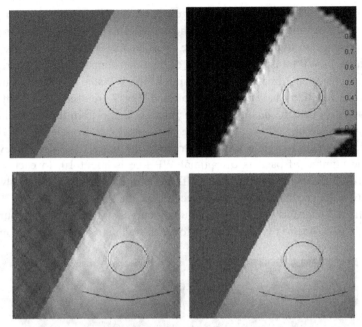

Figure 10. (a)-The original image containing curves. (b)- The reconstructed image from WP using Db3 with 64 coefficients for each packet. (c)- The reconstructed image from Curvelet transform. (d)- The reconstructed image from PWPC with two coefficients for each wedge.

## 6. Conclusion

The PWPC transform represents the curved features very well. The result shows that the quality of PWPC is better than wavelet or ridgelet transform. The speed of PWPC transform is faster than that of Curvelet. With the methods of choosing the significant coefficients of PWPC, the reconstructed images still maintain the curved features with only few coefficients. We see that, the wavelet transform has the advantages in low pass images. Therefore, the combination between PWPC and WT as well as the relationships between the coefficients are required for the next researches. We consider these problems as the core for recognition for nano images.

## References

1. S. Mallat & W. L. Hwang, "Sigularity detection and processing with wavelet", IEEE Trans. Inf Theory, vol 38, no.2 pp 617-643, 1992.

2.  Emmanuel Jeans Candes "Ridgelets: Theory and applications ", Stanford University 1999.
3.  Emmanuel J. Candes, David L. Donoho-Curvelets: A surprisingly Effective NonAdptive Representation for objects with edges– Vanderbilt University Press, Nashville, TN, USA 2000
4.  M. N. Do, *Directional multi-resolution image representations.* PhD thesis, EPFL, Lausanne, Switzerland, Dec. 2001
5.  R. H. Bamberger and M. J. T. Smith, "A filter bank for the directional decomposition of images: Theory and design," *IEEE Trans Signal Proc.*, vol. 40, no. 4, pp. 882–893, April 1992.
6.  F. G. Mayer, A. Z. Averbuch, and J.-O. Stromberg, "Fast adaptive wavelet packet image compression," *IEEE Trans. Image Processing,* vol. 9, no. 5, pp. 792-800, May 2000.

# CHAPTER 10

# TABLET PC APPLICATIONS IN AN ACADEMIC ENVIRONMENT[*]

DAT TRAN, WANLI MA, DHARMENDRA SHARMA AND SHUANGZHE LIU

*School of Information Sciences and Engineering, University of Canberra,
Canberra, ACT 2601, Australia*

Tablet PCs are a new generation of notebook computers which provide multimodal input options of pen, voice and keyboard. Recently, these portable and flexible Tablet PCs have attracted attention as a potential tool in academic environments. This paper reviews the current use of Tablet PCs in teaching computer science and software engineering courses, presenting lectures and papers, and creating peer-review comments. The paper also presents applications of Tablet PCs in teaching and research at our university, the University of Canberra, Australia. These applications include marking assignments and reports, and developing signature verification applications.

## 1. Introduction

Palm devices and Pocket PCs are tablet-like devices that have achieved a high level of success in the market place. They are small, specialized and designed to be carried around in your pocket. Tablet PCs, on the other hand, are general-purpose computers, with sensitive screens designed to interact with an accompanied pen. They run on the same processors as a laptop, have large hard drives, and have as much memory as any other computer [6].

Tablet PCs are hybrids of handheld devices, laptops and other information tools. They are powered by special tablet PC versions of operating systems. The paper focuses on the Microsoft Windows XP Tablet PC Edition and its related software. The Windows XP Tablet PC is a superset of Windows XP; therefore all applications that can run on a regular PC can also run on the Tablet PC. This includes anything from MS Office to the applications we write ourselves.

The current Tablet PC tools offered by Microsoft include Input Panel, Office OneNote, Windows Journal, Sticky Notes, and the Education Pack. Input

---

[*] This work is supported by University of Canberra Multidisciplinary Research Grant and Divisional Research Grant.

Panel dynamically converts handwriting input by a user to text. OneNote is a tool to enhance note taking; users can copy notes from other sources or insert documents from other Office programs such as Word and PowerPoint. Windows Journal is a basic note-taking tool that is used to capture handwritten notes and drawings, convert handwritten notes to text, import graphics files, and share notes with others. The Sticky Notes tool is used to write and store short notes, phone numbers, and other reminders. Sticky notes can be placed directly on the desktop as quick reminders or in MS Word to add electronic comments or reminders to documents [11]. The latest tool for the academic environment is the Education Pack which includes Ink Flash Cards and Equation Writer as the main programs [10]. With Ink Flash Cards, a student can create two-sided question-and-answer cards to test their knowledge. Equation Writer helps users handwrite a math equation and convert it to text with the touch of a pen; much more efficient than using Equation in Word.

Academic staff members at universities around the world have developed Tablet PC-based applications in their academic environments. Typical application includes lecture presentations, teaching computer science and software engineering courses and providing peer-review comments. For lecture presentations, the Classroom Presenter system [2] has been developed to enhance an instructors' flexibility in giving presentations, by allowing easy navigation through a presentation and the ability to write on the presentation itself. K. Mock presented his experience in teaching computer science and software engineering courses with a tablet PC [1, 9]. He used the Tablet PC in the classroom as a digital whiteboard, by connecting it to a data projector. Outside of the classroom, the Tablet PC is also a useful tool for grading assignments, creating lecture material, and capturing meeting notes. Pérez-Quiñones and S. Turner performed an informal study on peer-review comments using the Tablet PC, by observing how students used the pen on a Tablet-PC to provide feedback on an object-oriented design created by other students [14]. Peer-review has been found to be a good way to help students learn from each other and to increase their understanding of coding and design issues.

In this paper, we review the current applications provided by Microsoft and also those developed by professors at universities for academic purposes. We then present the Tablet PC applications developed at our university, using the Visual Studio.NET software package. With extra Windows controls designed for Tablet PCs, we can develop pen-based programs for teaching purposes as well as handwriting recognition and signature authentication for research purposes.

## 2. Tablet PC Tools

In this section we present some of the most commonly used tools designed for Tablet PCs: Input Panel, Office OneNote, Windows Journal, Sticky Notes, and the Education Pack. These tools are provided by Microsoft [10, 11].

The *Input Panel* tool dynamically converts handwriting to text. There are three modes for input: Writing Pad, Character Pad and On-screen Keyboard. Figure 1 displays the Input Panel using Writing Pad to convert handwriting input to text. The Input Panel also helps the user make corrections quickly and easily before inserting text.

*OneNote* is a note taking tool. It enables users to copy notes from a Microsoft Windows Mobile-based Pocket PC or Smartphone, record video notes, capture screen clippings, import meeting details from Outlook, and insert documents from other Office programs such as Word or PowerPoint. Interestingly, OneNote files can be saved as MHTML files, which other users can view with Microsoft Internet Explorer version 5.0 or later.

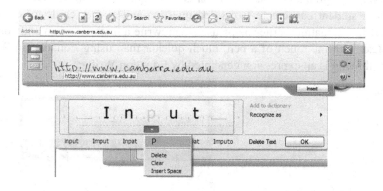

Figure 1. Handwriting-to-text conversion using the Input Panel tool in Writing Pad mode.

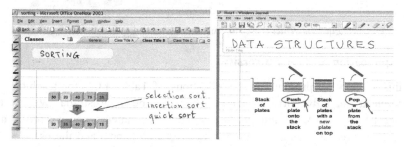

Figure 2. Pages in Office OneNote and Windows Journal, respectively.

*Windows Journal* is a basic note-taking tool that is used to capture handwritten notes and drawings, convert handwritten notes to text, import graphics files, and share notes with others. Windows Journal can be used as a powerful presentation enhancement, by making presentations more interactive with use of the pen, digital ink, and highlighter tools. Similar to Office OneNote, Journal files can be shared with non-Tablet PC users by exporting them as MHTML files.

*Sticky Notes* tool is used to write and store short notes, phone numbers, and other reminders. Sticky Notes can be placed directly on the desktop as quick reminders or used in MS Word to add electronic comments or reminders to documents. They are easy to use and quick to access. Users can also use a microphone to record information. A sticky note can contain both writing and recordings.

The latest tool for an academic environment is *Education Pack.* It includes five programs that can help users get organized and study effectively. The most interesting programs are Ink Flash Cards and Equation Writer. With Ink Flash Cards, a student can create two-sided question-and-answer cards to test their knowledge. Equation Writer helps users handwrite a math equation and convert it to text with the touch of a pen; much quicker than using Equation in Word. The following is an expression generated by Equation Writer:

$$\alpha \sum_{i=0}^{n} x^i + \beta \int_0^1 e^{-x} dx$$

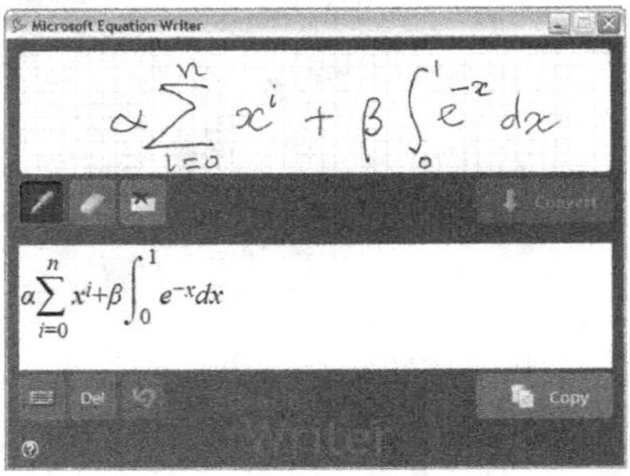

Figure 3. Equation Writer is used to generate mathematic expressions and equations.

## 3. Applications at Our University

In this section we present some applications of Tablet PCs, for teaching and research at our university, the University of Canberra, Australia. We use the Tablet PC for marking and grading student assignments and exercises and adding peer-review comments to drafts of research papers and theses. We also developed our own Tablet PC signature recognition system. Students can develop Tablet PC applications as a semester-long project using MS Visual Studio .NET. With the support of MS Visual Studio.NET, ink-enabled applications can easily be created. There are two ink-based controls for Windows applications which are InkEdit and InkPicture. The InkEdit control gets handwriting input and converts it into text. The InkPicture control displays handwriting inputs as they looked when created. Other controls on the Windows form can be ink-enabled using the InkOverlay class. The InkCollector class could be used to recognize the pen when it moves over the textbox and open up a larger input area when the pen hovers within its range. This control can automatically recognize the handwritten text and paste it into the textbox when the pen moves away [6].

## 3.1. *Marking, Grading and Peer-Review Comments*

In order to use the Tablet PC for marking and grading, students are required to submit their assignments, exercises and reports electronically via email or a Web page such as WebCT. Electronic submission makes it easy for instructors to check the submission dates for assignments. Marking, grading and providing comments to the submissions is fast and clear with the Tablet PC. Instructors can also keep a copy of marked submissions without the hassle of having to photocopy hard copies.

Reports, presentations and research papers written amongst a group of authors require several draft revisions. It is fast, clear and concise for authors to use a Tablet PC to provide comments and suggestions on the same draft. Figure 4 presents an example of using the Tablet PC to suggest comments on a research paper draft.

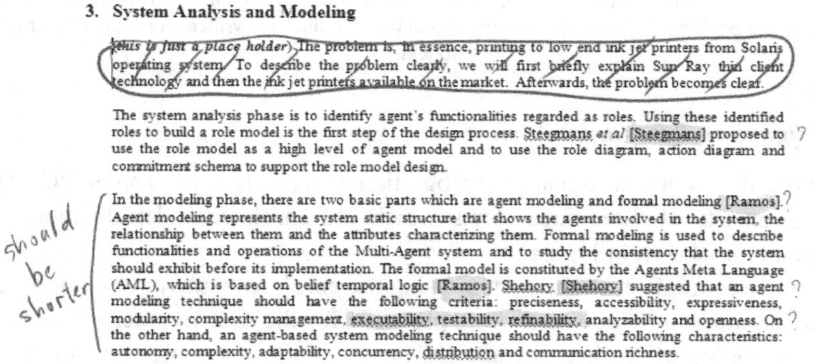

**3. System Analysis and Modeling**

*this is just a place holder).* The problem is, in essence, printing to low end ink jet printers from Solaris operating system. To describe the problem clearly, we will first briefly explain Sun Ray thin client technology and then the ink jet printers available on the market. Afterwards, the problem becomes clear.

The system analysis phase is to identify agent's functionalities regarded as roles. Using these identified roles to build a role model is the first step of the design process. Steegmans *et al* [Steegmans] proposed to use the role model as a high level of agent model and to use the role diagram, action diagram and commitment schema to support the role model design.

*should be shorter*

In the modeling phase, there are two basic parts which are agent modeling and formal modeling [Ramos]. Agent modeling represents the system static structure that shows the agents involved in the system, the relationship between them and the attributes characterizing them. Formal modeling is used to describe functionalities and operations of the Multi-Agent system and to study the consistency that the system should exhibit before its implementation. The formal model is constituted by the Agents Meta Language (AML), which is based on belief temporal logic [Ramos]. Shehory [Shehory] suggested that an agent modeling technique should have the following criteria: preciseness, accessibility, expressiveness, modularity, complexity management, executability, testability, refinability, analyzability and openness. On the other hand, an agent-based system modeling technique should have the following characteristics: autonomy, complexity, adaptability, concurrency, distribution and communication richness.

Figure 4. Comments are given on a research paper draft.

### 3.2. *Handwriting Recognition Applications*

The proposed handwriting recognition applications for teaching purpose include implementation of crosswords and puzzles. These applications were developed using MS Visual Studio .NET.

There are currently some applications for solving crosswords and puzzles, especially Sudoku puzzle [20] available on the Internet. However these applications require a user to use mouse and keyboard to solve those crosswords and puzzles. The Tablet PC provides a very convenient way to the user to solve those crosswords and Sudoku puzzle displayed on the Tablet PC screen. The user is able to use pen to handwrite letters or digits to cells in a crossword or in a Sudoku puzzle. The cells in these applications are created with the use of the InkEdit control available in MS Visual Studio.NET. The handwritings will then be converted to text. Figure 5 shows a Sudoku puzzle application for the Tablet PC. The handwritten digits in the first three cells are converted to digits after a preset recognition timeout.

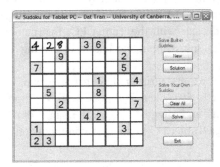 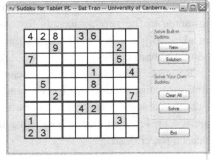

Figure 5. A Sudoku puzzle for Tablet PC. The first three cells are entered the handwritten digits of 4, 2 and 8, respectively. After a preset recognition timeout, the handwritten words are converted to text.

### 3.3. *Signature Recognition System*

We have developed a signature recognition system for the Tablet PC. The system consists of three subsystems which are enrolment, identification and verification as shown in Figure 6.

New users register to the system using the enrolment subsystem. For a new user registration, a Windows form is provided for the user to enter a username and two copies of his/her signature. The system extracts features from the entered signatures and builds a signature model using a modeling technique such as vector quantization, Gaussian mixture modeling or hidden Markov modeling. Signature models are stored in XML (Extensible Markup Language) format.

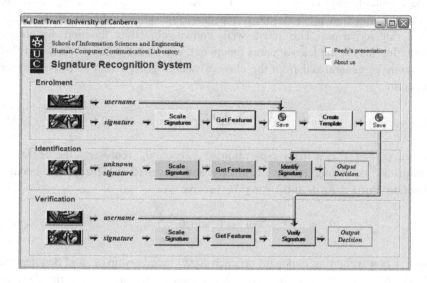

Figure 6. A signature recognition system.

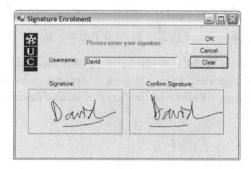

Figure 7. New user registration form for a signature verification-based application.

Vector quantization (VQ), regarded as the simplest modeling method, was applied to this system. The fuzzy c-means (FCM) clustering method [4] was used to create signature models known as vector quantization codebooks. The method is summarized as follows.

Let $X = \{x_1, x_2, ..., x_T\}$ be a set of $T$ feature vectors. Fuzzy clustering known as unsupervised learning in $X$ is a fuzzy partitioning of $X$ into $C$ fuzzy subsets or $C$ clusters where $1 < C < T$. The most important requirement is to find a suitable measure of clusters, referred to as a fuzzy clustering criterion. Objective function methods allow the most precise formulation of the fuzzy clustering criterion. The most well known objective function for fuzzy clustering in $X$ is the least-squares functional, that is, the infinite family of FCM functionals, generalized from the classical within-groups sum of squared error function

$$J_m(U, \mu; X) = \sum_{i=1}^{C} \sum_{t=1}^{T} u_{it}^m d_{it}^2 \tag{1}$$

where $U = \{u_{it}\}$ is a fuzzy $c$-partition of $X$, each $u_{it}$ represents the degree of vector $x_t$ belonging to the $i$th cluster and is called the fuzzy membership function. For $1 \leq i \leq C$ and $1 \leq t \leq T$, we have

$$0 \leq u_{it} \leq 1, \quad \sum_{i=1}^{C} u_{it} = 1, \text{ and } 0 < \sum_{t=1}^{T} u_{it} < T \tag{2}$$

$m \geq 1$ is a weighting exponent on each fuzzy membership $u_{it}$ and denotes the degree of fuzziness; $\mu = (\mu_1, ..., \mu_C)$ are cluster centers and, $d_{it}$ is the distance in the $A$ norm ($A$ is any positive definite matrix) from $x_t$ to $\mu_i$, known as a measure of dissimilarity

$$d_{it}^2 = \| x_t - \mu_i \|_A^2 = (x_t - \mu_i)' A(x_t - \mu_i) . \tag{3}$$

The basic idea in the FCM is to minimize $J_m$ over the variables $U$ and $\mu$, on the assumption that matrices $U$ that are part of optimal pairs for $J_m$ identify good partitions of the data. Minimizing the fuzzy objective function $J_m$ in (1) gives

$$u_{it} = \left[ \sum_{k=1}^{C} (d_{it} / d_{kt})^{\frac{2}{m-1}} \right]^{-1} \tag{4}$$

$$\mu_i = \sum_{t=1}^{T} u_{it}^m x_t \Big/ \sum_{t=1}^{T} u_{it}^m . \tag{5}$$

The FCM algorithm is known as the fuzzy vector quantization (FVQ) algorithm in pattern recognition and is used to train codebooks in the VQ approach.

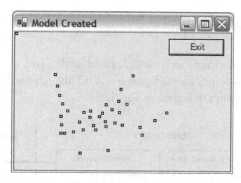

Figure 8. A vector quantization model for the signature in Figure 7.

After registration, the user can log on to the system using his/her registered signature for identification or verification.

For identification purpose, the user enters his/her signature on a identification form displayed after clicking a button.

The unknown signature $X$ will be scaled and extracted features to calculate $N$ likelihood functions $P(X \mid \lambda_i)$, $i = 1, ..., N$. The highest likelihood value is chosen and the unknown signature is identified as the signature of the corresponding user

*Choose the signature model $\lambda_{i*}$ if $i^* = \arg \max P(X \mid \lambda_i)$ .*

For verification purpose, the user's signature plays the role of a password. The user logs on to the system using his/her registered username and signature, via a verified login form. The entered signature will be compared with the signature model whose identity is claimed. If the match is above a given threshold, the identity claim is accepted. The verification method is summarized as follows.

In a statistical approach, the verification problem is usually formulated as a problem of statistical hypothesis testing. For an input signature $X$ and a claimed identity $S$, the task is to determine if $X$ was signed by the claimed writer $S$.

Assuming that $X$ contains signature features from only one writer, the signature verification task can be regarded as a basic hypothesis test between the null hypothesis $H_0$: $X$ is from the claimed writer $S$ against the alternative hypothesis H: $X$ is *not* from the claimed writer $S$. According to Neyman-Pearson Lemma, if the probabilities of both the hypotheses are known exactly, the optimum test to decide between these two hypotheses is a likelihood ratio test given by

$$S(X) = \frac{P(X \mid H_0)}{P(X \mid H)} \begin{cases} > \theta & accept \ H_0 \\ \leq \theta & reject \ H_0 \end{cases} \tag{6}$$

where $\theta$ is a predefined decision threshold and $S(X)$ is referred to as the similarity score of the input signature $X$. This approach provides a good theoretical formulation to signature verification.

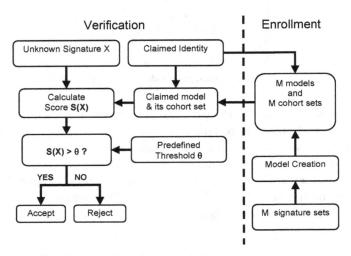

Figure 9. A typical signature verification system.

However, in practical verification problems, it is impossible to obtain the exact probability density functions for either the null hypothesis or the alternative hypothesis. A parametric form of the distribution under each hypothesis is assumed to estimate these probability density functions. Let $\lambda_c$ be the claimed signature model and $\lambda$ be a model representing all other possible signatures, i.e. impostors. Let $P(X \mid \lambda_c)$ and $P(X \mid \lambda)$ be the likelihood functions of the claimed writer and impostors, respectively. The similarity score is calculated as follows

$$S(X) = \frac{P(X \mid \lambda_c)}{P(X \mid \lambda)} \begin{cases} > \theta & accept \ H_0 \\ \leq \theta & reject \ H_0 \end{cases} . \tag{7}$$

For the verification stage, the impostor model was approximated by a background signature model. We used the same training data to build the claimed signature model and background signature model [16, 17]. We trained these 2 VQ models for each signature with codebook sizes of 16 and 32 codewords, respectively. The 16 codeword model was used as the background model and the 32 codeword model was used as the claimed signature model. The background modeling method is useful for practical and portable devices such as palm-top computers, since a higher demand for computation and memory requirements may not be desirable for such applications [16].

For evaluation, the signature verification system was tested by more than 100 signatures in two classes and in a Science Festival. The verification equal error rate result was 17.5% for using a computer mouse to produce signatures and about 9.5% for using the Tablet pen. It is hard to produce good signatures using a computer mouse; therefore the verification equal error rate was higher than that using the Tablet pen. However, those are very promising results as the VQ modeling technique was used. A better version using Markov modeling technique is implementing to achieve a lower verification equal error rate.

## 4. Conclusion

In this paper, we have presented Tablet PC-based applications supplied by Microsoft and developed by academic staff at universities around the world. We have also presented applications at our university. With the use of MS Visual Studio.NET, we have developed a signature verification system using fuzzy vector quantization technique for modeling and new background modeling technique for verification. More applications are in development at other organizations and universities.

## Acknowledgements

The first author would like to acknowledge the support of the University of Canberra Multidisciplinary and Divisional Research Grants.

## References

1. R. J. Anderson, R. Anderson, B. Simon, S. A. Wolfman, T. VanDeGrift, and K. Yasuhara, "Experiences with a tablet pc based lecture presentation system in computer science courses," in Proc. of the 35th SIGCSE Technical Symposium on Computer Science Education, 56–60 (2004)
2. R. J. Anderson, R. Anderson, T. VanDeGriff, S. A. Wolfman, and K. Yasuhara, "Classroom presentation from the Tablet PC," in Proc. of the 8th annual conference on innovation and technology in computer science education, 238–238 (2003)

132

3. R.J. Anderson, C. Hoyer, S.A. Wolfman, R. Anderson, "A Study of Digital Ink in Lecture Presentation," in Proc. of CHI'04, ACM Press, 567–574 (2004)
4. J. C. Bezdek, "Fuzzy Mathemathics in Pattern Classification", PhD Thesis, Applied Math. Center, Cornell University, Ithaca, 1973
5. R. Condon, "Tablet PC's in Education," National Institute for Technology and Liberal Education, Electronic file, Retrieved 3 Jul 04, www.nitle.org/rsrc_issues_tabletpc.php
6. M. Egger, "Creating Tablet PC Applications with VS .NET," http://www.devx.com/codemag/Article/17439, 6 Oct 2003.
7. E. F. Gehringer, "Electronic peer review and peer grading in computer-science courses", Proceedings of the thirty-second SIGCSE technical symposium on Computer Science Education, Charlotte, North Carolina, United States, 139-143 (2001)
8. P. Lowe, "Bentley College students evaluate Tablet PCs," www.hp.com/hpinfo/newsroom/feature_stories/2004/04bentley.html, retrieved 20 Mar 2006.
9. K. Mock, "Teaching with Tablet PC," Journal of Computing Sciences in Colleges, 20, 2, pp. 17-27, 2004.
10. Microsoft Corporation, "Education Pack for Tablet PC", www.microsoft.com/windowsxp/downloads/tabletpc/educationpack/default.mspx, retrieved 19 Mar 06.
11. Microsoft Corporation, "Tablet PC", retrieved 19 Mar 06, www.microsoft.com/windowsxp/tabletpc/default.mspx
12. Microsoft Corporation, "Massachusetts Institute of Technology Changes the Face of Education using Tablet PCs," documents retrieved on 20 March 2006 from www.microsoft.com/resources/casestudies/ShowFile.asp?FileResourceID=1196, Nov 2002.
13. Notre Dame Tablet PC Initiative. Retrieved 20 Mar 2006 from http://www.nd.edu/~learning/tabletpc/
14. M.A. Pérez-Quiñones and S. Turner, "Using a Tablet-PC to Provide Peer-Review Comments,"
15. SHU Tablet PC Project. Retrieved 20 Mar 2006 from http://www.cs.shu.edu/tabletpc/
16. D. Tran, "New Background Modeling for Speaker Verification", in the Proceedings of the INTERSPEECH Conference, Korea, 4, 2605-2608 (2004)
17. D. Tran and D. Sharma, "New Background Speaker Models and Experiments on the ANDOSL Speech Corpus", Lecture Notes in Artificial Intelligence: Knowledge-Based Intelligent Information and Engineering Systems, 2, 498-503 (2004)

18. D. Tran and M. Wagner, "Fuzzy Gaussian Mixture Models for Speaker Recognition", Australian Journal of Intelligent Information Processing Systems (AJIIPS), 5(4), 293-300 (1998)
19. J. V. West, *Tablet PC Quick Reference*, Microsoft Press (2002)

# CHAPTER 11

# APPLYING AI TECHNIQUES FOR TRANSFERRING 3D FACIAL ANIMATION

THE DUY BUI

*College of Technology,*
*Vietnam National University, Hanoi, Vietnam*
*E-mail: duybt@vnu.edu.vn*

In this paper, we describe the use of Artificial Intelligent (AI) techniques to transfer the animation from one 3D face to a newly created face. The animation is produced with the use of the vector muscle model. With this muscle model, in order to generate natural facial expressions in a 3D face, muscles have to be placed in the correct positions in the face and other parameters of the muscles need to be assigned suitable values. This is a heavy human-involved and time-consuming procedure. Our approach replaces this process by a faster and easier one, facilitated by AI techniques, in which the animator only has to select the faces with the most natural expressions from his point of view. First, we use Radial Basis Function (RBF) networks to deform a source face model to represent a target face model using the specification of corresponding landmarks on the two face models. We introduce a novel method to specify and adjust landmarks on the target face model automatically. The landmark adjustment process is done by Genetic Algorithms (GAs). After all the landmarks have been placed in optimal positions, the RBF networks are used to deform the source face model as well as to transfer the muscles on the source face model to the deformed face model. Finally, Interactive Genetic Algorithms are used to refine the parameters of muscles in order to produce high quality facial expressions.

*Keywords*: Facial Animation; Genetic Algorithms; RBF networks.

## 1. Introduction

Human facial movements, consisting of lip movements and facial expressions, play an important role in face-to-face communication. Lip movements during speech provide a visual hint about what is being said. Facial expressions take place continuously during speech. They provide additional commentary to and illustration of the verbal information. Facial expressions are able to express emotions and moods. Recognizing the importance of facial expressions in a communication, researchers have been paying attention to 3D facial animation with the aim of producing facial movements on a 3D face model of an avatar or an embodied agent during the interaction between human and computer. There are several techniques to achieve this goal, which are: direct parameterized animation (e.g.[1-4]). A common limitation of these techniques is that they cannot reuse available data for animating new face models themselves. Each time a new face model is created for animation, either the animation must be produced from scratch or a process for manually tuning parameters is required.

The research question studied in this paper is how to transfer the animation from a given face model to a newly created one. Several approaches have been proposed for this purpose. Noh and Neumann[5] transfers the motion vectors between two face models using the specification of corresponding landmarks on the two models. Mani and Ostermann[6] transfers the Face Animation Table (FAT) from an MPEG-4 face model to another one. In the work of Kahler et al.,[7] the face mesh, the muscles and the skull mesh of a multi-layer muscle based face model are transferred to a new face model. All these approaches, however, require heavy human involvement to specify and adjust the correspondences between the source and the target face model, as well as to adjust the animation parameters.

In this paper, we describe the use of Artificial Intelligent (AI) techniques to transfer the animation from one 3D face to a newly created face. The animation is produced with the use of the vector muscle model was introduced by Waters,[3] and improved by Bui et. al.[8] With this muscle model, in order to generate natural facial expressions in a 3D face, muscles have to be placed in the correct positions in the face and other parameters of the muscles need to be assigned suitable values. This is a heavy human-involved and time-consuming procedure. Our approach replaces this process by a faster and easier one, facilitated by AI techniques, in which the animator only has to select the faces with the most natural expressions from his point of view. First, we use Radial Basis Function (RBF) networks to deform a source face model to represent a target face model using the specification of corresponding landmarks on the two face models.[9] The landmarks on the source face model are one-time manually specified and are reused for every target face model. We introduce a novel method to specify and adjust landmarks on the target face model automatically. The landmark adjustment process is done by Genetic Algorithms (GAs). The fitness function used in the GAs expresses the difference between the surface of the deformed face model and the target face model. After all the landmarks have been placed in optimal positions, the RBF networks are used to deform the source face

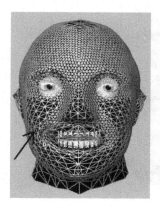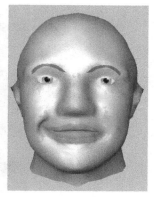

Figure 1.   Deformation on a 3D face created by a vector muscle.

model as well as to transfer the muscles on the source face model to the deformed face model. Finally, Interactive Genetic Algorithms (IGAs) are used to refine the parameters of muscles in order to produce high quality facial expressions.

The overview of the approach is presented in Section 2. In Section 3, we discuss the process of deforming the source face model to represent the target face model. The IGAs muscle tuning process is discussed in details in Section 4. Finally, some results are shown in Section 5.

## 2.  Overview

The 3D facial animation was produced with the vector muscle model introduced by Waters,[3] and improved by Bui.[8] Each vector muscle can be described mainly by a set of ten parameters:

- coordinates of the head of the muscle (3 parameters)
- coordinates of the tail of the muscle (3 parameters)
- the value of fall-off start, fall-off finish and influence angle (3 parameters), which are used to define the influence zone of a muscle.
- the value of the standard to transform contraction level to (0..1)

Figure 1 shows an example of the deformation on a 3D face created by the smiling muscle (Zygomatic Major). Figure 2 shows how wrongly placed muscle can cause unnatural facial expressions. This shows that the importance of the position and parameters of a muscle in creating natural and believable facial expressions.

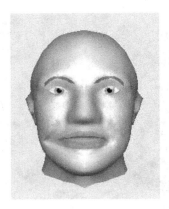

Figure 2.    Wrongly placed muscle causes unnatural facial expression.

The process of transferring 3D facial animation consists of two stages. At the first the stage, based on the landmarks on the source and target face, Radial Basis Function (RBF) networks are used to deform a source face model to represent a target face model.[9] We introduce a novel method to specify and adjust landmarks automatically. The adjustment process is done by Genetic Algorithms (GAs). After all the landmarks have been placed in optimal positions, the RBF networks are used to deform the source face model as well as to transfer the muscles on the source face model to the deformed face model. At the second stage, Interactive Genetic Algorithms are used to refine the parameters of muscles in order to produce high quality facial expressions.

## 3. Deforming the Source Face Model

We deform a source face model to represent a target face model using RBF networks,[10] which are trained by the value of corresponding landmarks on the two face models. The landmarks on the source face are fixed, while we search for the landmarks on the target face to minimize the difference between the deformed face model and the target face model. This is described in more details in.[9]

A set of landmarks is predetermined on the source face model. Most landmarks are specified manually except several that can be detected automatically to cover all the features of the face. These landmarks are determined only once and are reused for every new target face model. For the landmarks on the target face model, we first determine several easy-to-detect landmarks, namely the top of the head, the tip of the nose, and so forth. The auto-detected landmarks will stay fixed whereas the rest of the landmarks will be adjusted; for convenience's sake let us call these "non-detected landmarks". We use the auto-detected landmarks and their correspondences on the source face model as the training set for the RBF networks to determine the initial version of the non-detected landmarks on the target face model. A deformed version of the source face model is created by RBF networks using the landmarks on the source and the target face model. The non-detected landmarks on the target face model are then adjusted with Genetic Algorithms to minimize the difference between the deformed and the target face model.

We follow[5] to use three RBF networks, which map a vertex on source face model to the $x$, $y$, and $z$ components of a vertex on target face model:

$$(x, y, z) \longmapsto (RBF_1(x, y, z), RBF_2(x, y, z), RBF_3(x, y, z)).$$

Each $RBF_i$ is given by

$$RBF_i(x, y, z) = \sum_{j=1}^{n} w_{i,j} h_{i,j}(x, y, z)$$

where the $w_{i,j}$ are the weights of the network that need to be determined or learned on the basis of a training set. The $x$, $y$, and $z$ components of source landmark points and target landmark points are used as the training sets for the three networks. For the basis functions $h_{i,j}$ we follow the successful approach given by:[5]

$$h_{i,j}(v) = \sqrt{\| v - \mu_{i,j} \|^2 + s_{i,j}^2} \quad , \quad v = (x, y, z)$$

where $\mu_{i,j}$ is called the center of $h_{i,j}$ and $s_{i,j}$ is given by

$$s_{i,j} = min_{k \neq j} \| \mu_{i,k} - \mu_{i,j} \| .$$

This choice for $s_{i,j}$, as suggested by,[11] leads to smaller deformations for widely scattered center points and larger deformations for closely located points.

In order to prevent overfitting and improve generalization, a regularization term $\sum_j w_{i,j}^2$ is added to the error term for each $RBF_i$, cf.[12]

Recall that several landmarks on the target face model can be detected automatically. The rest of the landmarks are "non-detected" ones. We use Genetic Algorithms to adjust the non-detected landmarks on the target face model to minimize the differences between the deformed and the  target

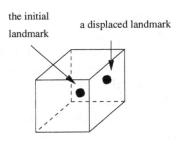

Figure 3. The initial position of a point and a modified version of it.

face model. The Genetic Algorithms search for the optimal variant of the landmarks to reduce the error function described in the previous section.

The GAs process starts with a random set of solutions, which are represented as chromosomes. Because we want to constrain the search to be only around the initial landmarks, each solution of the GAs process is a variant of the landmark points on the target face model, which is the modification of the initial landmark points. In this modification, each variant of the landmark point is any point inside the cube with specified length and the initial landmark point as the center (see Figure 3). Solutions from one population are taken and used to form a new population. Then the new solutions are selected according to their fitness. The more suitable they are, the better chances they have to reproduce. In this case, the fitness function is the inverse of the error function that minimizes the difference between the deformed and the target face model.

**The Chromosome** A chromosome is the concatenation of binary representations of all non-detected landmarks on the target face model. Each landmark is represented in the chromosome by the distance between this landmark and the original landmark.

Each landmark can be described by three coordinates $v_1, v_2, v_3$. Starting from an initial version of the landmark, various versions of the landmark can be obtained by modifying each coordinate in a specified range. Let $Rmin_1$, $Rmax_1$, $Rmin_2$, $Rmax_2$, $Rmin_3$, $Rmax_3$ be the ranges of value for these coordinates. The coordinate of a landmark can be represented as:

$$(p_1, p_2, p_3)$$

where $0 \leq p_i \leq 1$,

$$p_i = \frac{v_i - Rmin_i}{Rmax_i - Rmin_i} \quad i = 1..3$$

and, consequently, we have

$$v_i = p_i(Rmax_i - Rmin_i) + Rmin_i.$$

We then convert $p_i$ to a binary string. Using $2^n$ as upper limit[a], we represent $p_i$ as $\lfloor 2^n p_i \rfloor$ in its binary format:

$$c_{i1}, c_{i2}, ..., c_{in} \qquad c_{ij} = 0 \text{ or } 1.$$

We concatenate the binary representation of the three coordinates of all landmark points to form a chromosome.

**The fitness function** The fitness function is the inverse of the error function, which assesses the differences between the deformed source face model and the target face model by calculating the distance between them at even-distributed sampling points:

$$\text{fitness(solution)} = \frac{1}{E(\text{deformed\_face(solution)}, \text{target\_face})}$$

where deformed\_face(solution) is the deformed face model using the solution as the landmarks on the target face model.

**Crossover** We use multi-point crossover, which is illustrated in Figure 4. For multi-point crossover, several crossover positions are chosen at random with no duplicates and sorted in ascending order. Then, the chromosome elements between successive crossover points are exchanged between the two parents to produce two new offsprings. The section between the first element and the first crossover point is not exchanged between individuals. The idea behind multi-point, and indeed many of the variations on the crossover operator, is that parts of the chromosome representation that contribute the most to the performance of a particular individual may not necessarily be contained in adjacent substrings.[13] Moreover, the disruptive nature of multi-point crossover appears to encourage the exploration of the search space, rather than favoring the convergence to highly fit individuals early in the search; thus making the search more robust.[14]

---

[a]By trial and error, $n$ ranging between 5 to 10 gives best convergence and best result for the GA.

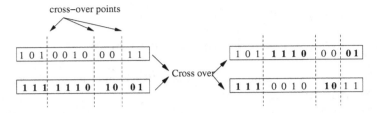

Figure 4.   Multi-point crossover.

**Mutation**   Solutions are mutated by applying random flipping to the component of the chromosomes (0 to 1 and 1 to 0). We start with a mutation rate of 0.3. We increase this mutation rate when the error stays stable, and decrease it when the GA process produces smaller errors (better results). This mutation rate is constrained to be in the range of 0.3 to 0.5.

## 4. Adjusting the Parameters of Muscles with an IGAs Process

While conventional Genetic Algorithms use external determined fitness functions,[15,16] Interactive Genetic Algorithms are guided by the user's intuition preference, subjectivity, sensation, perception, cognition and other psychological processing functions.[17] Instead of rating chromosomes on certain values (fitness), Interactive Genetic Algorithms rate chromosomes interactively based on evaluations of a user. Interactive Genetic Algorithms are useful for searching through an object space when assessment criteria are not well defined enough to form explicit rules.[18] Some applications of Genetic Algorithms are interactive design aid system,[19] montage face image generation[20] and line drawing.[21]

In this phase, the muscles are adjusted interactively by group using Interactive Genetic Algorithms (IGAs) as the underlying technique. We concern about six groups of muscles, which are used to produce six basic expressions: happiness, sadness, surprise, anger, fear and disgust. For each group of muscles, expressed faces created by different versions of the muscles in the group are repeatedly shown to animator. The animator selects the faces which show the most natural expression from the animator's point of view. The IGAs process calculates new faces and shows the animator these new faces again. This selection process finishes when the animator is satisfied with the facial expression performance of the face. The algorithm can be described as follows:

**For** expression $E=Happiness, Surprise, Sadness, Anger, Fear, Disgust$
   **Repeat** (Interactive Genetic Algorithms)
     Show different versions of expression $E$
     The user chooses some "favored" faces
     The system calculates new faces
   **Until** the user satisfies with the faces
   The version of the muscles that creates that best satisfied face is saved.

A snapshot of the system is shown in Figure 5.

The IGAs process starts with a set of solutions, which are represented as chromosomes. Each solution is a version of the being-adjusted group of muscles on the 3D face, which is the modification of the initial version of the group of muscles. In this modification, each parameter of a muscle is modified in a specified range. For example, the head of a muscle will be modified to be any point inside the cube with specified length and the initial head of the muscle as the center (see Figure 3). Solutions from one population are taken and used to form a new population. Solutions which are then selected to form new solutions (offspring) are selected according to their fitness - the more suitable they are the more chances they have to reproduce.

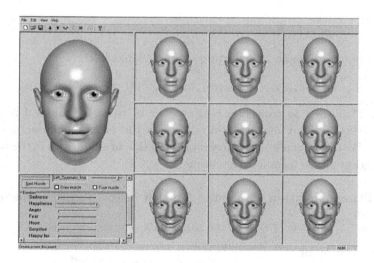

Figure 5.   A snapshot of the IGAs muscle tuning system.

**The Chromosome** A chromosome is a string of binary representation of all parameters of all the muscles in the being-adjusted group. Each muscle is represented as ten parameters:

$$p_1, p_2, .., p_{10}$$

Starting from an initial version of the muscle, numbers of versions of the muscle are created by modifying each parameter in a specified range. Let

$$Rmin_1, Rmax_1, ..., Rmin_{10}, Rmax_{10}$$

be the ranges of values of these parameters. The coordinate of a feature point can be represented as:

$$(b_1, b_2, ..., b_{10})$$

where

$$0.0 \le b_i \le 1.0$$

$$b_i = \frac{p_i - Rmin_i}{Rmax_i - Rmin_i}$$

$$p_i = b_i(Rmax_i - Rmin_i) + Rmin_i \qquad i = 1..10.$$

A part of chromosome representing a muscle looks like:

$$c_{11}, c_{12}, ..., c_{1n}, c_{21}, ..., c_{10n} \qquad c_{ij} = 0 \text{ or } 1$$

where $2^n$ is used to convert a real number between 0.0 and 1.0 to a binary string [b]. That means $c_{i1}, c_{i2}, ..., c_{in}$ is the binary representation of $\lfloor 2^n b_i \rfloor$. We concatenate the binary representation of all muscles in the being-adjusted group to form a chromosome.

**The fitness function** The fitness function reflects the selections of the animator:

$$\text{fitness(solution)} = \begin{cases} 0.9 & \text{if the solution is selected by} \\ & \text{the animator} \\ 0.1 & \text{if the solution is not selected} \\ & \text{by the animator} \end{cases}$$

[b]From our experience $n$ ranging between 5 to 10 gives best convergence and best result for the GA

This fitness function warranties that the selected solutions will be selected to form new generation with very high possibility. The fitness of 0.1 for the solutions which are not selected by the animator still allows these solutions to be selected to form new generation but with very low possibility.

**Crossover**    We use multi-point crossover, which is described in Section 3.

**Mutation**    We start with a mutation rate of 0.3. We increase this mutation rate when the IGAs process seems to converge, and decrease it when the process produces new faces. This mutation rate is constrained to be in the range of 0.3 to 0.5.

## 5. Result

Figure 6 shows the landmarks on the source face model and the adjusted landmark points on the target face model. As can be seen from this figure, the landmarks on the target face model are adjusted to the right position. The deformed face model generated by RBF networks using these landmarks is shown in Figure 7. The deformed face model has the overall shape, forehead and cheek surface, chin shape as the target face model. Eyes, nose and mouth are in correct position. The shape of the deformed face model's lips, however, does not completely match the shape of the target face model's lip. This is because the difference between two pairs of lips is hard to measure even if they look very different. Another example of the exportation's result is shown in Figure 8.

After the deformed face model is created, the muscles are also transferred from the source face model to the deformed face model. Using these muscles, we can create facial expressions on the deformed face model, which are shown in Figure 9. The muscles, however, are not in the perfect positions in the the deformed face model. Some more fine tuning is still needed.

We will now show the result of muscles tuning up process with IGAs. These muscles are used to create happiness and sadness. The happiness created by the initial version of the muscles is shown in Figure 5. The muscles are then interactively adjusted with the IGAs system. Figure 5 and 5 present the intermediate versions of the muscles during the IGAs process. Figure 5 shows the final adjusted result. How the muscles that create sadness are adjusted is shown in Figure 11. Muscles that create other expressions are adjusted in the same manner. As can be seen from the figures, the muscles are step by step adjusted to the right positions with appropriate parameters. The final result is good from a perception of an animator. This can hardly be achieved without the underlying technology of IGAs.

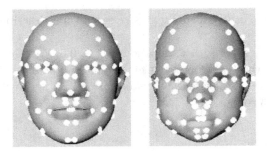

Figure 6. The landmarks on the source face model (left) and the target face model(right).

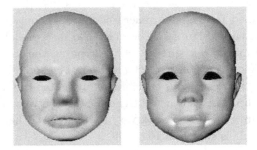

Figure 7. The deformed face model (4650 polygons) (left) and the target face model (4142 polygons) (right).

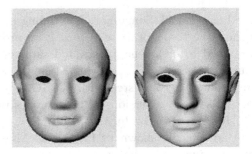

Figure 8. Another example of the deformed face model (4650 polygons) (left) and the target face model (7736 polygons) (right).

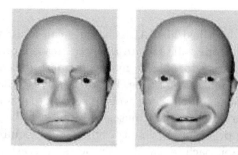

Figure 9. Facial expressions on the deformed face model: sadness (left) and happiness (right).

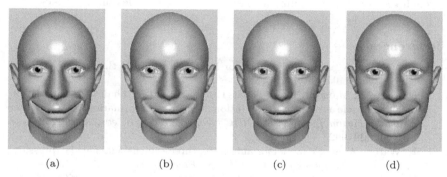

| (a) | (b) | (c) | (d) |

Figure 10. Tuning up the muscles for happiness: (a) - initial placement; (b),(c),(d) - step by step result from IGAs tuning system.

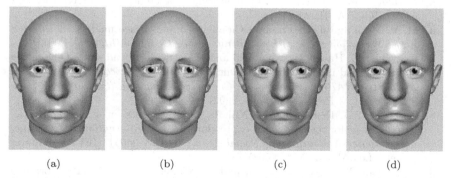

| (a) | (b) | (c) | (d) |

Figure 11. Tuning up the muscles for sadness: (a) - initial placement; (b),(c),(d) - step by step result from IGAs tuning system.

## 6. Conclusion

In this paper, we described how AI techniques can assist the exportation of facial animation from a 3D face to a newly create face. The animation is produced with the vector muscle model first introduced by Waters[3] to create facial expressions in real-time. In order to create natural facial expressions in a 3D face, muscles have to be placed in the correct positions in the face. Other parameters of the muscles also need to be assigned appropriate values. This procedure is time-consuming and requires heavy human involvement. Our approach replaced this process by a faster and easier one, facilitated by AI techniques, in which the animator only has to select the faces with the most natural expressions from his point of view. Our approach takes about 10 minutes to adjust all the muscles on a 3D face.

## References

1. F. I. Parke, A parametric model for human faces, PhD thesis, University of Utah, ([Salt Lake City], 1974).
2. P. Kalra, A. Mangili, N. Magnenat-Thalmann and D. Thalmann, Simulation of facial muscle actions based on rational free form deformations, in *Computer Graphics Forum (EUROGRAPHICS '92 Proceedings)*, eds. A. Kilgour and L. Kjelldahl1992.
3. K. Waters, A muscle model for animating three-dimensional facial expression, in *Computer Graphics (SIGGRAPH '87 Proceedings)*, ed. M. C. Stone1987.
4. D. Terzopoulos and K. Waters, *The Journal of Visualization and Computer Animation* **1**, 73 (1990).
5. J. Noh and U. Neumann, Expression cloning, in *SIGGRAPH 2001, Computer Graphics Proceedings*, ed. E. FiumeAnnual Conference Series (ACM Press / ACM SIGGRAPH, 2001).
6. M. V. Mani and J. Ostermann, Cloning of mpeg-4 face models, in *International Workshop on Very Low Bit rate Video Coding (VLBV01)*, 2001.
7. K. Kähler, J. Haber, H. Yamauchi and H. P. Seidel, Head shop: Generating animated head models with anatomical structure, in *Proceedings of the 2002 ACM SIGGRAPH Symposium on Computer Animation (SCA-02)*, ed. S. N. Spencer (ACM Press, New York, 2002).
8. T. D. Bui, D. Heylen and A. Nijholt, Improvements on a simple muscle-based 3d face for realistic facial expressions, in *16th International Conference on Computer Animation and Social Agents (CASA-2003)*, (IEEE Computer Society, Los Alamos, CA, 2003).
9. T. D. Bui, M. Poel, D. Heylen and A. Nijholt, Automatic face morphing for transferring facial animation, in *Proceedings 6th IASTED International Conference on Computers, Graphics, and Imaging (CGIM 2003)*, (ACTA Press, Anaheim/Calgary/Zurich, 2003).
10. D. S. Broomhead and D. Lowe, *Complex Systems* **2** (1988).

11. M. Eck, *CAD und Computergraphik* **13** (1991).
12. C. M. Bishop, *Neural Networks for Pattern Recognition* (Oxford University Press, Oxford, 1995).
13. L. Booker, Improving search in genetic algorithms, in *Genetic Algorithms and Simulated Annealing*, ed. L. Davis (Pitman Publishing, London, 1987) pp. 61–73.
14. W. M. Spears and K. A. DeJong, An analysis of multi-point crossover, in *Foundations of genetic algorithms*, ed. G. J. E. Rawlings (Morgan Kaufmann, San Mateo, 1991) pp. 301–315.
15. D. E. Goldberg, *Genetic Algorithms in Search, Optimization, and Machine Learning* (Addison-Wesley, Reading, MA, 1989).
16. L. Davis, *Handbook of Genetic Algorithms* (Van Nostrand Reinhold, New York, 1991).
17. H. Takagi, Interactive evolutionary computation: Cooperation of computational intelligent and human kansei, in *Proceeding of 5th International conference on Soft Computing*, 1998.
18. K. Nishio, M. Murakami, E. Mizutani and H. N., Fuzzy fitness assignment in an interactive genetic algorithm for a cartoon face search, in *Genetic Algorithm and Fuzzy Logic Systems*, 1997.
19. Y. Nakanishi, Applying evolutionary systems to design aid system, in *ALIFEV*, 1996.
20. C. Caldwell and J. V.S., Tracking of criminal suspect through face-space with a genetic algorithm, in *4th International Conference on Genetic Algorithms (ICGA'91)*, 1991.
21. E. Baker and M. Seltzer, Evolving line drawings, in *Graphics Interface'94 Proc.*, 1994.

# CHAPTER 12

# TNT: TRANSPARENT NETWORK AND TRANSPORT LAYER NORMALIZER

CAO ANH TUAN

*Vishwakarma Institute of Technology, 666, Upper Indira Nagar, Bibwewadi, Pune – 411037, India*

VARUN KAPOOR

*Vishwakarma Institute of Technology, 666, Upper Indira Nagar, Bibwewadi, Pune – 411037, India*

Security administrators use *network intrusion detection systems* (NID systems) as a tool for detecting attacks and misuse, using passive monitoring techniques. However, there are sophisticated attacks which use ambiguities in protocol specifications to subvert detection. In these attacks, the destination endpoint reconstructs a malicious interpretation, whereas the passive NID system's protocol stack interprets the protocol as a benign exchange. There is a dire need for a new software element at the entry point of the network, which transparently modifies network traffic, so as to remove all possible ambiguities. This will ensure that all internal hosts and the NIDS interpret the traffic in a uniform way, hence removing all chances of an attack sneaking past the NIDS, unnoticed and unmonitored. In this paper, we will present the design and implementation of a normalizer whose job is to eliminate evasion and insertion attacks against an NIDS at the transport and network layers.

## 1. Introduction

NID systems rely on their ability to correctly predict the effect of observed packets on an end-host system in order to be useful. However, as attacks are increasing in sophistication it is becoming difficult to determine when an internal network has been compromised. Examples of these are **Insertion and Evasion attacks** - attacks that use ambiguities in protocol specifications to subvert detection [4].

Examples of these ambiguities are IP fragment reconstruction and the reassembly of overlapping out-of-order TCP byte sequences. The role of the normalizer is to pick one interpretation of the protocols and to convert incoming flows into a single representation that all endpoints will universally interpret.

The normalizer is located at the edge of the network and is meant to be the first internal machine to see the traffic flowing into the site (before any of the internal end-hosts or NIDSs see it) after the site's firewall/router has determined that a packet's intended destination lies within the internal network [6]. It is an in-kernel module which intercepts TCP/IP traffic from the external network, normalizes this traffic by removing the possible ambiguities, performs logical reassembly and forwards this traffic to its intended destination on the internal network. The normalizer also receives traffic from the internal network, but since its normalizations are half-duplex (for performance reasons), it does minimal connection state processing using this data and forwards it to the external network.

The normalizer's approach to converting ambiguous TCP streams into unequivocal, well-behaved flows lies in the middle of a wide spectrum of solutions. This spectrum contains stateless filters at one end and full transport-level proxies – with a considerable amount of state – at the other. Stateless filters can handle simple ambiguities such as non-standard usage of TCP/IP header fields with little overhead. However, they are incapable of converting a stateful protocol, such as TCP, into a non-ambiguous stream. Full transport-layer proxies lie at the other end of the spectrum, and can convert all ambiguities into a single well-behaved flow. However, the cost of constructing and maintaining two full TCP state machines – scheduling timer events, roundtrip time estimation, window size calculations, etc. – for each network flow restricts performance and scalability. The normalizer's approach to converting ambiguous TCP streams into well-behaved flows attempts to balance the performance of stateless solutions with the security of a full transport-layer proxy. Specifically, the normalizer maintains a small amount of state for each connection but leaves the bulk of the TCP processing and state maintenance to the end hosts. Thus, through interposition, the normalizer can guarantee protocol invariants that enable downstream Network Intrusion Detection Systems to work with confidence.

## 2. Shortcomings of an NIDS

An NIDS, which predominantly consists of network sensors, is basically a machine in promiscuous mode that logs all traffic that appears on its LAN segment, and alerts the network administrator of any traffic that it classifies as dangerous, based on a pattern-matching engine which is constantly updated with important patterns to watch out for. NID systems identify attacks using passive monitoring techniques to recognize patterns of misuse as they occur within the protocol streams that pass through the firewall, as well as those that originate within the network's perimeter. As such, they have become the second line of defense within an organization, after firewalls. Unfortunately, there are still some weaknesses that remain unpatched in this layer of defense, which are as follows:

1. An NIDS is, by nature, a device that functions passively, and hence is inherently fail-open.
2. Because of the location of the NIDS within the network topology, it is possible that the NIDS sees some packets which the end-host may not.
3. Because they mainly depend on pattern-matching, and do not process the traffic through a TCP/IP stack, packets can intentionally be crafted in such a way so as to confuse the pattern-matching system, while still correctly being reassembled at the end-host, which may result in the end-host getting attacked.
4. There are some more powerful NIDSs that do perform full reassembly in an attempt to approximate the effect of each packet on an end-host, but sadly, this is just that, an approximation. Studies have shown that different Operating Systems handle cases like overlapping fragments and support for newly introduced TCP and IP options differently, thus making it virtually impossible for the NIDS to know exactly how a particular packet will be reassembled at a given end-host [4].

All these problems led to the rise of a new class of sophisticated attacks, called **Insertion** and **Evasion** attacks. Insertion Attacks are attacks where the NIDS accepts a packet that the end-host rejects. The exact opposites are Evasion Attacks, where the NIDS rejects a packet that the end-host will end up accepting. In both these cases, the NIDS and end-host see 2 different data streams, wherein the NIDS is shown a harmless string, while an attack is being carried out right under its nose.

In this paper, we outline the solution to these, and many more such important problems, in the form of the design and implementation of a Transport and Network Layer Traffic Normalizer. This is an active interposition mechanism that resides at the entry-point of the network and transparently modifies all incoming traffic, so as to remove all possible ambiguities at the TCP and IP levels, which will result in a uniform interpretation of network traffic by all internal hosts and the NIDS.

## 3. History and Related Work

Network security always has been, and probably will always continue to be, an intellectual battle between network administrators and attackers. While an attacker will first try every possible way to infiltrate the system without being detected, and then attempt to escape from the system without leaving a trace behind, the network administrator directs all his efforts towards using every resource available at his disposal to develop tools to detect, prevent and analyze forensically, every intrusion attempt. These pressing needs gave birth to the concept of an NIDS, which helped to serve as a burglar alarm for network administrators, by inspecting all network traffic to identify suspicious patterns that may have indicated a network or system attack.

The definitions of Insertion and Evasion were first mentioned in the paper 'Insertion, Evasion, and Denial of Service: Eluding Network Intrusion Detection' [4]. The word 'Ambiguous' was defined by Ptacek and Newsham as "if an important conclusion about a packet cannot be made without a secondary source of information". The term 'Normalization' first appeared in the paper 'Network Intrusion Detection: Evasion, Traffic Normalisation, and End-to-End Protocol Semantics' [2]. In this paper, Mark Handley and Vern Paxson introduced *norm*, a user level normalizer for IP, TCP, UDP and ICMP, that used libpcap to capture packets, and a raw socket to forward them. It had been tested under FreeBSD, and was released publicly in the summer of 2001, via *www.sourceforge.net*. The basic idea of traffic normalization was simultaneously introduced in the form of a *transport scrubber* [1]. A *transport scrubber* supports downstream passive network-based intrusion detection systems by converting *ambiguous* network flows into *well-behaved* flows that are unequivocally interpreted by all downstream endpoints. A current implementation of the transport scrubber exists as a modified FreeBSD kernel. These two approaches focused on defending against attacks that primarily depended on ambiguous TCP retransmissions, as defined above.

Although *norm* could normalize a TCP traffic stream at 100,000 packets-per-second using a memory-to-memory copy, it was, after all, a user-level implementation, and its authors, Mark Handley and Vern Paxson, in their paper, suggested that an in-kernel implementation of the normalizer would provide better performance, which is one of the improvements we have made over *norm*. Aside from being in-kernel and avoiding copying data back and forth between application-space and kernel-space, we have also implemented all our IP and TCP reassembly "logically". This further contributes to the fulfillment of our overall goal of upholding high performance of the network, described in more detail in section 5.8 [High Performance]. Also, as compared to *norm*, we are a more transparent entity in the network, thus implying less configuration hassles for the network administrator, and more security through a lack of our presence being detectable by machines from both, the external and internal network. More details on this can be found in section 5.1 [MAC Transparency]. Finally, we wanted to propose a good solution for companies wanting a self-contained and independent hardware box that would be ready-to-deploy in a production network as one component of a site's overall security setup, and we have achieved that through our design, which works off of its own customized mini-network stack and abides by our state-diagram, which serves to enforce all our security policies in a reliable and efficient manner.

Another line of thinking was introduced as a solution to the previously-mentioned problems of NIDSs in the paper 'Active Mapping: Resisting NIDS EvasionWithout Altering Traffic'[16], which focused on "eliminating TCP/IP based ambiguity in a NIDS' analysis with minimal runtime cost, by efficiently building profiles of the network topology and the TCP/IP policies of hosts on the network, and then making the NIDS use the host profiles to disambiguate the interpretation of the network traffic on a per-host basis."

The disadvantages of the Active Mapper, as compared to our normalizer are:

1.  They have a need, in general, to be aware of IP and MAC addresses, which, as they themselves admit, can lead to real-world problems when it comes to dealing with issues like NAT and DHCP. We, however, face no such problems, since we are transparent at the TCP, IP and MAC layers, and only classify traffic as internal or external based on the interface on which it comes in.

2.  Maintenance and integration with a site's existing security setup seems to be a problem with them, since they need to be given permission on internal hosts' ACLs, so as to send them probe packets and build up their profile database, and then they need to modify the NIDS' code to use this profile information gathered by them. This modification to the NIDS is rarely ever feasible in a real-world production network. Our normalizer has no such issues and can just be plugged into the network and will start functioning correctly, invisible to everyone.

3.  Maintaining a profile database of the network topology and individual host behaviour is not only an impractical task (as mentioned in [2]), but also a security concern, since the Active Mapper getting compromised and this vast amount of information falling into the wrong hands could be dangerous for the site. Furthermore, the Active Mapper requires the NIDS to be configured to ignore traffic to and from the mapping machine. If an attacker

gets control of the Active Mapper, these kind of special privileges can lead to him having free reign over the internal network, which is a possibly catastrophic circumstance.

4.  The Active Mapper cannot solely depend on the profile built up, since they themselves have mentioned that in the case of internal machines' Network Stacks being modified from the stock version provided by default with the Operating System, their profile information will be inconsistent. They also cannot work correctly in the case of customized proprietary network stacks, which are becoming a very common occurrence in today's world of start-ups, all having developed their own Network Stacks or even specialized Kernels from scratch.

5.  Ambiguous retransmissions cannot always be fixed by them, in which case they do need something like our normalizer in the picture to augment their functioning. We need no such augmentation and, as previously mentioned, are totally self-contained in our functioning.

6.  Finally, and very importantly, they suffer from the same problems an NIDS does, due to their requirement of being located at a network point that is topologically equivalent to the link the NIDS is watching. This problem manifests itself if an attacker can get the Active Mapper to go down, because since the Mapper is fail-open, the network is still open to attack, whereas our normalizer is an active device in the path of all flows, so if it goes down, all access to the network from the external world is also restricted (fail-closed). This is a desirable property when security is more important to a site than accessibility.

One of the most common misconceptions in Network Security today is that a passive NIDS can effectively protect an organization from these attacks [12]. Unfortunately, this belief is misplaced for the reasons described in the previous section. As shown in paper [1], researchers already proved that passive NIDSs can only effectively identify malicious flows when used in conjunction with an active interposition mechanism. Through interposition, a Traffic Normalizer can guarantee protocol invariants that enable downstream intrusion detection systems to work with confidence. In the following sections, we will present our unique approach towards achieving this goal in an effective and computationally efficient manner.

## 4. Design

Our design was guided by, and was meant to conform to, the following principles:

## 4.1. *Design Goals*

1. **Generic and Reusable Design:** The key distinction of our work is a totally generic design whose policies are guided by an optimized state diagram, which, accompanied by a customized-mini stack, totally bypasses the in-built kernel stack.

2. **Security Without Compromising High Performance:** Regarding the security aspect, we guarantee to remove Insertion and Evasion attacks against an NIDS, which then helps the NIDS work with high assurance and confidence. To uphold the high performance of the network, we keep a minimum amount of state, performing only "logical reassembly" of incoming packets, with absolutely no movement of data, and leave all complex TCP processing to the end-hosts, while still being able to extrapolate the state of the TCP connections on both ends by examining the TCP headers of packets passing through us. This is explained in more detail in section 5.8 [High Performance].

3. **Robustness In The Face Of Attacks:** Our normalizer is an active element in the forwarding path of all traffic into and out of the site, so it plays an important role in the availability of the network. Therefore it was designed to not only survive, but also continue to function correctly, in the face of both direct (as mentioned in section 5.1 [MAC Transparency]) and indirect (as mentioned in section 5.6 [Self-Defense]) attacks.

4. **Independent and Self-Contained Implementation:** Eventually, our network stack, combined with a customized memory management module and slightly tweaked network device driver code, would be all the software our normalizer would need to work as a stand-alone hardware box of its own.

## 4.2. *Design Features*

1. **Active interposition mechanism** → Is a "bump in the wire" [1], so all traffic must pass through it, hence it cannot be evaded. This also makes it fail-closed.

2. **Totally Transparent** → Even at the link layer level, thus requiring absolutely no re-configuration of any element of the network. This also makes it virtually impossible for attackers to direct attacks at our normalizer at the TCP,IP or MAC layers, as explained further in section 5.1 [MAC Transparency].

3. **Customized mini-stack** → We totally bypass the kernel stack from just before the IP layer, using our specialized IP and TCP packet-handlers.

4. **Optimized State Diagram** → The backbone and guiding force for all of our normalizer's policies.

5. **Scalability** → Is half-duplex and implemented In-Kernel, keeps a small amount of state, performs minimal processing, and leaves all complex window management and all timers to the end-hosts.

6. **Reliable RST** → Innovative technique to ensure that end-hosts and NIDS maintain same state, especially in the case of connections being reset [2].

7. **Triage** → Robust mechanism for self-defense against Stateholding Attacks [2].

8. Provides a solution to the problem of the highly tricky and hard-to-detect IP Identifier and Stealth Port Scans [2].

9. Unique way of reliably instantiating valid state in the event of cold start.

10. At all points, we have ensured that TCP/IP semantics of packets sanctioned by us to enter the internal network, do not violate the RFC specifications in any way.

## 5. Implementation Details

The normalizer is implemented as a loadable kernel module for the Linux 2.4 kernel [13], which can easily be installed and removed using a single command. The normalizer module receives sk_buffs containing incoming IP packets as input from the first Netfilter hook. This ensures that we are receiving the packets from a safe point in the kernel [7]. Once we get this packet, we steal it and send it through our own customized mini-stack. From this point onwards, we do not use the kernel stack at all.

### 5.1. *Mac Transparency*

MAC transparency helps reduce the need for unnecessary tedious configurations by the network administrator and also ensures that users and attackers are unaware of our presence.

This was done by modifying the receive chain of packets in the Linux 2.4.20 kernel. When our normalizer module is not installed, this modification to the receive chain makes the machine behave like a *logical bridge*, just blindly forwarding packets from the external to the internal network, and vice – versa.

We had already insured that the normalizer machine itself was absolutely inaccessible by any other machine on the network, by not giving it an IP address. Thus, no packets can be directly addressed to the normalizer, and it will hence only process traffic at the IP and TCP layers for machines other than itself.

MAC transparency takes this self-defense against direct attacks one step further by making sure that any Ethernet frame whose protocol field does not specify IP, is sent untouched to the network on the other side of the normalizer, ensuring that we do not process anything at the MAC layer, and as a result, inoculating ourselves against any possible attacks at this level.

Thus, ARP poisoning and other such MAC layer attacks are impotent when attempted against our normalizer. Also, protocols that have a link-layer dependency or component, like ARP, RARP and DHCP can work totally unbroken and unchanged in the presence of our normalizer.

The normalizer consists of two main modules:

1.   IP level normalizations module
2.   TCP level normalizations module

## 5.2.  *IP Level Normalizations Module*

This module gets input from the first Netfilter hook as mentioned above. We begin by walking through the IP header [3] of these packets, normalizing fields which may cause ambiguities. If the packet is fragmented, we *logically reassemble* this packet from its fragments, hashing each packet to its proper slot in a hash queue. Next, if the amount of memory consumed by fragment reassembly has surpassed a configurable upper limit, we perform IP triage to defend ourselves against a Stateholding attack. Once we get a complete IP packet, we check the protocol in its header, and in case it is TCP, we pass it to the next module.

## 5.3.  *TCP Level Normalizer Module*

This module receives complete IP packets, either as a single sk_buff (an unfragmented IP packet) or as a list of sk_buffs containing fragmented IP packets. Initially, we check whether this packet's header is malformed or contains an incorrect checksum, in which cases, we drop it. Also, we ensure that all incoming SYN or RST TCP segments enter the internal network with no payload whatsoever.

### 5.4. *Safe and Consistent Retransmissions*

By performing full TCP and IP reassembly in a light manner, and thus enforcing a single interpretation of each data stream, our normalizer guarantees that its output to the internal network is totally contiguous and free of holes, and in the case of retransmissions, it assures that the data it resends, is an exact copy of what it had sent out previously, leaving absolutely no scope for ambiguous retransmissions.

### 5.5. *Cold Start Problem*

In order to ascertain that we can be inserted seamlessly into any existing network, we have tackled the Cold Start problem ingeniously. This is done by following these 2 simple rules:

1. If a packet on an unknown connection seen after cold start is from the internal network, instantiate state, since the internal network is trusted.
2. If a packet on an unknown connection seen after cold start is from the untrusted external network, transform the packet into a keep-alive ACK packet and forward it inside. If there actually was a connection before cold start, the internal host will reply to this keep-alive, and hence state will reliably be instantiated, according to the previous rule.

### 5.6. *Effective Self-Defense*

One more handy feature of our normalizer is the fact that it can defend itself effectively against indirect DOS and Stateholding attacks, by following a policy of triage. According to this policy, we monitor the amount of in-use memory for TCP connections currently being tracked, and if this memory crosses a configurable upper threshold, we discard state for connections that haven't shown activity in a long time.

The information about relative activity of connections is maintained in a simple and efficient manner, by hashing all our connection states to a hash queue, and on every access of a particular connection, moving that connection's state to the front of its queue. Thus, triage victims are selected in a Least Recently Used fashion by just deleting the state of the connection at the end of each queue for each hash slot.

Also, our state diagram dictates that all state is to be instantiated based on the internal machines' reactions only, so as to prevent the normalizer falling prey to a SYN flooding attack.

## 5.7. *State Diagram*

The major part of our design phase went in creating our optimized and reduced state diagram, which tries to take care of all possibilities of retransmissions in different situations, and makes sure traffic flowing into the network is totally innocuous. We have also dealt with small but important details, like half-close, simultaneous-open and simultaneous-close efficiently and simply. Further, the stringent rules enforced by our state diagram block many stealthy and dangerous pre-attack scans, the most notable ones being *nmap*'s stealth NULL scan, stealth XMAS scan and stealth FIN scan [9].

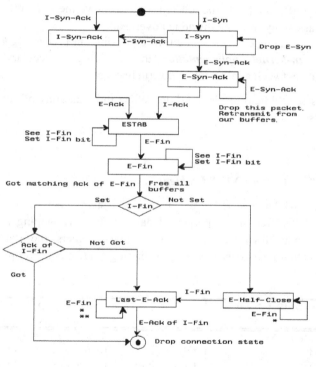

## 5.8. *High Performance*

Because of being an active part of all flows, our basic design goal had to be to uphold the high performance of the network, which we have achieved by:

1. Holding a minimal amount of state. Whereas Linux's TCP data structure occupies 424 bytes (*struct tcp_opt*), we achieve our goal by holding ONLY 60 bytes (*struct tnt_tcp_conn*) of state per connection.
   That is 7 times less state than the Linux Kernel!!!
2. Performing the basic minimum amount of required processing to function correctly, by leaving all complex window management and timer processing to the end-hosts.
3. Doing all our reassembly, at both the IP and TCP layers, *logically*. We don't strip and prepend headers, or defragment and refragment IP packets, or physically reassemble and compress fragments into 1 big sk_buff, like the kernel does. But we achieve the same effect as kernel reassembly, without the added overhead.
4. Normalizing only incoming traffic, making our processing *half-duplex*.
5. An *in-kernel implementation*, thus reducing unnecessary copying of data between application and kernel-space.

These facts should help inspire confidence that the scalability of our normalizer is not an issue.

## 6. Testing

### 6.1. *The "Root" of all NIDS Problems*

As [2] and [4] have stated, when an end-system receives *overlapping* IP fragments that differ in the purported data for the overlapping region, some endsystems may favor the data first received, others the portion of the overlapping fragment present in the lower fragment, others the portion in the upper fragment.

| Operating System | Overlap Behavior |
|---|---|
| Windows NT 4.0 | Always Favors Old Data |
| 4.4BSD | Favors New Data for Forward Overlap |
| Linux | Favors New Data for Forward Overlap |
| Solaris 2.6 | Always Favors Old Data |
| HP-UX 9.01 | Favors New Data for Forward Overlap |
| Irix 5.3 | Favors New Data for Forward Overlap |

The table above is a summary of the research done in [4] to point out IP fragment overlap behaviour for various OSs, and has been used here verbatim to further explain the problem of ambiguous retransmissions.

This leads to a problem that is not easily reliably solvable by an NIDS, because of the exponential explosion of possibilities for it to analyze. As a result, this translates into a very easily generatable cause of failure of an NIDS, thus rendering it ineffective.

(All packets in the test below were generated with the help of an open-source, free packet-generator called packETH [17], which was also used for the majority of our basic-correctness testing, with the help of which we were able to test all flow paths through our customized state-diagram (section 5.7) and verify that things worked as expected.)

To demonstrate the problem of ambiguous retransmissions and to test that our normalizer correctly solved this problem, we hijacked an existing telnet session and sent a hole that looked like this....

    \_ \_ \_ \_ **R O O T**

Then, we retransmitted this overlapping segment....

    \_ **S E R G R U B**

and finally patched up the hole by sending

    **U**

**Without our normalizer installed**
**Windows** reassembled     **U S E R R O O T.**
**Linux**    reassembled     **U S E R G R U B.**

**With our normalizer installed**
**Windows** and *Linux* reassembled **U S E R G R U B.**

This was a very important proof-of-concept test for us, since every ambiguous reassembly attack that an NIDS is susceptible to, can be reduced to this simple test, thus proving the usefulness of and need for our normalizer.

### 6.2. *Nmap Tests*

To test the correctness of our state-diagram (section 5.7), we used the full gamut of tests provided by nmap, and were successfully able to block all their stealthy and dangerous pre-attack scans, the most notable ones being their stealth NULL-scan, stealth FIN-scan, and stealth XMAS-scan.

As concrete proof of our generic and complete approach to normalizing traffic, we were also able to defeat nmap's most diligent OS fingerprinting scan, without making any extra efforts, or intending to do so. We just ran their OS fingerprinting scan through our normalizer, and all the normalizations we had already performed took care of blocking it automatically, without us having to make a single change anywhere.

### 6.3. *Fragroute Tests*

Fragroute by Dug Song [10] is a tool that "intercepts, modifies, and rewrites egress traffic destined for a specified host, implementing most of the attacks described in the paper "Insertion, Evasion, and Denial of Service: Eluding Network Intrusion Detection" [4].

This tool has been able to break several commercial NIDSs deployed in the real-world, by providing implementations for all the different categories of attacks made famous in Ptacek and Newsham's seminal paper on the shortcomings of IDSs and the ways in which they could be exploited, and was therefore invaluable to us and formed the backbone of our testing methodology. Other related works like [2] and [16] have also used this as one of the primary tools in their test setup, thus establishing fragroute as the common benchmark for any work in this field to be validated against.

Our test setup consisted of 2 machines representing the external network, 5 machines representing the internal network, and the our normalizer residing between these 2 networks.

We installed fragroute on the external machines, which along with valid traffic, would also inject bogus and malicious packets into the internal network, according to the rules specified by us. Thus, we simulated a multitude of known reasons-of-failure for an NIDS, and were successfully able to defeat and defend against all of the possible attacks that can be generated by fragroute's ruleset (including combinations of ambiguous and overlapping retransmissions, insertion and evasion attacks), which is, in itself, no small feat.

### 6.4. *Benchmark Tests*

#### 6.4.1. *Internet Downloads*

We connected to the internet on a 128 kbps broadband connection, through the normalizer machine, and ran some basic download tests with and without our normalizer module installed. The timings are as shown in the table below.

| Size (in MB) | Time Without Our Normalizer | Time With Our Normalizer |
|---|---|---|
| 2.55 | 7:42 | 7:57 |
| 3.71 | 12:05 | 12:18 |
| 3.77 | 12:10 | 12:21 |
| 6.33 | 18:46 | 18:53 |
| 10.86 | 25:12 | 25:22 |

### 6.4.2. *Real-time Performance Testing*

To back our performance claims, we also listened to Yahoo!'s real-time internet streaming radio, Launchcast with and without our normalizer module installed and the results are shown below.

| Song Duration (in minutes) | TB Without Our Normalizer (in seconds) | TB With Our Normalizer (in seconds) |
|---|---|---|
| 3: 02 | 5 | 7 |
| 4:29 | 8 | 9 |
| 5:37 | 9 | 10 |
| 7:41 | 10 | 10 |
| 16:23 | 12 | 7 |

TB: Total Buffering

## 7. Future Work and Enhancements

Our first enhancement is to be *totally independent* of the kernel stack. To do this, we need to design our own memory management module. In the case of Linux, this would imply having to write our own version of an sk_buff, because we found that Linux's sk_buff [5] contained too many fields that were of no use to us, so that is a totally unnecessary overhead. Also, we would have to provide a set of our own access functions for our new data structure.

Due to our dependence on the native Linux network device driver code [8], this version of our normalizer sometimes shows limited performance. Hence, we would like to modify our NIC device drivers [11] to customize the reception and transmission queuing policies to achieve better performance in these pathological cases.

Once we fulfill these 2 goals, our normalizer would then *truly* be working with our *own full-fledged customized network stack*.

The implementation introduced in this paper is basically the framework for an industry-level product, which will deliver much higher performance and will be capable of surviving in environments of 1Gbps and beyond. To turn this dream into a reality, we realize that nothing short of hardware implementation will do. Right from the design phase, we have made a conscious and deliberate effort to minimize the amount of external interference and configuration needed for our normalizer to run. This was done keeping in mind our ultimate end-goal of being a transparent Plug-n-Play device on the wire.

## 8. Conclusion

An NIDS is like a network sensor, which is used to detect various attacks or patterns of misuse. If this sensor can be fooled, many attacks may go unmonitored and unnoticed. Since our normalizer guarantees the proper functioning of the NIDS, this is a huge threat we mitigate. Furthermore, the NIDS log is reviewed by the network administrator for forensic analysis, to try and see what went wrong. Our normalizer will help by showing very clearly, exactly what happened, by removing all ambiguous or confusing traffic. Our normalizer fixes an inherent problem in all NIDSs, which is to log many false positives (false alarms) and false negatives (failure to alert). In spite of being an active part of all flows, the normalizer manages to uphold the high performance of the network, which is a huge point in its favor. Finally, due to the increasing inability of NIDSs to faithfully detect various new attacks, companies have to reinvest and spend more money by shifting to Host-based IDSs, which are more expensive and difficult to maintain. Thus, our normalizer can ease this financial burden on companies, by making what they already have invested in (i.e. NIDSs), work with high assurance and correctness.

## References

1.  David Watson, Matthew Smart, G. Robert Malan, and Farnam Jahanian, "Protocol Scrubbing: Network Security through Transparent Flow Modification, IEEE/ACM Transactions on Networking, Vol. 12, No. 2, April 2004.
2.  M. Handley, C. Kreibich, and V. Paxson, "Network intrusion detection: evasion, traffic normalization, and end-to-end protocol semantics," in Proc. 10th USENIX Security Symp., Washington, DC, Aug. 2001.
3.  W. R. Stevens, TCP/IP Illustrated, Volume 1: The Protocols, Addison-Wesley, 1994.

4. T. H. Ptacek and T. N. Newsham, "Insertion, evasion, and denial of service: Eluding network intrusion detection," Secure Networks, Inc., Tech. Rep., Jan. 1998.

5. Thomas F. Herbert, The Linux TCP/IP Stack: Networking for Embedded Systems. Charles River Media, 1st edition, May 2004.

6. Elizabeth D. Zwicky, Simon Cooper & D. Brent Chapman, Building Internet Firewalls, O'Reilly Media, Inc.; 2nd edition, January 15, 2000.

7. Guo Chuanxiong, and Zheng Shaoren, Analysis and Evaluation of the TCP/IP Protocol Stack of LINUX, [Online]. Available: http://edu.jsvnet.com/~xguo/IP_Stack_Analysis_2000.pdf

8. Robert Love, Linux Kernel Development, Novell Press; 2 edition, January 12, 2005

9. Fyodor, *nmap*, 2001. [Online]. Available: http://www.insecure.org/nmap/

10. Fragroute, D. Song. [Online]. Available: http://www.monkey.org/~dugsong/fragroute/

11. Jonathan Corbet, Alessandro Rubini, Greg Kroah-Hartman, Linux Device Drivers, O'Reilly Media, Inc.; 3 edition, February 7, 2005.

12. Sarah Sorensen, Intrusion Detection and Prevention: Protecting Your Network from Attacks. [Online]. Available: www.juniper.net/solutions/literature/white_papers/wp_idp.pdf

13. Daniel P. Bovet, Marco Cesati, Understanding the Linux Kernel, O'Reilly Media, Inc.; 2 edition, December 2002.

14. Douglas E. Comer and David L. Stevens, Internetworking with TCP/IP (volume 1), Prentice Hall; 3rd edition, June 15, 1998.

15. Andrew S. Tanenbaum, Computer Networks, Prentice Hall PTR; 4 edition, August 9, 2002.

16. Umesh Shankar & Vern Paxson, "Active mapping: Resisting NIDS evasion without altering traffic", Security and Privacy, 2003.

17. Packeth – Ethernet packet generator [online]. Available: http://packeth.sourceforge.net/

# CHAPTER 13

# AN INTEGRATED EMBEDDED WEB-SERVICE FRAMEWORK FOR ELECTRONIC DEVICE COMMUNICATION

HUYNH ANH VU

*School of Computer Engineering, Nanyang Technological University, Block N4, Nanyang Avenue, Singapore 639798*

NGUYEN HUY DUNG

*School of Computer Engineering, Nanyang Technological University, Block N4, Nanyang Avenue, Singapore 639798*

RAM GOPALAKRISHNAN

*School of Computer Engineering, Nanyang Technological University, Block N4, Nanyang Avenue, Singapore 639798*

This paper proposes a general low cost framework to enable remote monitoring and controlling tasks in different environments, which leverage the strengths of uIP and web service technology. In this work, we further extend capabilities of uIP, the core tool to realize web services for embedded devices, to define a new standard for electronic devices to communicate using web services. The web service is provided as API to support three key operations with electronic devices including configuration, monitoring status and real-time controlling. This offers great flexibility and reusability as operations can be done remotely through the internet or mobile devices. In addition, the framework can be deployed fully or partially depending on the scale of target environments.

## 1. Introduction

Currently, the ability to monitor device status and issue commands to embedded devices over the Internet is desirable. Traditional instruments have low connectivity or use the relatively inflexible field bus systems for short range distances [1]. Therefore, embedded devices with a full built-in TCP/IP suite could prove to be a significant step in today's networked world. However, placing the entire TCP/IP suite into 8/16 bit devices with limited resources is a challenging task. Therefore, the uIP protocol suite, which is the absolute minimal set of features needed for a full TCP/IP stack, is the general network

169

solution for these devices [2]. Running an embedded web server on the top of uIP enables these small devices to directly communicate with other nodes in the network via the traditional HTTP GET method and simultaneously perform its normal monitoring/controlling tasks. This establishes the foundation to integrate web service technology into embedded devices. Nevertheless, this uIP protocol suite is not robust enough to be deployed in environments that require critical, systematic management. Hence, we are adopting a framework model to make the deployment and management of such systems easier while still maintaining stable and secure operations.

Based on uIP Protocol suite and XML Web Services, this paper proposes the general framework that provides core web service as APIs to support three general operations with embedded devices, namely device configuration during the set up phase, diagnostics and management for monitoring tasks and real-time service interfaces for control tasks, all of which are performed remotely. This framework can be used in home environments or large scale environments such as manufacturing automation and hospitals

The organization of this paper is as follows. Section 2 briefly discusses the uIP protocol suite and its characteristics. Section 3 gives a general overview of web service technology and how cross device communication through web services is made possible. In section 4, we present the architectural view of our proposed embedded web-service framework. An example of its application for large scale hospital with a remote patient monitoring system is introduced in section 5. Next, we evaluate the performance of the framework in section 6. Section 7 concludes the paper by emphasizing the work that has been done and the scope for future development.

## 2. Embedded Web Server

The ideal application of the uIP protocol suite is in small embedded devices running low-end 8-bit or 16-bit microcontrollers. These devices are usually offered at low cost and perform simple tasks. Therefore, they have very limited memory (RAM, ROM) as well as low speed operating clocks. In order to include communication ability to these devices, we must utilize minimum resources in the system for communication tasks. The uIP protocol suite is able to achieve this with the code size of a few kilobytes and required RAM of a few hundred bytes [2]. This is significantly smaller than the generic TCP/IP in most modern day operating systems. Nevertheless, uIP can communicate with these full featured TCP/IP stacks. Moreover, an additional web server program on the top of uIP protocol suite allows small embedded electronic devices handle information submitted by nodes in the network and then reply to these nodes. As a comparison, we note that the traditional field bus system lacks this ability [5]. Hence, the web servers make embedded systems a living entity by its own on the network by communicating status and control information with other nodes in the network.

In this work, the general open source code uIP [1, 2] is ported to Renesas M16C28 microcontroller. The entire stack to communicate over the Ethernet LAN is shown in Figure 1.

The bottom layer is the network controller card, RTL8019AS that interfaces with the physical layer in the LAN.

| Application |
| :---: |
| HTTP Protocol |
| ICMP, IP, AR Protocols |
| Ethernet Driver |
| Ethernet RTL8019AS Network Control Interface |

Figure 1.  Layers in uIP protocol stack.

The second layer is the Ethernet driver that sends and receives packets to/from the physical link by writing to the register set of the RTL8019AS. The buffer control logic inside RTL8019AS will handle the rest of the communication [3]. The next two layers implement only ICMP (Ping), simple IP, AR, and TCP protocols [1] in the full featured TCP/IP stack. The last layer is the HTTP protocol which enables M16C28 as a tiny web server. All the firmware implementation is burnt into the M16C28's built-in ROM.

Compared to the standard implementation of the traditional TCP/IP stack, uIP does not have an operating system to support it. It has an event driven interface where the application is called in response to certain events. The entire process, including application and uIP, is to poll for arrival of packets from the network or timeout so that uIP knows what happens and in turn calls the application based on events. To reduce the memory usage, uIP does not buffer outgoing packets for retransmission purposes. Instead it calls the application layers to reproduce that piece of information and send out after that [1, 2].

To extend the capability of the embedded web server, we make use of the existing XML web service technology as a standard communication link through Hyper Text Transfer Protocol (HTTP).

## 3. XML Web-Service

Today's Internet combines a number of inter-connected computers, ranging from the peer-to-pear model and client/server model to various kinds of others distributed models. Among those, a popular system model is to keep information in centralized databases, with gatekeepers (web servers) controlling access. Users send requests to these servers to gain access to available services. The web server, in reply, invokes (remote) objects on its local or another server's environment to perform necessary actions (request and reply protocol) [13], [14]. With this interaction model between servers, the Internet and existing electronics devices are loosely coupled, as a fundamental feature of distributed systems. They are two isolated islands of information and functionality [9]. What we require is a generic framework that will allow developers and users to exploit both the power of electronics devices and the global network, making truly distributed computing a possibility.

Furthermore, this framework must facilitate the separation of data from the way in which the data is presented (metadata)—it must natively support free flow of information between devices [8, 12]. But traditional Hypertext Markup Language (HTML) can only allow users to have access to information. They do not enable users to leverage it. This is where Extended Markup Language (XML) serves as a better choice.

XML is a Recommendation from the World Wide Web Consortium, (http://www.w3.org), the multi company group that defined XHTML and its predecessor, HTML. It is a vehicle for information that brings usable data to the desktop and is a universal data format that does for data what HTML does for Web content—it provides the necessary markup. It has proved to be a good choice for defining data [11, 14].

XML is the enabling technology for the Microsoft.NET Web Services - a fundamental building block in the move to distributed computing on the Internet. Generally, a Web Service is simply an application that can be integrated with other Web Services using Internet standards. It's a URL-addressable and discoverable resource that can returns information to clients who want to use it programmatically [13]. Among important features of Web Services are its open standards, self-contained, self-discovery [14]. The focus on communication and collaboration among people and applications has created an environment where XML Web services are becoming the platform for application integration.

Unlike current component technologies, Web Services do not use object model specific protocols such as DCOM, RMI, or IIOP. Web Services take a different approach: they are built on XML, SOAP, WSDL and UDDI specifications using ubiquitous web protocol (HTML, XML). Any system supporting these Web standards will be able to support Web Services.

Based on these abilities, XML web services prove themselves to be a good supplement for the uIP protocol suite. In this work, we propose an effective way to put them to work together in the integrated framework.

## 4. Integrated Embedded Web-Service Framework

The vertical architecture of the framework as well as the application program on the top of this framework is shown in Figure 2.

### 4.1. *Physical Layer*

This layer comprises of all hardware related components of the framework. They are typically smart transducer nodes that can interface with the outside world. These transducers are controlled by small microcontrollers. They are either sensors collecting status of a system or actuators performing predefined tasks. Now, we add communication capability to these nodes by embedding the web server using the uIP protocol suite. As uIP does not consume much of the nodes' resource, it does not impact the node's capabilities but rather we significantly boost the connectivity of these nodes. Each node has an IP address and this implies that any other connected device could communicate with this node through traditional HTTP GET.

### 4.2. *Service Layer*

Once smart transducer nodes gain connectivity, they could be connected to one or many service providers that form the layer two of the framework. Communication between these service providers and transducer nodes is through a LAN. While transducer nodes themselves could provide very limited services i.e. only raw data through HTTP GET method due to its processing and memory constraint, addition of service providers will enhance the overall capabilities of the framework and further abstract transducer nodes from higher layers.

#### 4.2.1. *XML web-services*

The underlying XML web services come as standard API to communicate with smart transducer nodes in the physical layer.

As we have mentioned above, every smart transducer is a connected entity in the network. Therefore, the XML web service enables users remotely control and administer those entities with great ease.

174

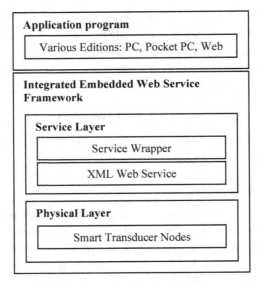

Figure 2. Layers of framework.

### 4.2.2. *Service wrapper*

This component is intended for deployment of the system in a large scale environment.

In a large scale environment like hospitals, the demand for stability, performance and information security is set to a very high standard [10], [11]. The native XML web services combined with smart transducers may not be adequate.

The basic function of service wrapper is to expose all web service methods that the XML web service offers to enable users remotely exploit those services. Furthermore, this service wrapper will handle the authentication, authorization against every web service call to the transducers. Additional reasons for this wrapper include the ability to change service provider and up-gradation of the system without impacting end users.

Security issues are also handled in this component. To prevent unlimited calls to smart transducers, like in a Denial of Service (DoS) attack that may degrade the system, the SOAP header is included in all service calls containing the caller's IP address that will limit the number of service call from a specific address at a time. In addition, a limit on the maximum number of concurrent connections can be configured by system administrator to enhance performance.

### 4.2.3. *Provided services*

Typically, there are three types of services [4]: device configuration services, diagnostic services and real-time services. Higher layers use each of these services for different purposes. Device configuration services are ways for higher layers to set-up the device during the set-up phase. This comprises of checking the presence of the device, setting up default device's parameters, etc. Diagnostic services allow higher layers to monitor the status of the device. This includes the monitoring of various device parameters. These could be key parameters such as blood pressure and pulse rate in the case of a medical diagnostic device. The service provider may periodically monitor this status and notify higher layers if a certain event occurs. Real-time services enables higher layers to issue commands to remotely control the device which in turn results in a modification of the device's parameter or perform an action.

## 4.3. *Information Flow*

The information flow inside the framework is depicted in Figure 3.

A key advantage that can be seen from the diagram is the flexible device management in an enterprise environment. The device now can be administered wirelessly, a major change compared to other traditional wired environments.

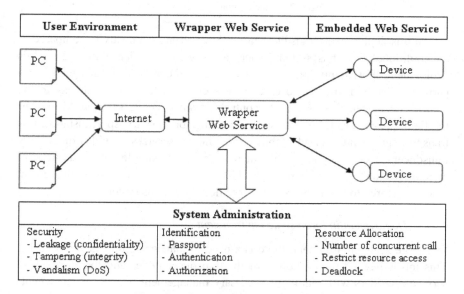

Figure 3. Information flow in the framework.

### 4.4. *Deployment of The Framework To Different Environments*

A key benefit of the integrated embedded web service framework is its flexibility in deployment on different kinds of environment. Depending on what is the targeted environment, part or entire layers of the framework are deployed. The following section presents deployment scenarios in home and large scale environments.

#### 4.4.1. *Deployment in home environment*

In this type of environment we *could* bypass the need of the service provider layer. A home user interacts directly with transducer nodes like in Figure 4.

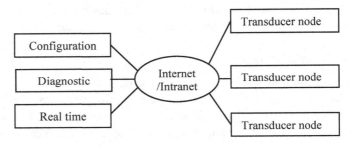

Figure 4. Home environment deployment.

In this deployment, transducer nodes have strong connectivity compared to the traditional field bus system. There are several benefits addressed by this deployment. For a multiple field bus system, the system is designed for a particular use and difficult to extend. It is essential to have a gateway to the control transducer if users want to control it from a remote location. Moreover, the field bus such as CAN or RS485 is usually for short transport distance, low transport speed and poor adaptability [5]. Though services provided directly by transducer nodes in our deployment are quite simple, the addition of communication capabilities through HTTP GET, is a significant improvement when compared to the abilities of the traditional field bus system.

#### 4.4.2. *Deployment in large scale environment*

In a large scale environment, there is a need to manage resources and security. This job is beyond the capability of the transducer nodes and therefore added service providers will handle all necessary management besides enhancements provided by it to the existing services.

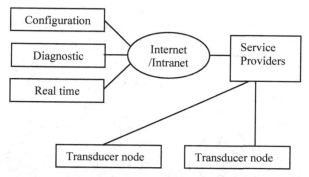

Figure 5. Large scale environment deployment.

This kind of deployment is similar to the vertical integration of field bus system proposed in [6]. However, we use generic transducer nodes, i.e. we need not manufacture nodes that are specific to a particular system; instead, we could reuse the nodes that are deployed in the home environment. Hence, the framework has high reusability and is generic in nature.

## 5. Remote Patient Monitoring System

To demonstrate a particular application of the framework, we present here a prototype of the system which could be used in hospitals in the future. There is an increasing requirement for manpower in hospitals and therefore, a system that enables doctors and nurses remotely monitor patients is desirable. The system connects various medical equipments in the hospital so that sharing information becomes easier. Furthermore, this is a platform for many other advanced features such as intelligent emergency alerts could be integrated into the system. Figure 6 illustrates our proposed system for the hospital environment.

In this prototype, the system allows doctors to constantly monitor a patient's heartbeat and oxygen saturation in blood through various devices such as personal computers in the hospital, pocket PCs or via web interfaces. The monitoring device uses photoplethysmographic principle to capture the heartbeat and oxygen saturation in patients' blood [7] and this device is installed at each patient's station (a smart bed). Moreover, the system also provides a standard set of APIs to allow other external software to interact with existing equipments in the hospital. Clearly, this deployment of the integrated embedded web-service framework into a large scale environment is indicative of its generic nature and widespread application. Table 1 shows the one to one correspondence between the framework and this system.

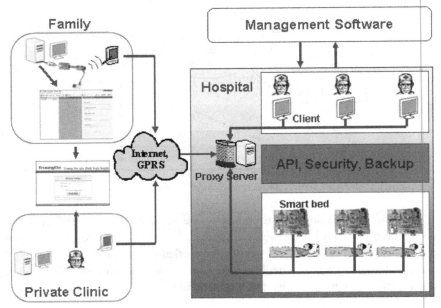

Figure 6. Remote patient monitoring system.

Table 1. A one to one correspondence between the framework and the system.

| Framework | System |
|---|---|
| *Physical layer:* Smart transducer node | *Smart bed:* heartbeat and oxygen saturation |
| *Service layer* | *Proxy Server* |
| *Provided services:* Standard API set to interact with device and for management software developers. | *Device configuration:* check existence of device on the network *Diagnostic service:* monitor patient |

## 6. Performance Evaluation

We examined the performance of the framework by measuring the response time of the proxy server when there are an increasing number of concurrent connections in the above remote patient monitoring system.

In the first experiment, we tested the response time of the proxy server from the same pocket PC issuing consecutive requests for information. Figure 7 shows the response with respect to different requests. The bottleneck of the first request resided in the transmission from the smart bed to the proxy server. After the data was cached inside the proxy server as it knew the data was most relevant, the subsequent requests had shorter response times.

In the second experiment, we increased the number of applications connecting to the proxy server and repeating requests for data. Figure 8 shows the response time with respect to the number of connections. In this case, the relevant data had been cached by the proxy server. It is not surprising that the time delay is rising as the number of connections increase. This is because the connections are queued to get a response from the server.

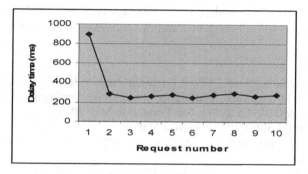

Figure 7. Time delay from proxy server.

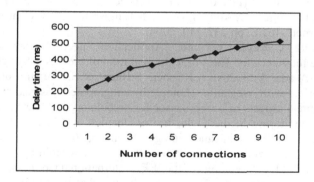

Figure 8. Time delay versus number of connections.

## 7. Conclusion

Overall, we have presented a framework that allows electronic devices to communicate in the network while keeping the cost of deployed systems as low as possible. The added advantage of improved communication ability and economic feasibility is due to the highly compact uIP combined with flexible web services. The framework has high scalability, reusability and compatibility. It can be deployed in various environments from small home environments to large scale enterprise environments. Currently, home appliances are the main target devices for this framework. In the future, with improved research on intelligent embedded systems, more sensitive medical devices such as non-invasive blood pressure monitor, glucose controller or industrial equipments will also be able to integrate this system using the framework thereby enabling them to perform more sophisticated tasks. In order to address these time critical application, research is underway on the service layer which resides in the service providers to facilitate better security and resource management.

## References

1. Adam Dunkels, "Full TCP/IP for 8-Bit Architectures", In Proceedings of the first international conference on mobile applications, system and services (MOBISYS 2003), San Francisco, May 2003.
2. Doxygen 1.3.3, uIP 0.9 Reference Manual.
3. National Semiconductor, DP8390D32490D NIC Network Interface Controller.
4. H. Kopetz, "The Three Interfaces of a Smart Transducer", In Proceedings of the Forth IFAC International Conference on Field Bus Systems and Their Applications (FeT'01), Nancy, France, 15th-16th November 2001.
5. H.Jiao, L.Jianguo, G. Min, "Embedded Temperature Web Controller Based on Internet", IEEE, pp 237-240, 2004.
6. M.Venzke, C.Weyer, V.Turau, "Application Specific vs Standard Web Service Interfaces for The Vertical Integration of Field Bus Systems", IEEE
7. H. H. Asada, P.Shaltis, A.Reisner, S.Rhee, R.C. Hutchinson, "Mobile monitoring with wearable photoplethysmographic biosensors: Technical and clinical aspects of a ring sensor for ambulatory, telemetric, continuous health monitoring in the Field, in the Hospital and in the Home", IEEE Engineering in Medicine and Biology Magazine, 2003.
8. Chan, A. T. S. and D. K. T. Wan , "Web services mobility in a pocket.". ICWS 2005, In Proceedings of the IEEE International Conference, 2005.
9. Fu, X., T. Bultan, et al., "Synchronizability of conversations among Web services", Software Engineering, IEEE Transactions Volume 31(Issue 12), pp 1042 – 1005, 2005.
10. Geer D., "Taking steps to secure Web services." Computer Volume 36(Issue 10), pp 14 – 16, 2003.
11. McGregor, C. and J. Scheifer, "A framework for analyzing and measuring business performance with Web services". E-Commerce, 2003. CEC 2003. IEEE International Conference, 2003

12. Tosic, V., H. Lutfiyya, et a., "On requirements for management of mobile XML Web services and a corresponding management system", Telecommunications in Modern Satellite, Cable and Broadcasting Services,7th International Conference, 2005
13. Wyke, R. A., R. A. Wyke, et al., XML Programming (Core Reference), Microsoft Press., 2002.
14. Coulouris, Dollimore, et al, Distributed Systems: Concepts and Design, Pearson Education, 2005

# CHAPTER 14

# USING ONTOLOGY TO HELP ACHIEVE MOBILE, MULTI-SKILLED EMPLOYEES

DANG THANH-TUNG [*†], CÁTHÁL WILSON, CON SHEAHAN

*Enterprise Research Centre, University of Limerick, Limerick, Ireland*


BEN FLOOD

*Center for Telecomunications and Value-Chain-Driven Research, UL, Limerick, Ireland*


DANG BAO-LAM

*Department of Design of Machines and Robots, Hanoi University of Technology, 1 Dai Co Viet str. Hanoi, Vietnam*

Migration of employees has posed a big problem for SMEs. Migration has many advantages but leads to difficulties for SMEs, too. One disadvantage caused by the migration of employees is that experience and knowledge lose when experienced employees leave. Training new employees consumes an enormous cost [1]. This paper discusses the problem how to compile the knowledge and reuse it to help mobile employees. The ontology methodology is chosen as a tool for modeling and storing knowledge. Ontology-based assistance is based on the work context, which employees are working on. Case-based reasoning technique is used to identify a suitable solution. The case study is a company that produces special ceramics for industrial applications. The project is developed in cooperation with experts from the company. The feedback from employees during implementation and exploitation in the company is the key factor for the project's success.

## 1. Introduction

One of key problems that every SME has to face is how to reduce total expenses, without interfering with the plants capability for satisfying external demands. To satisfy customer's demands, a number of things have to be carried out within the SME framework, every product or service that an SME provides

---

[*] The author's work has been funded by the Irish Research Council for Science, Engineering and Technology (IRCSET).
[†] Email contact to a corresponding author: dang.tung@ul.ie

consists of a number of elementary operations, which are associated with one another.

Generally it is possible to execute each basic operation by a number of methods. It is the nature of any plant that a large number of operations are repeated many times during a day or may appear in multiple processes. SME's generally prefer to use their own capacity if possible to perform these operations rather than redistributing them to external vendors. As a result multi-skilled employees are common within the SME sector. Many factors gathered during carrying out the study in SMEs, like the large number of tasks, a wide range of task's types, the possibility of someone missing and stopping production is not acceptable, lead to a conclusion that there must be employees capable of filling vacant roles. The management of the studied company has come to the conclusion that employee's migration from one job to another is a common reality and it is not necessarily a bad thing, a certain amount of staff turnover is good for a plant. The key advantage of a certain amount of staff turnover is that it allows changes to be made to an advancing production process without having to overcome issues with staff that are set in their ways. This does pose some problems however, training new employees is a high-cost operation as a result of the time of key employees and supervisors being consumed.

Training is typically carried out via video, tutorials or hands-on experience. There are disadvantages with all these methods. As a result of that only basic situations are captured in the video, tutorial and hands on training, many non-standard or unexpected situations are missed. Default solutions are generally not available for situations that are not identified as standard ones and are not captured in tutorials or the video. Training under the supervision by experts takes up a lot of valuable people's time and is not as practical and effective as self-training based on the employee-to-employee approach. The main ineffectiveness of the supervisor's training method is that almost employees need a proactive assistance in solving unexpected situations; meanwhile the supervisor is not able to assist on time and in every situation. Many non-standard situations can repeatedly occur. Each situation can be solved or processed differently by different employees. Consequently, there is a considerable amount of experiences that is available for every employee and can be useful for solving unexpected or non standard situations.

Real advice from practitioners who worked on the same process or situations would be more helpful than any general guide. Advices are deduced and recommended on the basis of previous experiences in relation to the concerning situations. Every employee in an organisation is both a provider and a user of experience. Employees communicate their experience to a common medium, then retrieve experience in a future from this common medium. Such self-training approach in combination with a feedback provided by experienced employees enables employees faster adapting new roles in the organisation or solving new situations that they have to face for very first time.

This paper suggests a solution to use ontology to represent and store relevant knowledge to assist employees in training for whatever situation they must work. According to the definition by [2], ontology is a specification of a conceptualization, i.e. a collection of the objects, concepts, and other entities that are assumed to exist in some area of interest and the relationships that hold among them. A short introduction on the ontology is available in [6] and [7].

The rest of this paper is organised as follows. Section 2 discusses the issue of multiskilled employees in SMEs. Section 3 describes the case for study – some scenarios taken from the studied company. Section 4 discusses ontology-based assistance for employees. Section 5 discusses some issues associated with realisation and exploitation of the research project in practice.

## 2. Multiskilled Employees in SME's

Reduction of labour expenses leads to a situation where employees have to migrate between different positions in the company to fill different roles. New roles and new tasks require new knowledge and skills for the employees. For these reasons it makes sense to exploit the experiences of previous employees to assist the ones undergoing training. That strategy allows maximizing economic effectiveness and reducing high cost demands associated with worker migration within the company. It is clear that know-how and experiences are worthwhile assets that every SME can own. When employee's leave, experiences or knowledge gathered by those employees themselves could be lost too. In order to prevent this happening there are 3 key tasks that must be carried out.

1. identify relevant experiences and knowledge that is worthwhile keeping for new employees to study,
2. identify a method to compile these relevant experiences and knowledge, and store them in a manner suitable for reuse,
3. identify an appropriate method of presenting the data collected to new employees/users.

It is also important to clarify the difference between some notations like skill and experience, knowledge and information. Undertaking any task or operation requires a certain skill. For example, in order to execute operations like milling, grinding, the concerning employee has to own some skill or have previous experiences with milling or grinding. Employees also own some skills that they have gained by on-the-job training, education. Skill is also required for working in some positions in the organization. For example, a machine operator needs some skills for working with machines to set up, to load or to operate efficiently. However, skill is *not transferable*; it is defined by the setting in which it is used. Employers usually tend to find employees with adequate skills familiar with all jobs technical dimensions in the company. That strategy is not cost-effective, due to the wide range of job's character involved in small organization like SME.

Experience, unlike skill, is not fixed for a specific context. Experience is *transferable* from setting to setting. It is generated and collected by the past behavior of employees, not the current knowledge. Experience can be, in general, called up and used in any situation. Being experienced with something means it is able to do it again, regardless the technical skill required to undertake the job. Our research focuses on experience management. Experience management is formed in [12] as a process of reusing experience, learning from experience and improving practices for employees. The goal is to offer automatic and proactive assistance in multiple contexts to employees.

*Information* that employees are asked to provide the computer aid system is data in context, or contextualized data. Information generally includes facts, observations, sensations, and messages. Information is content which provides an understanding of relationship between individual situation and associated experiences. *Knowledge*, in contrast, is the human experience deduced on the basis of gathered information.

Before discussing how to deal with the above tasks, some fundamental assumptions and features relating to worker migration need to be mentioned in order to restrict and simplify the problem for solving.

In general, each process involved in manufacturing consists of multiple smaller steps called basic operations. The first assumption is that the employee is capable of executing all of the basic operations. The problem for employees is often choosing the best combination of basic operations and the identification of the nuances of the problem that are generally only obtained through experience, for fulfilling the assigned task. There can be many alternative ways to fulfil a goal, and experience can often be the difference between carrying out a task the right way and carrying it out the wrong way. The purpose of using ontology is to bypass this experience requirement by presenting the process/job information from the experienced to the inexperienced employees.

Another issue is that not every migrated employee needs help. There might be employees (skilled employees) that have some skill allowing them to perform the assigned task, though their method may not be the best one. Recruits in a new position, or those who have to face a new task for the first time, might need complete guidance and assistance, but employees with a little experience may be interested in how to carry out the assigned task better than their current approach.

The important assumption in our work is the willingness for employees to operate the computer aid system. Because every employee in an SME is both a provider and a user of experience, cooperation between the computer aid system and employees is vital for the project's success. Employees provide their experience and additional information to a common medium. Employees are also able to retrieve experience in a future from this common medium for further usage. In order to make the system work, real data provided by employees must be converted to a format, which a computer can understand. The technical problem of the collection and transformation of real data to a computer-understandable format is sophisticated. For example, getting data like duration of operation, temperature, pressure, etc. requires a connection between the real measurement and the computer system. Manual entry of data is necessary, but should be carried out in such a way (as much as possible) that it does not disturb the process of fulfilling the assigned task. This would require some time initially to capture situations and experiences in the ontology, but once this is achieved, it would only be a matter of keeping it up to date when new situations occur.

## 3.  The Case Study

The case selected for study is "a Ceramics Production Plant". The plant is an MTO (Make-To-Order) operation and employees must be flexible to fulfill various kinds of tasks during a working day. One of tasks that must be carried out constantly is "Kiln Operation". The following text is a note entered by one employee as an approach to set Kiln programs and all the steps that have to be carried out in order to eliminate alarms and other events. Since obviously not everyone will be familiar with the operation of a kiln, several simple instances have been selected from this note for illustration.

### 3.1.  *Context/Job*

The Kiln is used to process a large number of parts and is the primary piece of equipment within this plant due to its process capability and its value as an asset. The below tables contain the data and quantities of parts that can be placed on each batch (These numbers have been altered for confidentiality reasons).

Table 1. List of ceramic elements.

| Ceramic Elements | | |
|---|---|---|
| ELEMENT TYPE | CLAY NO. | GLAZED NO. |
| FFE | 4 | 4 |
| FTE | 4 | 4 |
| HFE | 8 | 8 |
| THE | 8 | 8 |
| QTE | 30 | 20 |
| LFFE | 3 + 1 FTE | 4 OR 2 LFFE AND 2 FTE |
| LFTE | 3 + 1 FTE | 4 OR 2 LFTE AND 2 FTE |
| SFSE | 5 | 5 + 1 FTE |
| SFEH | 5 | 5 + 1 FTE |
| BULBS (LARGE) | 6 + 4 FTE | 6 |
| BULBS (SMALL) | 7 + 4 FTE | 6 |

Table 2. Component quantity for batch machine.

| Dust Press Parts | |
|---|---|
| COMPONENT | MAXIMUM QUANTITY |
| Beads | 1 Sagger (c. 4000 beads) |
| Bridges | 180 |
| Flats | 180 |
| James Thomas Blocks | 30 blocks / 60 halves |
| Pillar | 20 pillars / 40 halves |
| Connector Block | 40 |
| MAK Plug | 20 plugs / 40 halves |

## 3.2. *Role of the Operator*

The role of the operator is to:
- Set the programs as described above,
- Reset the machine if any alarms go off or get one of the authorised/trained personnel to sort the issue if they themselves are not capable.
- The operator is also responsible for loading and unloading the machine.

## 3.3. *Setting Kiln Programs*

- STEP 1: Call up 'F4 Programs', on the bottom bar.
- STEP 2: When prompted, enter password – *******, and press 'Enter'.
- STEP 3: In the top left panel of the F4 display, change the program number shown to '3' by clicking on the left – hand or the right – hand arrow as relevant, using the mouse key.

- STEP 4: Click on the large rectangular button next to: **Temperature/ Calculation** – Wait for status indicator to go from red to green, (click again if it fails to go green).

Repeat for:
  - ○ Pressure
  - ○ Gradient

*Ensure in each case that the indicator has gone green before clicking again.*

- STEP 5: Visually confirm that Program 3 is active by checking on the set temperatures (max zone = 900 degrees C) under the 'F1 controller', and leave the PC.
- If the program is not active, repeat the STEP 1 – STEP 5, until successful.

**Different Programs Include (in step 1):**
- ➤ Program 1 – Cool Down.
- ➤ Program 2 – Biscuit.
- ➤ Program 3 – Glaze.
- ➤ Program 4 – Dust Press.
- ➤ Program 5 – Stand by.

**Kiln Speed Setting:** The correct kiln speed (transit time) for the biscuit and glaze firing programs for regular elements is as follows:
- ➤ BISCUIT:   Program 3 – speed 85 minutes.
- ➤ GLAZING: Program 3 – speed 89 minutes.
- ➤ BULB ELEMENTS:   Program 3 – speed 150 minutes.
- ➤ DUST PRESSED FIRINGS: Program 4 – speed 210-220 minutes.

**To alter the kiln speed setting – proceed as follows:**
- STEP 1: Call up the "Menu" option on the PLC.
- STEP 2: Now call up "Transit time" within the menu.
- Step 3: The inverter frequency (in Hz), and real time speed (in minutes) will be displayed.
- STEP 4: To change the speed, touch the box labelled "Manual", and the background should go black. To increase the time, press the "Down" box, and observe the inverter frequency dropping, this will reduce the motor speed and therefore increase the time taken for the elements to pass through the kiln.
- STEP 5: When the required frequency is displayed, this should also reflect the correct kiln speed. Check the real time speed - reading, this updates every 30 seconds approximately.

- STEP 6:
  - ➤ If the speed is in the range of that required – as outlined above the correct frequency has also been reached.
  - ➤ If it is **above** this range hit " Down" again and wait.
  - ➤ If it is **below** this range hit "Up" again and wait.

*Continue until the correct range is reached.*

- STEP 7: Once the correct speed reading is has been reached and is stable, hit the "Manual " button again, and the black background disappears.
- STEP 7: Once the correct speed reading has been reached and is stable, hit the "Manual "button again, and the black background disappears.
- STEP 8: Go back to "Menu".

### 3.4. *Kiln Max. Temp. Alarm*

In this case, the Control System incorrectly thinks that the maximum temperature setting of the kiln (approx. 1350 degrees C) has been exceeded. The max temperature device inside the control cabinet is clearly labeled, and a reset button can be seen in the top left hand corner through the hole in the plastic cover.
Press this button to cancel the max. temperature alarm.

### 3.5. *Kiln Draft Alarm*

This occurs when the draft in the kiln is too low.

- STEP 1: If this alarm is activated on the PLC, access the "menu", on the PLC screen. One of the options then displayed is "regul. pressure / temp", select this option and then select "reg.pres.kiln". This displays an information screen regarding kiln pressure, and one of the features shown is a number relating to flap %.
- STEP 2: If the kiln draft is low, then this flap should be opened up to increase the draft. This is done by selecting the "manual" box on the screen and then selecting the "up" arrow.
- STEP 3: When the increase in the flap opening % is sufficient (usually 29%) to cancel the kiln draft (as indicated by the cancellation of the alarm on the PLC screen), press the "Gas On" button.
- STEP 4: This will initiate the safety checks by the gas test unit within the control cabinet. The first light (amber) indicating 'test' will illuminate, and if no safety problem is found in the gas line, then the second (green) light will illuminate.

- STEP 5: At this stage, the 'tightness control lamp' on the front panel should be on. If the gas is still off, press the 'Gas On' button again, and it should immediately come on.
- STEP 6: Raise the temperature of the kiln slowly by initiating program 5 on the PC.

*If any problem other than the above is present, the cause and cure must be found to allow the gas to reset.*

### 3.6. *Alarms*

Alarm Strobe Light Indicators:
**Red** – Burner Malfunction.
**Blue** – Conveyor Malfunction
RED LIGHT:
- STEP 1: Check Program Display – F1: Control and / or F3 'Kiln Display', To Determine location of possible burner malfunction.
- STEP 2: The burner may be reset manually at the source – and this is the preferred method.
- STEP 3: Visually inspect for the flame through the peep hole at the malfunctioning burner.
- STEP 4: Check the instruction with regard to the No. being displayed – press the "i" reset button.
- STEP 5: If the No. "52" is flashing – the operator must reset the burner at the control panel. In this case: reset the burner by turning the black knob of the desired burner group 03 – 10 back and forth once. Press the green reset button of the desired burner group 03-10.
- STEP 6: Reset the flashing alarm light on the "Kiln Alarm Display"

BLUE LIGHT: etc.


### 4. How to Assist – The Problem Formulation

This section discusses how to realise the three basic tasks stated in Section 2, to fulfil the main purpose – to assist employees, to advise what employees should do in each situation to achieve the production goal via the best and most efficient method possible.

## 4.1. *Process Representation*

The question about whether or not the process representation is necessary has been the subject for discussion between practitioners and project's developers. The process representation is crucial for knowledge maintenance and management, as well as important for communication between employees and the computer aid system. A good representation allows the computer aid system easily communicating with employees, i.e. processing requests, information without extra interpretation or translation. Finding a method for representation, which is able to generate suitable a model for computer processing as well as for practitioners understanding, is not easy. As a result, a number of difficulties related to the representation issue have been identified.

From developer's point of view, a technical representation of processes is suggested as a solution. Each process, basic operations and all other associated features are described by using a number of standard attributes, logical operations and numerical or fuzzy values. But, in order to do that, employees or practitioners are required to have a certain technical background familiar with the technology used in the project, e.g. ontology editor, logical rules editor. That means there will be more additional work for employees. That will discourage employees to cooperate with the computer aid system and consequently the main goal of the project will never be achieved.

From practitioners' point of view, verbal and other formats of representation that are easily understandable for human being like using diagrams or pictures are preferred. All processes included in manufacturing are described by XML diagrams and they are created and edited by practitioners from the studied company. An additional tool is needed for processing diagrams manually edited by practitioners. However, a large number of processes, complicated relationships between processes; sophisticated operation structure inside each process lead to the decision that building complete representation for all processes is not effective as regards to the project's purpose. Instead of that, a simpler approach has been decided for representation as follows.

Manufacturing processes are described by chains of **events**. An event represents a concrete situation, on which an employee was working. Event includes the request for assistance, the action that an employee executed; the effects observed after realization of the selected action and relationships between the current situation and other ones.

**Event** = {*context, request, action, effect, commitments*}.

Events are dependent each other. For example, if an employee takes alternative A1 to undertake operation X1, then the following alternative to perform next operation X2 will be B1. If alternative A2 is chosen to execute operation X1, then next operation to be executed will be X3, not X2, and one of alternatives {C1, C2} will be selected to accomplish this operation.

The context of situation defines the relationships between events. Only the context of a current situation is considered as an input for searching for a suitable advice. Other features like employee's role in the organization, skill or experience are still considered as less relevant for the computation. Anonymousness also encourages employees to participate in the experiment and to provide feedback and their own experience.

Using events to represent things that occur inside the manufacturing simplifies the communication barrier between practitioners and developers. The fact is that the computer aid system is able to assist even when it has no knowledge about the manufacturing processes. The complication of the representation issue, due to the requirement of owning knowledge about production processes for developers, or having technical background familiar with the technology used in the project for practitioners, is therefore considerable reduced.

## 4.2. *Identification of Relevant Data*

Data collection and gathering play a crucial role in the system. In order to generate quality advices, more data, feedback and experiences are required to collect. Employees therefore are asked to give complete information describing situations on which they were working, including their selected actions, effects captured after realisation of the action and other observations, comments or explanation. However, employees may not always be aware or confident of identifying which data is useful and relevant for future usage. When the system is initially introduced it asks employees to provide all data available that they consider relevant. Based on the analysis of questions that employees ask the system, the system is able to identify the primary problems for which solutions have been requested. It will also be possible to identify the relevant data from viewing requests.

The first category is made up of frequent requests. For example, a request to know how to alter the kiln speed setting is easily answered by listing all steps that the previous employee did, from the beginning until the objective is achieved. For this category of requests it is sufficient to record all actions employees did on each operation and a collection of standard approaches is built up.

The second category of requests and solutions is made up of those what require more knowledge and experience to solve. For example, to produce 1000 pieces of product A, an optimal solution is to process 4800 Bridges in the batch due to the fact that there is a constant demand and the fact that ramping up the kiln temperature to the much higher setting for dust press components must be justified. The request could be how many bridges is an optimal for batching or what is an appropriate pressure and temperature. Employees need advice and guidance on what to do in such cases so the batch size is sufficient to justify changing the settings to the machine. Requests for this type of information will be flagged by the system to ask employees to provide the required data, for example, number of pierces in batch and the reasons for setting this value as in the above example.

Besides employing experts to identify relevant data, there is an automatic data rating system that automatically filters and updates the data importance. Stored data are rated according to how many times they are reused for calculation or updated. Data rating system identifies the importance and relevancy of data in relation to concrete situations. For a frequently occurred situation, the relevancy of each piece of data describing that situation is repeatedly evaluated. During the exploitation of the system, excess data that is not used will be filtered out and erased. Ranking process is off-line and it is a part of the database maintenance that will be discussed later in Section 4.4.

The idea to leave the information acquisition process being open so that employees could decide on what data is relevant or important is based on the fact that experts and developers are not entirely familiar with all manufacturing processes. Employee's feedback enriches the experience database by bringing more alternatives for consideration; sequentially, more solutions will be available for deliberation.

### 4.3. *Information Gathering and Storing*

The ontology is used as a basic formation for recording data provided by employees. The employee's task is to fill up individual properties in each instance. They are also able to create new instances to represent unregistered attributes or new situations. In order to avoid a problem with the terminology, there is a list of keywords and terms to be used for representation of situations or attributes. The 3 primary items that will have to be provided or updated include:

- Circumstances describing the situation in which employees ask for help,
- Types of requests or problems that employees need assistance,

- Results and effects after realisation of the selected action, some reasons or explanations about selecting the action that was taken.

New types of information request will lead to adding new properties to the ontology. Some properties could be automatically added, e.g. the number of pieces in a batch (similar to the previous example), if the format of these properties are easily identifiable. For most cases however, an expert system is required to evaluate the requests and decide on new properties needed to update the ontology.

There is a question about the state-of-the-art of data or information. Out of date information or false data lead to incorrect solutions, for that reason, employees are obliged to provide only up-to-date information but they are free not to provide information if it's acquisition is not available.

### 4.4. *Database Maintenance*

Employees are under no obligation to fill in these forms unless it is specified by the job description or supervisor as something that has to be done. As a result of their being no obligation it may be difficult to get employees to fully complete these requested forms. It is also possible that employees may create too many new instances, demonstrating the same thing. Clearing redundant instances is based on similarity between multiple instances. Using a unique list of terminology allows comparing properties of each instance, if they do not have numerical values. Instances that are 100% identical will be removed from the ontology. For instances which are described by numerical properties, comparison their similarity can be done by using some standard distance measurements, for example Euclid distance. Fuzzy comparison is also applicable for cases where properties are described by non-numerical values. Employees are asked to evaluate the analogy between single instances. Their feedback will be used to re-design the similarity measurement. More information about fuzzy sets, fuzzy numbers and other operations is available in [14], [15].

Missing data properties, which have numerical values, could be approximated on the basis of values of the same property involved in similar cases. As a result of the limited framework of this paper the discussion about similarity calculation, instance comparison, and updating missing values by approximation are omitted. Methods chosen for implementation in our project are based on the statistical methodology and datamining. More information about these techniques is available in [3], [4].

Data is considered useless, if it is not requested later for either a calculation or evaluation. If an employee enters some properties, but in later instances these properties are omitted or not filled by others, then these properties will be considered less relevant or useful for a calculation. Each property is rated by the system, in relation to a developing situation the properties rating depends on three variables: the total number of cases describing this situation, a subset of cases where the property is filled in (considered as relevant data by others) and a subset of cases in which the value of this property is used for calculation. If the rating is lower than any bound, the system will automatically remove this property from the ontology.

Property rating is also served as a factor for evaluation of data relevancy. Irrelevant data will not be involved in future requests asking employees to provide information.

### 4.5. *Knowledge-Based Assistance*

The kernel focus is to exploit the collection of data in order to assist employees in doing their jobs better. Answering requests belonging to the first category (mentioned in Section 4.2) could be done by querying the ontology to find a solution with the same context as the one an employee is currently working on. The context here is specified by the role of employee in the company, the task on which s/he is working on, including previous and successive associated tasks. To improve the performance, a set of most frequent requests and their solutions are collected. Their default solutions can be entered by a system administrator or anybody working in these areas.

The problem for solving is more complicated when the system comes to dealing with non-standard requests. Case-based reasoning (CBR) is applied for solving these requests, since it does not require specific knowledge about the production processes involved in the company. Employees are interactively asked to give more data for consideration in order to identify the problem for solving. Based on the given data, similar cases are extracted, included their solutions and some reasons or explanations why these solutions were exploited. If there is no instance with the exact context given by an employee, cases of lower similarity can be used. The recommended solution is calculated by adaptation or approximation of the selected solutions. Fundamental information about the CBR technique can be found in [4]. This paper gives a very thorough overview of the foundational issues related to CBR, describes some of the leading methodological approaches within the field.

For illustration, again look at the example in Section 4.1 and consider a simple scenario as follows. A request is given for an optimal batch size in the Kiln for production of 10000 products of type A. But the ontology includes only instances with data for 1000 and 6000 products of type A entered by some employees before. For the case with 1000 products, an optimal size is 2400 pieces/batch. In the second case with 6000 products, the optimal batch size is 9600 pieces/batch with the reasons that there is a constant demand for these pieces and the quantity being produced must be sufficient to justify raising the temperature of the kiln as it will take time for it to cool for processing of other items afterwards and there is also the expense of the extra gas, both solutions are suggested to an employee for deliberation. The number of the batches to fill the kiln is also 80 and it is more efficient to operate with the kiln full. However, if such a request occurs frequently, employees maybe asked to provide more information about each stage of production, included related data (execution time, capacity limitation, commitments between machines and components, and so on). An expert system is required to update the ontology by adding a new functionality to respond to such a request, i.e. to calculate an optimal (or best) batch size for production of any amount of product.

In our project, the CBR technique has to deal with two key problems similarity comparison between instances and creation of a new solution based on previously-used ones. To resolve the first problem, the system interactively asks employees to clarify the current work context. A set of similar instances is sequentially reduced, until only a few instances remain. Enquiry includes different questions for different scenarios; each question has a different weight, i.e. a parameter that reflects how the answer to this question influences the similarity comparison.

Many properties are described by non-numerical variables, for that reason, similarity comparison between cases is calculated based on using fuzzy sets [14], [15]. A fuzzy number is used to express the similarity between each employee's answer and a value of the corresponding property. The total similarity is achieved by combination of all partial similarities and their weights.

A method for the adaptation of old solutions is simple; solutions of most similar cases are suggested to employees for consideration. Reasons and explanations about why these solutions were selected help employees to make better decisions. If employees decide on a new different solution as apposed to the suggested ones, they should give some explanations or opinions of taking such a step. The feedback is valuable for use of this solution later.

In summary, answering non-standard requests is an interactive process with feedback from employees. Data provided by employees serve as a filter to restrict the range of candidate solutions (similar cases) and an expert system is used to correct and update the functionalities of the ontology.

In addition to providing assistance by interactive communication with employees, the system is able to deduce by itself some rules or patterns based on a data collection. This process works unseen and frequently repeats when data is updated. The pattern can be, for example, frequent mistakes or wrong setting approaches that lead to an alarm's activation. Patterns can also be common approaches used to produce certain types of products or similar orders. Another target is to identify the common (or best) machine configuration, since each employee might configure machines in different ways. To identify the best approach, employees might have to provide more information, for example, set-up time, execution time, quality of products, etc. These discovered patterns will automatically be added to the recommendation suggested to employees, if the context related to these patterns matches the context of situation on which the employee is working.

## 5. Realisation and Some Issues for Discussion

The first version of the system described for demonstration consists of basic components as follows. An OWL ontology [6], [7] is used and it is created by the Protégé tool [8]. The structure of the ontology is formed in cooperation with some experts from the studied company. The studied company also provided a number of scenarios and real data for testing purpose. The assistant system is implemented in Java and is accessed using Jena [9], which is a tool used to access OWL ontology from Java. The user interface allows interactive communication with employees to assist their work. Employees also have a responsibility to give feedback to the system (situation description, selected solution and effects of its realisation). Experts from the studied company will evaluate the quality of the recommended solution.

Employees are asked to voluntarily participate in the project. When an employee meets a new situation, for example, an employee moves to a new position in the organisation, gets a new task, or faces a new problem during working, he/she can ask the system to give an advice. Any decision made by an employee and any action taken for solving the difficulty is recorded. Employees can provide an explanation of their decision making so that later users can understand the relationship between a situation context and a chosen solution. Provided explanations help employees to deduce their own experience in relation to certain groups of situations.

Each event occurred in the company and all circumstances associated with that event are evidenced and stored. Employees have to follow a standard procedure for adding new data records into the ontology, as well as a process for getting assistance. The approach that employees and the computer aid system communicate each other was described in Section 4.5.

During implementation some issues have been identified and require further analysis and study. The first difficulty is as a result of the different ways (phrases) that employees use to describe a working situation, request or other requirements. A person who has knowledge of the different production processes used in this company must edit the list of questions. The more detailed questions will create problems for inexperienced employees to answer. Detailed questions however will force the inexperienced employees to learn information so they can solve them. General questions do not allow precision problem solving and lead to poor solutions. Experts also specify the weights of the questions and the links between them for various scenarios. To reduce expert's interventions, self-learning technique is used to auto-adjust these weights to improve the similarity comparison.

The second problem is how to get missing data to react to new requests. Experts cannot predict every type of request, so the ontology has only a limited amount of concepts, properties and data. For new types of request, intervention of experts is necessary. Although default solutions for new types of requests might not be optimal, they will at least give inexperienced employees the basic guide of how to deal with a particular situation. Open information acquisition process where every employee has a possibility to contribute their own experiences and information that they considered as relevant brings positive results. Achieved results prove the right choice to leave the system to be open for everybody. However, there is needed to update and regularly filter the database of redundant and irrelevant data, in order for the system to work effectively.

Other issues like combination CBR and Rule-based reasoning (RBR) or improving fuzzy classification techniques in the studied case have been considered and are under development. It is also necessary to mention the performance problem of using Java and OWL ontology. Java might not be the best choice as an implementation tool due to its slow running speed. As a result of the relatively small data volume being used and the other advantages that the OWL ontology can provide (e.g. reasoning, inverse relation, multiply properties), the selected tools are sufficient for the studied case.

## 6. Conclusion

This paper discusses the problem on how to help mobile employees do their jobs better, and reduce the cost of creating a multi-skilled workforce. Multi-skilled mobile operators are commonplace in SMEs where it is essential to keep low production cost. Employees are assisted by being given solutions calculated based on previous solutions entered by previous operators. A catalogue of standard or frequent requests is then created to give employees a quick guide for solving standard production situations. CBR is applied to solve non-standard requests or situations. Besides recommendation of old or customized solutions, some other techniques like pattern discovery, data mining are used to find common patterns within a data collection. Newly discovered patterns help to identify trends of employees work and they are new values added to the recommended solution suggested to employees.

The first version was developed for demonstration, based on cooperation with experts from the studied company. Some information cannot be published as a result of the short framework of this paper. The primary limitation is that there is too much manual work involved in the system so far. It is planned to replace interactive communication with an adaptable user's model, where user's (or employee's) position, skill and own experience are considered for searching for suitable advices. However, it is still not possible to remove manually given feedback and intervention by experts.

## Acknowledgments

This work has been funded by the Irish Research Council for Science, Engineering and Technology (IRCSET).

## References

1. Pellucid - A Platform for Organisationally Mobile Public Employees - EU 5FP RTD IST-2001-34519. http://www.sadiel.es/Europa/pellucid/
2. T. R. Gruber. *"A translation approach to portable ontologies"*. Knowledge Acquisition, 5(2):199-220, 1993. Available on: http://ksl-web.stanford.edu/KSL_Abstracts/KSL-92-71.html
3. Afifi, A.A., and Clark, V., *"Computer Aided Multivariate Analysis, Third edition"*. Chapman & Hall, 1999.
4. http://www.statsoft.com/textbook/stathome.html
5. Aamodt and E. Plaza, *"Case-Based Reasoning:Foundational Issues, Methodological Variations, and System Approaches"*, Artificial Intelligence Communications, IOS Press, Vol. 7:1, pp. 39 – 59, 1994.

6. http://www.w3.org/TR/owl-ref/
7. http://www.w3.org/TR/owl-guide/
8. http://protege.stanford.edu/
9. http://jena.sourceforge.net/
10. Frankovic B. and Budinska I., *"Advantages and disadvanteges of heuristic and multi-agent approaches to the solution of scheduling problem"*. In Proc. of the IFAC Conference on Control System Design, Bratislava, Elsevier, ISBN 0-08-043546 7, pp. 372-378, 2000.
11. Frankovic B. and Budinska I.: *"Single and multi machine scheduling of jobs in production sytem"*. In Tzafestas, S.G. (Ed.): Advances in manufacturing, Decision, Control, and Information Technology, Springer Verlag, London, pp. 25-36, 1999.
12. R. Bergmann. *"Experience Management"*. Lecture Notes in Artificial Intelligence Series, vol. 2432. Springer, 2002.
13. R. Dieng-Kuntz, N. Matta, editors. *"Knowledge Management and Organizational Memories"*. Kluwer Academic Publishers, 2002.
14. Dubois D., Prade H., Yager R. (Eds.) *Fuzzy Sets for Intelligent Systems*, Morgan Kaufmann Publishers, Inc., 1993.
15. Chen Sh.-J., Hwang CH. -L., Hwang F. P., *Fuzzy Multiple Attribute Decision Making*, Springer-Verlag, Berlin, 1992.

# CHAPTER 15

# AN APPROACH TO ESTIMATE SOFTWARE COSTS WITHIN A NARROW CONTEXT

NGOC-BAO NGUYEN, VIET-HA NGUYEN

*College of Technology*
*Vietnam National University, Hanoi*
*Email: {baonn, hanv}@vnu.edu.vn*

This paper proposes a new approach to estimate software costs using case-based reasoning. In this approach, the costs of a new software project are estimated by firstly retrieving the similar previous project and then adapting its costs to the current conditions. The approach focus on the estimation within a narrow context. The project is described as an ontology which allows the managers to estimate with various level of requirement analysis during the development. Moreover, the statistical analysis of previous works (i.e. the COCOMO model) are utilized to reflect the software development domain knowledge.

*Keywords*: software project management, cost estimation, case-based reasoning, ontology, COCOMO

## 1. Introduction

Early and accurate cost estimation is an important factor influencing the profitability of every industry, including software development. However, the task of cost estimation in software development is different from that in other fields due to some particular characteristics of software: First, software is an intellectual product, and thus hard to be thoroughly understood and represented. Second, because of the continual emergence of new technologies, it is too complex to define a universal metric to calibrate all kinds of software. Those characteristics of *a weak theory domain* make software costs difficult to be estimated. In fact, the software cost estimation task will never be an exact science.[1]

Over the years, a number of software cost estimation models have been proposed in attempts to minimize the errors of the estimation.[1,2] However, most of them are based on mathematical models (i.e. statistical models), which seem too theoretical and rigid. Moreover, the proposed models are only available in late phases of the development when requirement analysis is well-defined. Consequently, many project managers find those models hard to be directly applied to their real works.

In this paper, we propose a new approach to estimate software costs using Case-Based Reasoning (CBR)[3]- a problem solving paradigm particularly suitable for weak theory domains. In this approach, the costs of a new software project are estimated by firstly retrieving similar previous project, and then adapting its costs to the current context. The CBR approach is attractive since there are evidences that experts can perform acceptable estimation basing solely on their specific experiences (i.e. expert judgment).[4]

We believe that the CBR approach is mostly effective in a narrow context, thus our approach is particularly designed for estimating within a certain software developing environment (e.g., the scope of a software company). The project is represented as an ontology to give the managers the flexibility in estimation with various level of requirement analysis. Moreover, the domain knowledge is reflected in the estimated results by utilizing the analysis of software development derived from existent statistical models.

The rest of this paper is organized as follows: In section 2, we summarize some key estimation methods used in software industry. Section 3 presents our proposed approach to estimate software costs using case-based reasoning. The approach is illustrated by some examples given in section 4. Section 5 provides some discussion and considers related works in the fields. In section 6, we summarize our findings and suggest directions for future research.

## 2. Background to Software Estimation

There are a number of software estimation methods which have been developed and validated in literature as well as in industry. Generally, the conventional methods can be divided into two main categories: *decomposition techniques* and *empirical models*.[1]

Decomposition techniques mean splitting the process or the software itself into small pieces for estimation and then adding the component estimates up to form the overall results. Although those methods are in somewhat similar to the way people deal with complex problems, the demand of decomposition implies that the techniques cannot be applied early. Furthermore, in software developmentation, the costs of system level activities such as integration and document are usually considerable and difficult to be predicted. As a result, decomposition approaches usually lead to underestimated costs.

Empirical models, on the other hand, build a general software model and estimate the software projects as a whole. Boehm, *et al.*[2] identified several current empirical software estimation models including PRICE-S,[5] SLIM,[6] COCOMO II[7]... Most of them were based on mathematical functions with a general form of $E = A + B \times (ev)^C$, where $E$ is the estimation results; $A$, $B$, $C$ are coefficients derived from regression analysis of historical data and $ev$ is the estimation variable (i.e. size in SLOC or FP).[1] Those models take the advantages of consistency and objectiveness. Unfortunately, due to the extreme variety in software development, a model derived statistically from a context cannot be useful in others without any calibration to local environment. Although some adjustment techniques (see[7-9]) were added to avoid that situation, they are too complex and difficult for practitioners (as well as customers) to understand and manipulate. In addition, like decomposition techniques, the need of detailed data (e.g., size) in empirical models also prevents the users from flexibly estimating.

More recently, attention has been turning to a variety of machine learning approaches which are trained on local data to estimate the software costs. Srinivasan used an inductive learning system to produce a set of rules for estimating.[10] Dolado applied a genetic programming (GP) approach to investigate the size-effort relationship and build dynamic software process equations.[11] Gary estimated by constructing a back propagation neural network.[12] However, such methods require an extremely large yet convergent historical data. Furthermore, the estimation are incoherent and lack of explanatory value.

## 3. Costs Estimating using CBR

Case-Based Reasoning (CBR) is a problem-solving method first appeared in the work on dynamic memory of Schank.[3] In this section, we make use of the CBR idea to propose a new approach for software costs estimation. In this approach, the costs of a project are estimated by adapting the costs of a similar project which has been completed. The approach can be flexibly used during the development and particularly applied within the scope of an organization.

### 3.1. *The Estimating Framework*

The estimation framework in our approach is built based on the CBR process proposed by Aarmodt and Plaza.[13] It is described as a cycle of four steps as shown in figure 1.

206

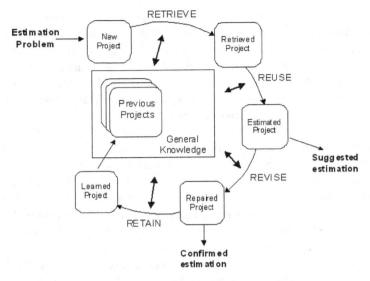

Figure 1.    The estimating framework.

The costs of a new project (i.e. a case) are estimated by firstly *retrieving* the most similar project from a set of previous ones. Then, the known costs of this project are *reused* by adapting to the circumstance of the estimating one. The *revise* step evaluates, normally by human, the estimation suggested previously whether it fits the real world environment. The last step is *retaining* where completed projects are stored into the knowledge base for future uses. All the four steps may be supported by the domain knowledge of software development to improve their performance.

In the followings, we will describe in more details three activities of our estimation approach, which are the project representation, the retrieval of similar project, and the adaptation of previous costs.

### 3.2. *Project Representation*

As the life cycle processed, the requirements of a project become more and more well-defined. We represent projects by an ontology, an explicit specification of a shared conceptualization;[14] so that the estimation can be performed at different levels of the requirement analysis.

Figure 2 shows the details of the project ontology representing a software project in our approach. In this figure, [PROJECT] is the top level concept consisting of two sub-concepts: [COSTS] and [COST DRIVERS]. The [COSTS] represents a set of values managers desire to estimate while [COST DRIVERS] represents factors (named cost drivers) believed to influence those values. There are a lot of factors may influence the final costs;[1,2,15] yet since our goal is to estimate within a specific circumstance, we just account for the features of the product (i.e. the software itself), not the features of the developing environment.

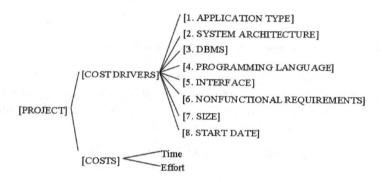

Figure 2.   The project ontology.

Each cost driver is again considered as a concept which is classified to several sub-concepts and instances in a hierarchical structure. Figure 3 illustrates an example of the ontology of cost driver [PROGRAMMING LANGUAGE] where elements in upper case present sub-concepts and elements in lower case present instances.

Previous studies[16,17] suggested that to obtain a reasonable estimation, at least a size factor should be taken into account. However, most of past approaches tend to use the same sizing model during their estimation. In this work, depending on the details of the requirement analysis, the size of a project can be flexibly considered in different levels of sizing models (e.g., User Functional Requirements, Function Points, SLOC...).

### 3.3. Retrieval

The aim of retrieval is to extract the nearest project from the historical database. To indicate which project is the nearest, we define the following similarity metric.

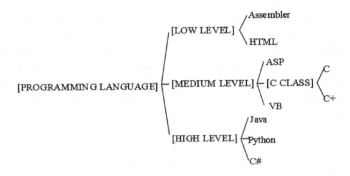

Figure 3. The ontology of a cost driver.

In the estimating process, some cost drivers may be not defined yet. Despite of that, the project similarity can still be calculated basing on the other available cost drivers. We use an weighted average function to calculate the similarity between two projects:

$$SIM(T,S) = \frac{\sum_{i=1}^{n} |sim(T_i, S_i)| \times w_i'}{\sum_{i=1}^{n} w_i'}, \qquad (1)$$

where $SIM(T,S)$ is the similarity between projects $T$ and $S$; $sim(T_i, S_i)$ is the similarity of their cost driver $i$ and $w_i'$ are a *extended weight* determined by:

$$w_i' = \begin{cases} w_i, & \text{if cost driver of two projects are defined;} \\ 0, & \text{otherwise.} \end{cases} \qquad (2)$$

where $w_i$ is the weight indicating the significance of cost driver $i$.

The similarity between two concepts is:

$$sim(T_i, S_i) = \frac{\sum_{j=1}^{m} \sum_{k=1}^{n} sim(t_j, s_k)}{mn}, \qquad (3)$$

where $t_j$ and $s_k$ are all instances, either directly or indirectly, under concepts $T_i$ and $S_i$ of cost driver $i$.

Likewise, the similarity between a concept and an instance is defined as:

$$sim(T_i, s_i) = \frac{\sum_{j=1}^{m} sim(t_j, s_i)}{m}, \qquad (4)$$

where $t_j$ are all instances under concept $T_i$.

The similarities between instances are calculated basing on the characteristics of individual cost drivers in software development.

The cost drivers No. 1-6 belong to categorical types and by now, the similarity of its instances is determined by referring to a similarity table. The values in this table are pre-defined basing on software engineering knowledge and normalized to be in the interval [-1, 1]. We are studying some fuzzy-based approaches to improve the similarity calculations for categorial cost drivers but they are out of the scope of this paper.

The similarity function of size is determined by:

$$sim(t_i, s_i) = [\frac{1}{2}(\frac{t_i}{s_i} + \frac{s_i}{t_i})]^{-\alpha}, \tag{5}$$

where $t_i$ and $s_i$ are size of two project in the same sizing model, $sim(t_i, s_i)$ is the similarity between them and $\alpha$ ($\alpha > 0$) is a scale factor .

In software engineering, the developing environment as well as the technologies are rapidly changed. The old projects may have little meaning in the estimation of the new one. Thus, we use an exponential form to present the similarity of start date:

$$sim(t_i, s_i) = \beta^{-\frac{t_i}{s_i}|t_i - s_i|}, \tag{6}$$

where $\beta$ ($\beta > 1$) indicates the growth rate in the software industry.

Although the similarity metric above seems to have so many degrees of freedom, since our calculations are just used for selecting the similar project from a limit number of the given ones, we believe that a more delicate metric would not give more accurate results though it complicates the estimating process.

## 3.4. *Adaptation*

We make use of the analysis derived from statistical estimation models to adapt the costs of the retrieved project. Particularly, the previous costs are adapted by COCOMO-like functions:

$$Time_{current} = aR^b \times Time_{previous} \tag{7}$$

$$Effort_{current} = cR^d \times Effort_{previous} \tag{8}$$

where $a$, $c$ are the differential coefficients of the project multiplicative adjustment factors; $b$, $d$ are the exponential scales of diseconomy [a]; $R$ is a size differential coefficient.

---

[a]The terms are used according to the COCOMO II model definition.[7]

Table 1.  Rating scheme for the COCOMO II scale factors.

| Scale Factors ($w_i$) | Very Low(5) | Low(4) | Nominal(3) | High(2) | Very High(1) | Extra High(0) |
|---|---|---|---|---|---|---|
| Precedented-ness | thoroughly unprece-dented | largely un-prece-dented | somewhat unprece-dented | generally familiar | largely familiar | throughly familiar |
| Development Flexibility | rigorous | occasional relaxation | some relaxation | general confor-mity | some con-formity | general goals |
| Architecture/ risk resolution | little (20%) | some (40%) | often (60%) | generally (75%) | mostly (90%) | full (100%) |
| Team cohesion | very diffi-cult inter-actions | some diffi-cult inter-actions | basically co-operative in-teractions | basically coop-erative in-teractions | basically coop-erative in-teractions | seamless interac-tions |
| Process maturity | Weighted average of "Yes" answers to CMM Maturity Questionaire | | | | | |

Since the current and the retrieved project share some common features, we assume that the differences of the project multiplicative adjustment factors can be inferred from the differences of non-functional requirements. Thus, we use a non-functional requirements differential coefficient as a single representative, which is defined as:

$$\delta = 1 + sim(T_i, S_i), \qquad (9)$$

where $sim(T_i, S_i)$ is the similarity of the non-functional requirements.

The scale exponents $b$ and $d$ reflect the characteristic of the organization and calculated basing on the analyses of the COCOMO II model.

$$b = 1.01 + 0.01 \sum w_i \qquad (10)$$

$$d = (0.33 + 0.2 \times (b - 1.01)) \times b \qquad (11)$$

where $w_i$ are rated according to table 1.

Finally, the size differential coefficient is determined by:

$$R = \frac{t_i}{s_i}, \qquad (12)$$

where $t_i$ and $s_i$ are size of two projects measured in the same sizing model.

## 4. Examples

Assume that we are estimating a project $P$ with a knowledge base of 3 projects $P1, P2, P3$ in table 2. At an early state of the development, the size of $P$ is only available in Number of User Functional Requirements (UFR) and the interface has not been defined yet. The weights of each cost driver in figure 2 are assigned to the value of $\{10, 2, 4, 5, 1, 4, 5, 10\}$, respectively. The constants in equation (5) and (6) are chosen as common values of 2.00 and 1.67. Then the similarity between $P$ and $P1, P2, P3$ are calculated as shown in table 2.

Since $P2$ is the nearest project to $P$, it is chosen for adaptation. We assign 1.05 to the scale exponent $b$ in equation (10) and derive the other exponent $d$ in equation (11) as 0.35 (i.e. the constants of the typical COCOMO organic mode[15]). The size and non-functional requirements differential coefficient are calculated as $R = 0.80$ and $\delta = 1.40$. Then, the estimated results would be $Time = 18.13$ and $Effort = 221.51$.

At later states when the requirement analysis of $P$ is refined, we know more exactly that the Programming Language is ASP, the interface is web-based and the size can be determined in Function Point as 14 FPs. Then, the similarities are recalculated as shown in table 3. In this case, the nearest project is changed to $P1$. Using the same calculations as above, we will obtain a new estimation as $Time = 16.40$ and $Effort = 234.39$. Hopefully,

Table 2.  An example of costs estimation in early states.

| Project factors | $P$ | $P1$ | $(P_i, P1_i)$ | $P2$ | $(P_i, P2_i)$ | $P3$ | $(P_i, P3_i)$ |
|---|---|---|---|---|---|---|---|
| App Dom | man | library | 0.70 | store | 0.70 | net | 0.50 |
| Sys Arch | s.alone | dist | 0.80 | s.alone | 1.00 | c/s | 0.40 |
| DBMS | simple | My SQL | 0.80 | Access | 0.80 | none | 0.40 |
| Prog Lang | med | ASP | 0.80 | VB | 0.80 | Java | -0.40 |
| Interface | undef | web | 0.00 | graphic | 0.00 | web | 0.00 |
| NF Reqs | med | low | 0.60 | low | 0.60 | high | -0.40 |
| Size | 4UFR | 5UFR/ 15FP | 0.95 | 5UFR/ 18FP | 0.95 | 3UFR/ 8FP | 0.92 |
| Start Date | 03/06 | 03/05 | 0.60 | 06/05 | 0.68 | 03/05 | 0.60 |
| Proj Sim | | | 0.71 | | 0.74 | | 0.53 |
| Time | | 12.00 | | 14.00 | | 8.00 | |
| Effort | | 180.00 | | 200.00 | | 160.00 | |

Note: $(P_i, Px_i)$ indicates the similarity of cost driver $i$ between project $P$ and $Px$.

Table 3.  An example of costs estimation in later states.

| Project factors | $P$ | $P1$ | $(P_i, P1_i)$ | $P2$ | $(P_i, P2_i)$ | $P3$ | $(P_i, P3_i)$ |
|---|---|---|---|---|---|---|---|
| Prog Lang | ASP | ASP | 1.00 | VB | 0.60 | Java | -0.50 |
| Interface | web | web | 1.00 | graphic | 0.50 | web | 1.00 |
| Size | 4UFR/ 14FP | 5UFR/ 15FP | 0.99 | 5UFR/ 18FP | 0.94 | 3UFR/ 8FP | 0.86 |
| Proj Sim | | | 0.76 | | 0.72 | | 0.56 |

when the more detailed information is available, the more "precise" project is retrieved and the estimated results are accordingly more reliable.

## 5. Discussion and Related Works

The previous statistical methods estimate the costs as direct mathematical functions of project parameters; thus they require all factors of project as well as their incoherent relationship must be reveal and formulate. Our approach otherwise uses the project parameters just for approximately comparing and selecting similar projects. For those reasons, it keeps the project representation simple and gives more flexibilities to the estimating process. For instance, although the environmental factors are extremely complex and vague, when estimating within a narrow context those factors implicitly remain constant. Using CBR as a strategy of estimation, we don't have to account for them (though they are still presented in the final results).

It is known that software development is a wide and often-changing domain. To archive an acceptable estimation, most of previous approaches require tuning their model to the local environment.[8] In our approach, such tuning task is automatically performed by a "learning" process where new projects are captured to enrich the project database. The database itself reflects the characteristics of the developing environment, and as it is changed the estimated results will be adapted accordingly.

There has been several works in the area of applying CBR to software cost estimation such as Estor,[18] FACE,[19] ANGEL,[17] F_ANGEL[20] (an extension of ANGEL using fuzzy similarities). However, all of them use a flat structure for project representation whereas our projects are represented by a layer structure as an ontology. Using such a flexible representation, managers are able to execute the estimation with various level of requirement analysis.

In,[16] Sarah, et al. introduced a CBR approach to early software cost estimation. In,[21] Belen, et al. presented the CBROnto architecture which combine CBR and Ontolgy ideas. Those models seem work as CBR frameworks where all of case features share a common similarity function (i.e. the Euclidean distance) or the similarity determining tasks is left to the users. In this work, on the other hand, we construct an approach specifically tailored for software development field. The project structure as well as the similarity calculation are predefined based on our studies of the software development. Moreover, the analysis derived from previous statistical models is also utilized in the estimating process. By this way, the domain knowledge of software development is automatically presented in the estimation.

# 6. Conclusion

In this paper, we presented an approach to estimate software costs using case-based reasoning. The approach is particularly used for estimation within a narrow context, for example the scope of an company. It does not require elaborate requirement analysis as some predecessors and can be flexibly applied in various phases of the development. The estimated results are clear and coherent in that they are directly derived from previous projects. Moreover, by concerning specific characteristics of software development, the approach seems to be more "software-oriented" than some other analog-based alternatives.

The current problem in our approach is the cost drivers as well as their similarity calculations were still roughly built. As for future works, those issues should be analyzed more thoroughly with the consideration to some existing standards. Mechanisms of parameter learning and database refining should also be investigated to improve the system performance. Furthermore, we are planning to implement our approach to an application which can be used and validated in real software developing environments.

## Acknowledgement

This work is partially supported by the National Fundamental IT Research Project.

## References

1. R. S.Pressman, *Software engineering: a practitioner's approach (5th ed.)* (McGraw-Hill, Inc, New York, NY, USA, 2001).
2. B. Boehm, C. Abts and S. Chulani, *Ann. Softw. Eng.* **10**, 177 (2000).
3. C. K. Riesbeck and R. C. Schank, *Inside Case-Based Reasoning* (Lawrence Erlbaum Associates, Inc, Mahwah, NJ, USA, 1989).
4. M.Jørgensen, G. Kirkeboen *et al.*, Human judgement in effort estimation of software project, in *Beg, Borrow, or Steal Workshop, International Conference on Software Engineering*, (Limerick, Ireland, 2001).
5. Park R, The central equations of the price software cost model, in *4th CO-COMO Users' Group Meeting*, 1988.
6. L. H. Putnam and W. Myers, *Measures for Excellence: Reliable Software on Time, within Budget* (Prentice Hall Professional Technical Reference, 1991).
7. B. Boehm, B. Clark *et al.*, *American Programmer* , 2 (1996).
8. M. Baldassarre, D. Caivano and G. Visaggio, *icsm* **00**, p. 105 (2003).
9. M. A. Sicilia, J. J. Cuadrado-Gallego *et al.*, *KYBERNETIKA* **35** (2004).
10. K. Srinivasan and D. Fisher, *IEEE Trans. Softw. Eng.* **21**, 126 (1995).

11. J. J. Dolado, Limits to the methods in software cost estimation, in *The 1st International Workshop on Soft Computing Applied to Software Engineering*, eds. C. Ryan and J. Buckley (Limerick University Press, 1999).

12. G. D. Boetticher, Using machine learning to predict project effort: Empirical case studies in data-starved domains, in *The First International Workshop on Model-based Requirements Engineering*, (San Diego, 2001).

13. A. Aamodt and E. Plaza, *AI Communications* **Vol 7**, 39 (1994).

14. T. R. Gruber, *Knowledge Acquisition* , p. 38 (1993).

15. B. Boehm, *Software Engineering Economics* (Prentice-Hall, 1981).

16. S. J. Delany and P. Cunningham, *The Application of Case-Based Reasoning to Early Software Project Cost Estimation and Risk Assessment*, tech. rep., Department of Computer Science, Trinity College Dublin, TDS-CS- 2000-10 (2000).

17. M. Shepperd and C. Schofield, *IEEE Trans. Softw. Eng* **23**, 736 (1997).

18. S. Vicinanza, M. J.Pritula and T. Mukhopadyay, Case-based reasoning in software effort estimation, in *The 11th International Conference on Information Systems*, 1990.

19. R. Bisio and F. Malabocchia, Cost estimation of software projects through case based reasoning, in *The First International Conference on Case Based Reasoning*, 1995.

20. A. Idri, A. Abran and T. M. Khoshgoftaar, *Engineering Intelligent Systems* **159**, 64 (2004).

21. B. Diaz-Agudo and P. A.Gonzalez-Calero, An architecture for knowledge intensive CBR systems, in *EWCBR 2000*, (Springer - Verlag, 2000).

# CHAPTER 16

# EXPLOITING PROCESS PATTERNS
# FOR SOFTWARE PROCESS MODELS REUSE

HANH NHI TRAN, BICH THUY DONG

*University of Natural Sciences, VNUHCM - 227 Nguyen Van Cu, Q5,
HoChiMinh Ville, Vietnam*

BERNARD COULETTE

*University of Toulouse 2 - 5, allées A. Machado F-31058, Toulouse, France*

Process Pattern is an emerging approach to reuse process knowledge. This concept, though attractive, has not been well understood and exploited yet due to the lack of formalization and supporting methodology. In this paper, we present our work towards a more efficient application of process patterns. Our goal is making process patterns directly applicable in process modeling to facilitate process reuse. In order to achieve this objective, we firstly define a process meta-model integrating the process pattern concept. This meta-model provides a formal definition of process patterns and allows describing processes based on process patterns. Then we propose a method for building process models from process patterns. This method itself is described as a pattern-based process which can be tailored and automated to guide process designers in their work.

## 1. Introduction

Nowadays it is widely accepted that software product quality depends on the software process that is carried out. This emphasis on processes leads to the strong development of Software Process Technology that aims at providing the means to model, to analyze and to automate software processes.

Process Technology introduced firstly the notion of process model, an abstract representation of process expressed in a process modeling notation. Process models are used for process communicating, training and guiding. Software processes are intrinsically complex, and sometime unpredictable. Consequently, building a software process model is a cumbersome and time-consuming work [6,9]. Process model reuse (i.e. the ability to construct new processes by assembling already built ones) therefore is a crucial issue in process technology.

Modeling a software process is describing the way in which software development is organized, managed, measured, supported and improved. Thus, it requires a high comprehension of process designers. In this regard, we argue that pattern-based approach which allows to explicitly reuse process knowledge is more suitable for process reuse than black-box ones.

The idea behind process patterns is to capture proven processes for recurrent development problems. As for software product patterns, the interests of reduced development time and improved process quality make process pattern approach attractive to both research and industry communities. However, up to now this approach has not been applied at its full force because of the immaturity of research on this subject. Most of existing works have just concentrated on process pattern identification [1,5,13,19,25] little attention has been focused on process pattern formalization [8,11,20] and reuse methodology [20,21] .

Therefore, we have been investigating various issues involving process pattern concept. The ultimate goal of our work is to propose a methodology for exploiting process patterns in process modeling. Hence, we address the following concerns:

- What is exactly a process pattern and what kind of process knowledge it can capture?
- How should process patterns and processes based on them be represented?
- How should process model be developed by reusing process patterns?

This paper presents our approach in answering the above questions. In section 2 we clarify the concept of process pattern. Section 3 presents a meta-model for defining and representing process patterns. In section 4 we introduce a method for building process models based on process patterns. An example illustrating our approach is given in section 5. Section 6 discusses some significant related works. Our contributions and future works are presented in the conclusion.

## 2. Process Pattern Concept

When studying process patterns, we realize that this notion has been used with terminological and conceptual confusion. There exists related terms (e.g. "process pattern", "business process pattern" and "workflow pattern) that bear both synonymy[*] and overloading[†] phenomena. Even the meaning of the term "process pattern" is not clear. In most of cases [1,5,8,11,21], a process pattern is defined as a pattern describing a process to be executed to accomplish a given goal. However,

---

[*] The same concept is designated by different terms.
[†] The same term is used to designate different concepts.

some authors [19,25] consider any guideline that helps modeling processes to be a process pattern.

Another observation is that there exists a large variety of process patterns according to their intents (i.e. the using purpose of knowledge captured), abstraction levels (i.e. the details of the solution) and granularities (i.e. the part of process described by a process pattern). Nevertheless, it still lacks a definition that can cover this diversity of process patterns.

The inadequate and confusing definitions make difficult to understand what exactly a process pattern is, for what purposes it is best suited, how it should be identified, formalized and applied (c.f.[23] for a more detailed discussion on these issues). In order to clarify this concept, we proposed the following definition and taxonomy for process patterns.

## 2.1. *Process Pattern Definition*

In our opinion, process patterns are patterns for modeling processes. A process pattern then captures a (fragment of) process model representing a solution that can be applied in a given context to resolve a recurrent process modeling problem. Such problems can vary from describing development tasks to suggesting efficient process structures, organizations or execution.

This definition covers the concept of "process pattern" as well as "business process pattern" and "workflow pattern".

## 2.2. *Process Pattern Taxonomy*

In [24] we introduced a process patterns taxonomy based on the intent, the abstraction level, and the granularity of captured processes. Due to the space constraint, we just present here the classification based on abstraction levels. The abstraction level of a pattern is determined by the detail level of its captured process model. We propose three abstraction levels for process patterns as follows.

An *AbstractProcessPattern* captures a recurrent structure for modeling or organizing processes. The process model captured in such a pattern can contain tasks without any semantic actions. Thus, abstract patterns are generic and can be applied (by specializing) for any process. Workflow patterns [25] that provide different structures describing the control flow between activities are examples of abstract process patterns.

A *GeneralProcessPattern* captures a process model describing how to realize a general development task. More precisely, tasks of the captured process model have semantic actions on general products. A general pattern thus can be specialized further to be applied on different products. For example, the pattern *Review-an-artifact* can be applied for reviewing a code or a design document.

A *ConcreteProcessPattern* captures a process model describing how to realize a concrete development task on specific products (e.g. *Review-a-JavaCode* is a concrete pattern). The captured process model of a concrete pattern therefore is executable.

Distinguishing process patterns at different abstraction levels, indeed, helps to promote process reuse and clarify the way of defining, customizing and applying process patterns systematically.

### 3. A Process Meta-Model Integrating Process Pattern Concept

In this section, we present a meta-model defining software process concepts and particularly the concept of process pattern.

To deal with the variety of process patterns, our meta-model provides a general definition. The aspects of process pattern concept as well as the relationships among patterns are defined to facilitate patterns organization.

To allow representing processes based on process patterns, we define rigorous process concepts and relations between process patterns and process models. Especially, we introduce multi-abstraction levels into process representation to reflect our taxonomy on process patterns and to promote patterns reuse. The relations between process models at different abstraction levels are defined to clarify the way of defining process models and their capturing process patterns. Moreover, to facilitate supporting tools development in the future, the semantics of our meta-model is expressed in natural language and reinforced by OCL expressions[‡].

Finally, to attaint the standardization requirement, our meta-model is strongly inspired by the software process meta-model SPEM 1.1[15] and developed as an UML profile[§].

### 3.1. *ProcessModel*

*ProcessModel* concept is used to describe (part of) a process. It is composed of process tasks (*Task*), the required products (*Product*) and the participating roles (*Role*) of these tasks (Figure 1).

---

[‡] Due to the space constraint, we cannot present here the OCL rules.

[§] Initially we aimed at integrating the process pattern concept into SPEM1.1. But it is progressing towards a next version [17]. So, we based our meta-model on UML. In the future, just the part describing processes will be adjusted to conform to the stable version of SPEM.

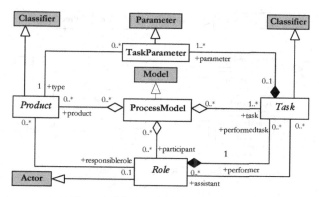

Figure 1. Meta-model for *ProcessModel*.

A *Task* is a unit of controlled work (i.e. scheduled) realized by a *Role* to create or modify *Products*. Each task has a *DevelopmentObjective* (e.g. Analyze Requirement, Verify Code, etc.) and is described by a *ProcessModel*. Necessary products for the execution of a task are described explicitly as its parameters (*TaskParameter*). A *SimpleTask* is composed of non-controlled activities (*Steps*) while a *ComplexTask* is decomposed into sub-tasks. Figure 2 shows the detailed description of a task.

We argue that the precise meaning of a task does not depend only on the action that it realizes but also on the products that it manipulates. For example, details concerning the realization of a *Review* task depend on the reviewed product: reviewing a code is different from reviewing a diagram. Therefore, we distinguish firstly the abstraction levels of products to determine the abstraction levels of tasks, which in turn are used to define the abstraction level of process model.

We describe tasks at three abstraction levels. An *AbstractTask* does not have any associated semantic action; it is just a "place-holder" for a real task. A *GeneralTask* creates or modifies one or several *general products* (i.e. product specified with a kind that can be specialized further for more specific goals). A general task thus has an associated semantic action but is not ready to be executed because the meaning of its actions depends on incompletely specified products. A *ConcreteTask* creates or modifies one or several *concrete products* (i.e. specific product that belongs to a product kind and is represented by a concrete formalism). It can be decomposed into elementary actions (*Step*) having precise semantics and is described completely in terms of used resources (*Resource*). A concrete task is therefore ready to be executed.

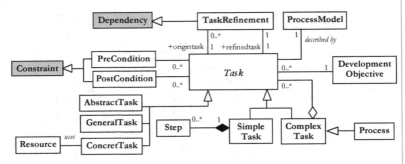

Figure 2. Meta-model for *Task*.

We also highlight the dependencies *TaskRefinement* between tasks at different abstraction levels. This relation allows refining a task to obtain more specific tasks by specifying more details on its semantic action and its manipulated products.

### 3.2. *ProcessPattern*

A *Process Pattern* captures a *Process Model* that can be reused to resolve a recurrent process development *Problem* in a given *Context* (**Error! Reference source not found.**). A *Problem* expresses the intention of a pattern and can be associated to a development task through the relation *«is applied for»*. A *Process Model* represents the solution of a process pattern. A *Context* characterizes conditions in which a process pattern can be applied (*Initiation*), results that must be achieved after applying the pattern (*Resulting*) and situation recommended of reuse (*Reuse Situation*).

We distinguish three types of process patterns according to abstraction level of their captured process model. An *AbstractProcessPattern* captures

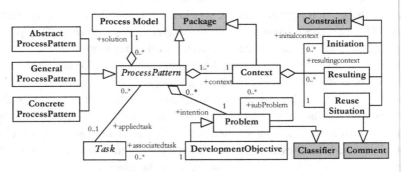

Figure 3. Meta-model for *ProcessPattern*.

a recurrent generic structure for modeling or organizing processes. A *GeneralProcessPattern* captures a process model that can be applied to realize a general task and a *ConcreteProcessPattern* captures a process model that can be applied to realize a concrete task.

Our meta-model describes important relations between process patterns. A *Sequence* relationship links two patterns if the predecessor produces all products required by the successor. A *(composite)* pattern *"uses"* another one if the latter can be applied for one (or more) task in the solution of the composite pattern. A pattern is *"refined"* from another if its associated task is refined from the associated task of the super pattern. Two patterns are *"alternative"* if they solve the same problem with different solutions.

## 4. A Pattern - Based Approach for Building Software Process Models

Constructing software processes is a complex and expensive work. Moreover, process models constructed in ad-hoc and intuitive ways are hard to be controlled and reused. The need of methods for conducting this task is therefore well recognized. From the engineering point-of-view, process constructing and managing itself is a process, called meta-process [15]. Defining rigorously this meta-process provides an explicit, systematic way for creating processes and facilitates automated support for process-engineering.

Hence, we propose a meta-process for modeling processes by reusing process patterns. This meta-process allows building and tailoring statically process models[**]. Figure 4 shows the main phases of our meta-process.

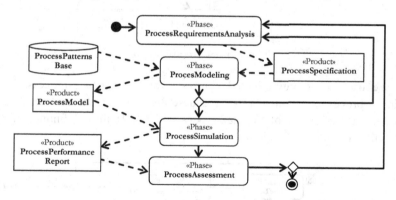

Figure 4. Meta-process Global Life Cycle.

---

[**] Discussion on process managing and evolving during its enactment is out of scope of this paper.

222

The specification of the process to be constructed is obtained during the *ProcessRequirementAnalysis* phase. Then, based on this specification, the *ProcessModeling* phase will create a process model. An approved model can be passed to the *ProcessSimulation* phase to be instantiated and simulated (or really executed) in a process environment. During this phase, remarks on process performance are registered and then fed to the *ProcessAssessment* phase to be analyzed. Analysis results can be used as feedback for improving process model.

For each phase, we identify the necessary meta-tasks and describe them as the general process patterns guiding how to construct process models. Our meta-process is thus represented as a pattern-based process. This representation makes it flexible and easy to be customized further for a specific process-engineering environment.

Figure 5 shows the workflow of the *ProcessModeling* phase. A model can be defined for a new process or can be improved from an existing one. Due to the space limit, just the meta-task *DefineProcessModel* will be described in details.

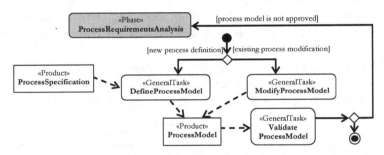

Figure 5. Phase *ProcessModeling*.

We use the activity-oriented approach for constructing process, i.e. to define a process we will identify and describe its tasks. In our meta-model, process is a special case of complex task (c.f. Figure 2), thus, defining a process is defining a root task (Figure 6).

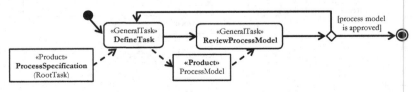

Figure 6. Meta-task *DefineProcessModel*.

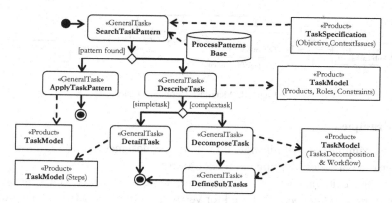

Figure 7. Meta-task *DefineTask*.

Now in Figure 7 we describe the meta-task DefineTask used to elaborate the model of a task. A TaskModel is composed of task description (products, participants, and constraints), task structure (sub-tasks or steps) and task workflow (execution orders of its sub-tasks or steps).

Our approach is characterized by reusing process patterns as building blocks for creating process models. Therefore, when defining a task, we firstly try to search (in a *Process Patterns Base*) a pattern that satisfies the task specification (*SearchTaskPattern*). If many patterns match the task objective, the most suitable pattern must be selected. The selecting criteria depend on many factors such as output products, team size, tools, etc. If there is no appropriate pattern at the same abstraction level of task, we can choose a more abstract pattern matching the task objective and context.

Once an acceptable pattern is chosen, the task model will be created from the captured process model of the pattern (*ApplyTaskPattern*). The application of a process pattern can be realized in two ways. The first one is to duplicate then tailor the captured process model to conform exactly to task specification. Another way is to make a reference link between the described task and the selected pattern. This solution is normally used when a totally suitable pattern is found or when process designer wants to refine the task model later.

If there is no acceptable pattern found, the task model will be built from scratch. The meta-tasks *DescribeTask* defines task description. Then, for a simple task, its steps and the workflow of these steps are defined by the meta-task *DetailTask*. For a complex task, we need to decompose it into sub-tasks (*DecomposeTask*) and then execute the meta-task *DefineSubTasks* to create the models for these sub-tasks. Figure 8 shows the meta-task *DefineSubTasks* with recursive calls for *DefineTask*.

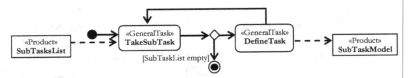

Figure 8.  Meta-task DefineSubTasks

## 5.  Example

In this example we will illustrate how a process designer defined a new process to verify Java codes by using our meta-process.

Suppose in the process patterns base there was a pattern capturing the *Fagan Inspection Process* [5] used for verifying software products. This process can be applied on different types of products (e.g. requirements, design, code, etc.) therefore we represent it with the general pattern *FaganInspectionPattern*[††] (Figure 9).

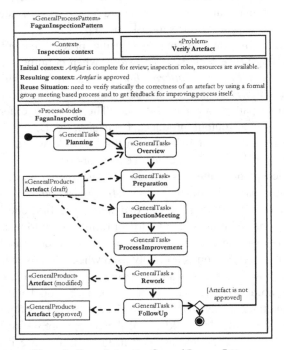

Figure 9.  *FaganInspection* General Process Pattern.

---

[††] For the sake of simplicity, here we just represent the principal elements of this process.

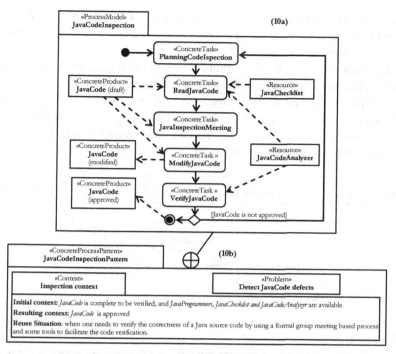

Figure 10. *JavaCodeInspection* Concrete Process Pattern.

After the *ProcessRequirementAnalysis* phase, the process designer obtained the process objective (i.e. objective of the root task) *"Verify Java Code"* and the organization constraint on the process to be constructed *"must be formal group meeting-based process"*. We describe in the following how he executed the meta-task *DefineTask* to elaborate the model of this root task (*Process Model*) and show the modified process model in Figure 10a.

He began with the meta-task *SearchTaskPattern* and got the *FaganInspectionPattern* as the most suitable for describing the task. This pattern just partially matches the process specification because it has the same objective and satisfies the constraints, but it is represented at a higher abstraction level for verifying general products. Therefore, the process designer needed to modify the pattern on applying it. To do so, he made a copy of the captured process model, then refined the general tasks by concrete tasks (e.g. the general task *Preparation* is specialized into the concrete task *ReadJavaCode*), and replaced general products by concrete products (e.g. the general product *Artifact* was replaced by the concrete product *JavaCode*). He also modified the process model by choosing just the pertinent tasks to be refined (e.g. the task *Overview* and *ProcessImprovement* in the original process model were omitted.

The process designer can capture this process model in a new concrete process pattern named *JavaCodeInspection* (Figure 10b). From now on, this concrete pattern can be applied directly in any process to model a task which verifies Java codes. For example, in Figure 11 the designer made a link between the *JavaCodeInspectionPattern* and the task *ReviewJavaCode* to reuse exactly the process model captured in this pattern.

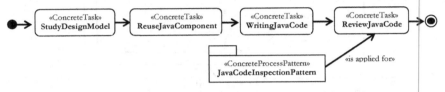

Figure 11. Process Pattern Reuse in Process Modeling.

## 6. Related Works

As introduced at the beginning of our paper, the research on process patterns is still modest.

Gnatz et al. proposed a process framework [8] that introduced the notion of process pattern as a modular way to document development knowledge. This work is noticeable for its explicit modeling of relationships between work products, modeling concepts, and notations which allows describing and integrating generic processes with specific development processes having concrete modeling concepts and notations. However, the process pattern structure as well as interrelationships of process patterns is not defined explicitly in the proposed framework.

Hagen et al. developed the language PROPEL [11] to describe explicitly process patterns and their relationships. The meta-model of PROPEL encloses the description of problems, contexts and solution of process patterns. Particularly, it defines explicitly the relationships between process patterns and thus helps organizing process patterns catalogues. But it lacks a rigorous semantics for the defined concepts in this meta-model.

Another significant works on process pattern formalizing is PROMENADE - a process modeling language developed by Ribo et al. [21]. The special features of PROMENADE is introducing a set of precedence relationships to enhance the expressiveness of language; defining the process pattern concept as a parameterized process template to provide a more generic process description; and proposing a set of high-operators for manipulating process models. Standardization is achieved by the mapping of PROMENADE features into a slightly extended UML.

There is an interesting related work of Rolland et al. [20] in the field of method engineering. This team developing a meta-model to capture *"way of working"* – a very close concept to process pattern, although the used terminology is different.

However, each of these meta-models proposes its proper conceptual model and notations to describe processes and process patterns. This variety of process pattern description makes difficult to align and to integrate process patterns from different sources. Besides, being academic works, these meta-models on a one hand do not profit from process modeling standards and tools actually used in industry, on another hand cannot strongly promote the application of process patterns. Another limitation of the above meta-models is that they do not explicitly deal with the diversity of process patterns abstraction levels. Indeed supporting the representation of process patterns at different abstraction levels can help promoting process patterns reuse and clarifying the way of defining, customizing and applying process patterns.

In the first draft submission for SPEM 2.0 [18], the process pattern concept is proposed as a *Capability Pattern* which describes reusable clusters of activities in common process areas. However, the internal structure of this concept and relationships between patterns are not defined. Moreover, in contrast to our approach, SPEM does not pay attention to the different abstraction levels of patterns. Our work thus still will be useful on integrating and adapting to SPEM 2.0 when it is stabilized.

With regard to process-building methods, there exists some industrial standards [4,12] suggesting a set of process-engineering activities. Nevertheless, these standards did not define explicitly a meta-process for guiding process designers. There are also noticeable academic works on meta-process such as the PRISM [13] model; the Process Cookbook [10] and the Meta-Process Framework [15]. All of these meta-processes however are coarse grained described and do not deal with the process reuse issue.

## 7. Conclusion

We have presented in this paper our work to exploit the process pattern concept for process models reuse.

We propose a process meta-model integrating the process pattern concept. Our approach aims at integrating process pattern to a widely accepted process meta-model, i.e. SPEM [15] of OMG. Especially, our meta-model covers a large variety of process patterns and allows representing process models and process patterns at different abstraction levels.

We also define explicitly a meta-process describing a systematic way to build process models by reusing process patterns. Our approach emphasizes process patterns reuse by abstraction mechanism. By applying the process patterns abstraction relations defined in our meta-model, we can derive general patterns from abstract patterns and refine general patterns into concrete patterns (or in a contrary direction, extract more abstract patterns from specific ones).

We are now implementing this meta-model as a UML profile by using the *Objecteering ProfileBuilder*. After this implementation, we can integrate the new profile into the *Objecteering UMLModeler* to model processes based on process patterns. In the future, in order to support process patterns application, we aim at implementing a tool to execute our meta-process to guide process designers in developing and reusing process patterns.

## References

1. S. W. Ambler, *Process Patterns: Building Large-Scale Systems Using Object Technology*, SIGS Books/Cambridge University Press,1998
2. B. Coulette, X. Crégut, T. B. T. Dong and D. T. Tran,    "A Metaprocess to define and reuse process components", IDPT02, Pasadena, USA,2002
3. A. Conte, M. Fredj, JP. Giraudin, D. Rieu, "P-Sigma : un formalisme pour une représentation unifiée de patrons", Inforsid, Genève, 2001
4. Capability Maturity Model® Integration (CMMISM), Version 1.1, CMU/SEI, 2002
5. M.E. Fagan, "Advances in Software Inspections", IEEE Transactions on Software Engineering, Vol. SE-12, No. 7, Page 744-751, 1986
6. Jean-Claude Derniame, Badara Ali Kaba, David Graham Wastell (Eds.): Software Process: Principles, Methodology Technology. LNCS1500, Springer-Verlag, 1999
7. D. Firesmith, B. Henderson-Sellers, The OPEN Process Framework. An Introduction. Addison-Wesley, 2001
8. M. Gnatz, F. Marschall, G. Popp, A. Rausch, W. Schwerin, "The Living Software Development Process" Journal Software Quality Professional, 5(3), 2003
9. C. Godart, P. Molli, O. Perrin, "Modeling and enacting processes: Some difficulties". In Proceeding of the International Process Techgnology Workshop, 1999

10. P. Kawalek and DG Wastell , "The Development of a Process Modelling Method", 2nd BCS Information Systems Methodology Conference, Edinburgh, 1994

11. M. Hagen, V. Gruhn, "Process Patterns - a Means to Describe Processes in a Flexible Way", ProSim04, Edinburgh, United Kingdom, 2004

12. ISO/IEC 12207, Information Technology Software LifeCycle Processes, 1995

13. N. H. Madhavji, et al., "Prism = Methodology + Process-oriented Environment," ICSE 1990, Nice, 1990

14. T.W, Malone, K. Crowston, G.A. Herman, (editors): Organizing Business Knowledge: The MIT Process Handbook,Cambridge, MA: MIT Press, 2003

15. M.N. Nguyen and R.Conradi. "Classification of Meta-processes and their Models". ICSE'94, Washington, 1994

16. OMG, Software Process Engineering Metamodel v1.1 Specification, OMG Document formal/05-01-06, 2005

17. OMG, SPEM 2.0 RFP. http://www.omg.org/cgi-bin/doc?ad/2004-11-4

18. OMG, SPEM 2.0 Draft Adopted Specification, http://www.omg.org/docs/ad/05-06-05.pdf

19. M. Penker, H.E. Eriksson, Business Modeling With UML: Business Patterns at Work, John Wiley & Sons, 2000

20. J. Ralyté, C. Rolland, "An Assembly Process Model for Method Engineering". CAISE'01, Switzerland, 2001

21. J. M. Ribó, X. Franch, "Supporting Process Reuse in PROMENADE", Research Report LSI-02-14-R, Politechnical University of Catalonia, 2002

22. C. Rolland, C. Souveyet, M. Moreno, "An Approach for Defining Ways-of-Working", Information Systems Journal,1995

23. H.N. Tran , B. Coulette, T.B.T. Dong, "Towards a better understanding of Process Patterns", SERP 2005, 2005

24. H.N. Tran, B. Coulette, T.B.T. Dong, "A classification of Process Patterns", SWDC-REK 2005, Island, 2005

25. W.M.P.Van der Aalst, A.H.M. ter Hofstede, B. Kiepuszewski, and A.P. Barros, "Workflow Patterns" Distributed and Parallel Databases, 14(3), pp 5-51,2003

# CHAPTER 17

# ONTOLOGY - MAS FOR MODELLING AND ROBUST CONTROLLING ENTERPRISES

DANG THANH-TUNG[(1),*,†], BEN FLOOD[(2)], CÁTHÁL WILSON[(1)],
CON SHEAHAN[(1)] AND DANG BAO-LAM[(3)].

[(1)] *Enterprise Research Centre, University of Limerick, Limerick, Ireland*
[(2)] *Center for Telecomunications and Value-Chain-Driven Research, UL, Limerick, Ireland*
[(3)] *Department of Design of Machines and Robots, Hanoi University of Technology, 1 Dai Co Viet str. Hanoi, Vietnam*

Currently, SMEs have to face a number of difficulties to survive in the market. Planning plays a crucial role for the management and control. SMEs operate on a dynamically changing environment, with many unexpected events. SMEs are differently organized; involve many complicated types of relationships between their basic entities. These factors lead to choose the MAS methodology as tool for modeling and controlling the running of SMEs. Each agent works on behalf of one business entity, and they are cooperative together to build the enterprise model. An ontology is chosen as a tool for representation of knowledge about enterprises. An ontology is used to form and store information describing an enterprise. It is a part of MAS and used for sharing information between agents. With the purpose to increase the robustness of enterprises, advance planning and scheduling (APS) is proposed as a methodology for solving planning problems. The research project is carried out in cooperation with an enterprise specialising in ceramic production for industrial applications.

## 1. Introduction to MAS and Ontology in SMEs

Unlike larger enterprises, which can operate in a stand-alone fashion, SMEs are dependent on inter-enterprise communications and short-term strategies. SMEs are under increasing pressure in the current European economic climate due to the introduction of low-priced products and services, provided by emerging markets in the accession countries. Modern SMEs must compete with these low prices, while maintaining the quality standards required by their customer bases.

---

* This work has been funded by the Irish Research Council for Science, Engineering and Technology (IRCSET).
† Email contact to a corresponding author: dang.tung@ul.ie

In order to plan and control the running of an SME, it is invaluable to have methods of composing knowledge about all aspects of production into a coherent framework, which can be used for informed reasoning in short term planning.

A fundamental aspect of SMEs is that they are typically holonic systems. A holonic system is a system that self-organises and evolves over time in order to optimise the efficiency of its own processes. The Multi-Agent System (MAS) methodology is suitable to modelling complex evolving systems, because of its modularity, ability to work autonomously, and its capacity to enable cooperation between entities in a system.

Another reason to choose MAS to model and manage an enterprise is its robustness. To distribute responsibility among personnel in an SME and to improve the ability of the enterprise to recover from failures the enterprise management strategy must be made up of separate components. Control actions, therefore, need to be delegated to separate sub-organisations to process. Because of various kinds of actions involved within the enterprise, e.g., capacity scheduling or material planning, different components will be required to model the enterprise. By using MAS, each agent will act on behalf of one of these components. It enables the control and management of the enterprise at various levels. Thus, the effects of failure can be eliminated at local levels using MAS before they impact other entities.

An ontology is a database with a special structure, allowing more types of relationships than the more traditional object databases. The basic elements of an ontology are variables with a subject element, an object element, and a property element. The structure of an ontology can be represented by a graph, in which the subject and object of each element are represented by nodes, and the property is represented by an edge.

Ontologies support reasoning tools on the graph structure that they are defined with. One key advantage of an ontology is that it can handle cycles in the graph describing the relationships between elements. An ontology presents an unique communication language for business entities. It eliminates incompatibilities of information exchanged between business entities. An ontology is machine readable and interpreted. This paper studies the advantages of using ontological databases, as part of an MAS, for reasoning and planning in an SME environment.

The rest of this paper is organised as follows. Section 2 describes the two main components of an ontology, the organisational ontology and the activity ontology. Section 3 describes the main components of a MAS for controlling SMEs. Section 4 discusses advance planning and scheduling. Section 5 describes an example scenario for one agent in a MAS. Section 6 discusses an ontology-based MAS model, using a case-study enterprise specialising in ceramic production for industrial applications.

## 2. Components of Ontology

### 2.1. *Organisational Ontology*

The organisational part of the ontology is used to compile information describing the organisation of the enterprise. The organisational ontology should be constructed as parsimoniously as possible to reduce its size, consequently accelerating its performance.

The SME structure published by [1] is used here as a basis for an organisational ontology. All relevant items are included in the ontology, namely: *Customers, Suppliers, Departments, Resources, Employees, Orders, Cost_Categories, Organisational_Contacts, Plan_Definitions, Precedent_Constraints, Unit_of_Measurements, Resource_Used, Resource_Required, Resource_Assigned, Stock_Level_Quantities, Due_Date, Duration_Distribution, Estimated_Duration.* Some of these items may not be relevant to specific enterprises, and can be left as empty field when filling the ontology with real data. The convention will be followed that italic font is used to denote variables.

Figure 1 shows the basic structure of the organisational ontology. Each element, or property, of the ontology has a number of sub-elements, and each element itself can be a sub-element. For example, *Order* has sub-elements *Product, Quantity, Due_Date*, etc. and *Resource* is a part of *Plan_Definition, Resource_used, Resource_Required, Precedent_Constraint*, and others. By using this hierarchical approach, the ontology is able to describe all relationships between elements, just as in object databases. The advantage, however, in using ontology is that the ontology is able to represent extra kinds of relationships.

An example of one of the types of relationships that an ontology can represent is the *inverse* relationship. In the inverse relationship, *Precedent_Constraint* has a *successor* and *predecessor* property that are inverse one to other. Other types of relationships that can be represented in ontologies, but not in object databases, are *multiple* relationships (e.g. *Resource_Required* could be two alternative resources), and *conditional* relationships (e.g. *Resource_Assigned* could be resource A, if condition X is satisfied, otherwise it will be resource B).

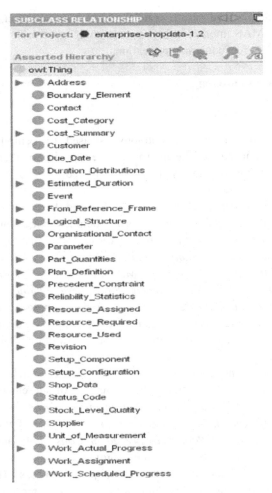

Figure 1. common data definitions in the ontology.

## 2.2. *Activity Ontology*

In the activity part of the ontology detailed information on each activity-execution, resource, and element in the enterprise is defined. The key requirement in the activity ontology is the specification of the workflow and the parameters associated with its execution.

For each activity the variables *Resource_Used*, *Duration_Distribution* or *Estimated_Duration,* and *Precedent_Constraints* must be defined. Each resource can operate in different state, so it is also necessary to define a *Resource_State* and *Probability_Distribution* for each resource to predict the state changes of the resource. The calculation of execution cost requires information about each partial cost that is recorded in the variables *Labour_Cost, Material_Cost* and *Resource_Used_Cost*.

It can be very difficult to specify partial costs for every activity. In many practical cases, the execution cost is estimated by merging all input costs (materials, components, and labour cost) and the cost of using resources. In our ontology, however, activity execution cost considers only the cost of using resources. Partial costs and other investments are defined under a special cost category, and they together create the variables *Cost_Summary* of the *Plan_Definition*. *Schedule_Cost* is a combination of *Cost_Summary* and *Execution_Cost*.

The inventory is another feature of the activity ontology. Important variables in inventory are *Part_Inventory* and *Material_Inventory*, giving information about the remaining components and materials in storage.

All of the these features are sub-elements in the *Jobs* property. The *Jobs* property is a collection of individual production workflows that can be processed by the SME to fulfil the *Order*. Each *Job* has a *Job_Definition*, which specifies what needs to be done in terms of *Due_Date, Part_Quantity, Resource_Required, Schedule_Cost,* and *Precedent_Constraint,* and a *Job_Status,* which specifies planning progresses and actual progresses toward accomplishing the job.

## 3. MAS

This section discusses MAS in the context of modelling and controlling an enterprise. Section 3.1 introduces the different types of agents and Section 3.2 discusses the organisation of the agents.

### 3.1. *Agents*

The enterprise is divided into disjoint blocks and then each of them is controlled by an agent. Interactions among agents are modelled by the relationships between these blocks. The customer agent (CA) represents each customer and acts on his behalf. Multiple CAs can be used in the system, each with different behaviour.

Marketing-Seller Agents (MSA) contacts CAs directly to receive orders. They are capable of negotiating about price, due date, delivery conditions, etc.

Master Production Agents (MA) make master plans for the whole company, based on predicted values. Capacity Planning Agents (CPA) calculate the best plan for all resources to produce the desired quantity of products such that the requirements of the CAs are satisfied. Material Planning Agents (MPA) create, on the basis of plans generated by CPAs, plans for material release and purchase. Supplier Agents (SA) act on behalf of suppliers, contacting MPAs to get requirements.

### 3.2. *Organisation of Agents*

All of the agents work cooperatively excect for CAs. CAs are autonomous and are responsible for invoking the system. MSAs register relevant data from orders placed by CAs forward them to MAs. MAs update the current plan with new data, and calculate predictions about future demands, distributing the updated plan to CPAs. CPAs are given a particularly difficult task, since a CPA must find a suitable plan to satisfy the requirements of all orders, including both newly arrived orders and older, unshipped orders.

If the prediction of the MA is close to the real order, the CPA does not have to re-schedule the production plan too much. If the prediction is poor, however, the rescheduled production plan will typically take longer, or worse, a suitable production plan might not be achieved. If a suitable production plan is not achieved the CPA asks the MA and the MSA to set new priorities for orders, so that the highest priority orders will be shipped.

Based on the plan generated and updated by the CPA, the MPA plans when to buy materials from the suppliers, and when to release materials to production. SA tells MPA whether or not they are able to satisfy the demand. Negative reply from SA (e.g. SA is not able to deliver material on time) will force MPA and CPA to update their plans with this information. Chain reactions can further extend and MA and MSA might be required to revise the order priorities again, or to negotiate with CAs to change some items of orders. Interactions among agents are depicted in Figure 2.

Figure 2 shows the feedback between agents that allows failures to be responded to immediately. Because many orders can arrive during one day, every day the production plan must be updated many times. However, by decomposing the enterprise into many entities, the production plan does not have to be changed as whole, but partially and by different agents. This decomposition allows for easy modification of the production plan and faster reactions to certain kinds of events (e.g. material delay, machine maintenance, etc.).

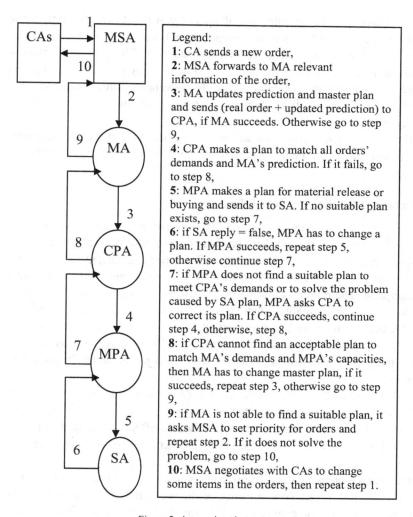

Figure 2. interactions between agents.

Practical experience has proved that the time for solving scheduling problems is much less (usually it has minute time units) than the time needed for its realisation (it might have hour or even day time unit). This means that finding a feasible planning solution (or even the optimal one, by running during the night time) is possible. However, realisation of the achieved schedule might not guarantee, for example, the deadline requirements or demanded amounts. In order to keep all the commitments of an order without any changes (since customers are not very willing to change orders), the production plan has to consider some reservation to cover such a situation. The prediction plays a significant role in fulfilling this goal. In order to optimise the reservations required to satisfy the customers' needs, advance-planning methods are required. The next section discusses advance planning and scheduling techniques (APS).

The next section will discuss advanced planning and scheduling technique used in our model to help the enterprise to maximally satisfy customer's demands.

## 4. Advance Planning and Scheduling

Enterprise resource planning (ERP) is one of the main techniques used to manage enterprises. Although there has been high uptake of ERP in industry, a lot of disadvantages of the ERP method have been identified [3], [4]. One weakness is that ERP is not able to flexibly react to changes occurring within the enterprise. The reason is that ERP is based on too many ideal assumptions that do not occur in reality, such as the assumption that every material is available before each schedule is implemented.

Another disadvantage is that ERP is a system for a single business entity. A system integrated from different entities requires a more flexible approach of planning.

The Advanced Planning and Scheduling (APS) technique aims to make the enterprise more robust to unexpected events. APS achieves this by generating plans with reservations designed to minimise the effects of possible failures. The disadvantage of this is that reservations increase the total expense. The goals in APS are as follows.

- Produce a suitable amount of products including some reservations so that all order's delivery commitments would be satisfied, to guarantee the maximal income the enterprise could earn if all orders will shipped in time and with the ordered amounts.
- Minimise the total expense to the enterprise for keeping to the production plan (to find such a schedule to produce the desired amount with as low cost as possible),
- Minimise the input cost, that is, to buy as much materials as needed and to employ production resources as effectively as possible, before considering exploiting external production resources or distributing sub-orders to external vendors.

The main difficulty in APS is in prediction. Many different factors have influences on the sale, for example, the unit price, product design, the sale season, the ways that customers could get to the products (buy online, via a network of braches, retails, …) and much more. Some of these factors (e.g. product design, online vs. offline selling) require a long-time analysis to identify their real effects on the final sale. Others are able to effect the sale immediately, for example, an offer of discount unit price or reduction of delivery time.

## 5. The Planning Problem for A Master Production Agent

This section is devoted to maximising expected profit over the potential plans that the MA can construct. The following notation is used.

- $\{C_i\}_{i=1,..,n}$ - a set of $n$ customers,
- $\{P_1,..,P_k\}$ - $k$ different kinds of products,
- $\{R_1,..,R_m\}$ - $m$ different production resources (machines, for example),
- $\{o_{i,t}\}_{i=1,..,n,\ t=1,2....}$ and $\{o^*_{i,t}\}_{i=1,..,n,\ t=1,2....} \in N^k$ – are real order and expected order for customer $C_i$ on day t ($t \in N$), respectively,
- $\forall i,j:\ o_{i,t} = \{x^1_{i,t},\ x^2_{i,t},...,x^k_{i,t}\} \in N^k$ - a $k$-element vector representing amounts of $k$ kinds of product that customer $C_i$ wants to buy,
- $\{arr_{i,t}\}_{i=1,..,n,\ t=1,2....} \in [0h,24h]$ - a time when the enterprise receives order $order_{i,t}$
- $\{d_{i,t}\}_{i=1,..,n,\ t=1,2....}$ - a deadline or delivery time for order $o_{i,t}$,
- $\{rate_{i,t}\}_{i=1,..,n,\ t=1,2....} \in N$ – rating of each order (*default values are equal to all orders*)
- $\{p_i\}_{i=1,..,k}$ - unit prices for every kind of product,
- $\{b_t\}_{t=1,2....} \in R^r$ - a state of reservation at day $t$ ($t \in N$), i.e. how many materials, subcomponents and final products are temporarily kept in the enterprise. $r$ is a dimension of vector $b_t$ and it covers all kinds of materials, components and final products that could be involved in the enterprise. $b_t$ is a function of time during day,
- $schedule_t$ – master production schedule for the enterprise at day $t$ ($t \in N$),
- $\{delay_t\}_{t=1,2....} \in R$ - a delay of material delivery at day $t$ ($t \in N$),
- $\{pro_i\}_{i=1,..,m} \in [0,1]^m$ - a probability that resource $\{R_i\}_{i=1,..,m}$ could break down,
- $\{repair_i\}_{i=1,..,m} \in R^m$ - time needed to repair resource $\{R_i\}_{i=1,..,m}$ after breaking down,

Sale is assumed to be dependent on the unit price and a time variable. Hence, expected order $o^*_{i,t}$ at day $t$ will be a function $f_1$,

$$o^*_{i,t} = f_1(p_1,...,p_k, t). \tag{1}$$

Identification of the dependency $f_1(.)$ is a typical *multivariate time series* issue. The main models for solving this problem are the *vector autoregression model (VAR)*, and *Auto-Regressive Integrated Moving Average (ARIMA)* [2]. Calculating a robust solution requires an estimate of the interval in which future sale will lie. Therefore the MA does not use the explicitly predicted value from (1), for planning, but uses the estimated sale with reservation.

$$o^{**}_{i,t} = o^*_{i,t} + \Delta_I \tag{2}$$

where $\Delta_i \in N^k$ denotes a vector of maximal excess that customer $C_i$ could actually bid more than the expected value, i.e. $(o_{i,t} - o^*_{i,t})$. Real data from customer's orders serve as a feedback for evaluation the accuracy of the estimated model used in (1) and values $\{\Delta_i\}$.

The $schedule_t$ is updated when any order $o_{i,t}$ arrives, by real data included in $o_{i,t}$, and a new prediction $(o^{**}_{i,t+1})$ for the next day. The MA can also consider a predicted sale more than one day in advance and make a plan for a longer time period. At any time $ti$ $(ti \in [0h, 24h])$ on day $t$, we can write:

$$schedule_t(ti+1) \leftarrow \{schedule_t(ti), o_{i,t}\mid_{arr=ti}, b_t(ti), o^{**}_{i,t+1}, \delta\} \tag{3}$$
$$\text{subject to: } \{d_{i,t}\}_{i=1,...,n},$$

where $\delta$ represents all considered errors. These errors can be delay of material delivery, production resource failure, or breakdown, that is:

$$\delta = \{\{delay_t\} \cup \{pro_i\}_{i=1,...,m} \cup \{repair_i\}_{i=1,...,m}\}.$$

The state of the reservation at time $ti$, $b_t(ti)$, is required for calculation of a master production schedule. Regular inventory-taking can be impractical because it consumes valuable time and labour. However, a feedback from the CPA provides the MA this actual data $\{b_t(ti)\}$, because the CPA is able to follow the progress of the production plan, until any unexpected event occurs.

The main objective for the MA is to find production plan to produce as many products as considered optimal, i.e. $\{o^{**}_{i,t}\}$, to cover the demands with sufficient flexibility to accommodate unexpected situations, without incurring excessive costs. Simultaneously the objective function for the MA must minimise reservation and overproduction,

$$\underset{o_{i,t}^{**}}{\arg\min} \quad \{\int_{t}^{\infty} \int_{ti=0}^{24} b_t(ti)\} \tag{4}$$

And $\underset{o_{i,t}^{**}}{\arg\min} \quad \{\sum_{t=0}^{\infty} \sum_{i=1}^{n} (o_{i,t}^{**} - o_{i,t})\}$

$$\tag{5}$$

Subject to: $\forall i,t: o_{i,t}^{**} \geq o_{i,t}.$

Condition (5) guarantee that all orders will be satisfied.

If the CPA is not able to construct a feasible plan to match the MA's master production plan, the MA asks the MSA to reset the order priorities and then the MA reschedules the master plan. A new variable considered in rescheduling is $\{rate_{j,t}\}_{j=1,..,n}$ that are specified by the MSA.

$$schedule_t(ti + 1) \leftarrow$$
$$\{schedule_t(ti), o_{i,t} |_{arr=ti}, b_t(ti), o_{i,t+1}^{**}, \delta, \{rate_{j,t}\}_{j=1,..,n}\} \tag{6}$$

The main aim of exploiting APS is to try to avoid situations where the MSA must reorder priorities.

Master production plans generated by the MA do not include details of jobs, resources and individual activity execution. The master plan provides the CPA general information about how many pieces of each product and how many components have to be produced, on each day, for a short period. Creating a detailed production plan to achieve this goal is a task for the CPA and the MPA. The scheduling problem described in Equation (3), subject to the objective function (4) and condition (5), could be solved by using some known techniques, e.g. constraint satisfaction problem (CSP), integer programming, or heuristic search (since $o_{i,t}^{**} \in N^k$, so it is easy to discrete the solution space). Other applicable techniques are: *Case-Based reasoning (CBR)*, practical for fast decision making, because it is easy to compare the similarity between orders coming from all customers on different days; *adaptive planning with a modifiable reference model* – i.e. the MA has a default plan for some basic scenarios, and some default policies to react to expectable events. The only task that the MA has to do is to adjust the appropriate parameters of these default models based on the real measure (real orders).

The APS corresponding to the CPA, the MPA and the SA are very similar to the APS for the MA, but include more features since it will have to consider the details of each activity, resource and other elements involved in the enterprise. Future research will focus on finding a robust solution for capacity and material planning.

## 6. Case Study and Discussion

The first phase of this project has been to implement a model to demonstrate the performance of MAS to control an enterprise. The ontology is built by using the Protégé software tool [7]. The agents are programmed in JADE [9]. Jena [8] is a tool for integration OWL ontology [5], [6] and Jade agents.

The case study enterprise is a company that produces special ceramics for industrial applications. Customers are various commercial companies, manufacturers and retail branches. The plant is an MTO (Make-To-Order) operation and therefore the production plan has to be updated regularly at any time when a new order arrives. The studied company organization consists of many departments and production entities. Each of departments and production entities is modeled by using one of agents defined in Section 3.1. The production capacity of the company is limited. As a result, the company's management has to deal carefully with the overcapacity problem in advance, in order to satisfy as many customers as the company can. Customer's satisfaction is one of the most important factors that the company must achieve. If orders are not shipped on time and with the ordered quantity, the company will lose customers. In order to avoid such a situation, the company's management decided to overproduce about 20% of ordered values. By other words, at any time the company is able to satisfy 20% of all incoming orders.

However, overproduction costs a small company like the studied one too expensively, if real orders do not achieve the expected values. The purpose of the experiment is to exploit MAS to simulate and to predict values of short-future demands. Based on the predicted values, a robust production plan is calculated. Values of real orders serve as a feedback for evaluation of production plans. Experimental results will be used for comparison between a production plan calculated by the company management based on their own experience and a production plan made by MAS on the basis of simulated and predicted values. The experiment was carried out as follows:

Orders generated by CAs are based on the one year sale information. The purpose is to show how the enterprise is able to satisfy these demands. MA tries to predict values of future orders on the basis of values of the current orders. A sale for one day in advance is predicted by using a method presented in Section 5. Only the product unit price and a time variable are considered for calculation, as assumed in Section 5. Incoming orders generated by CAs and predicted orders generated by MA create an input for the rest of agents calculation. All agents try together to find best plans to realize these orders. Similar to MA, the rest of agents CPA, MPA and SA are also able to make a prediction of future demands and try to make such a plan which is able to overcome an overloading situation. Yet, the main focus in the experiment is on the MA's performance. Evaluation of other agents' performance will be presented in our future research.

Orders are generated between random time intervals. Ordered quantities are taken from the one year sale information. Agents restart their calculation, update the prediction model and share information about their capacity when a new order is generated.

Two key indicators used for evaluation of the master production plan made by MA are the total cost of overproduction during a certain interval of time and the percentage of orders satisfied on time. Calculating the total cost of reservation requires detailed knowledge of the CPA's production plan and it is not possible so far due to incomplete knowledge about the production processes involved in the case study.

Experimental results showed that the company can save up to 5% of the total expense if APS is applied for making a plan. Production plans based on the management own experience generate almost higher overproduction than plans made by MAS. Explanation can be that customer's demand is a sophisticated function of multiple variables and factors. Exploiting experience, although that is valuable experience provided by experts, is not adequate for solving a complicated task like prediction of demand. The total saving is multiplied if MPA and SA get a precise model of how future material's demands will be developing. In the studied case, materials are ordered in advance for long-term production. However, optimal solutions made by MPA and SA suggested to reduce ordered quantities of materials and a frequency of supplying. From practitioner's point of view, such a solution might not be suitable for the studied company due to a large distance between single suppliers and the enterprise.

However, experimental simulation also showed some weaknesses of APS, or disadvantages of the making-products-in-advance method, in general. Because the studied company is a Make-To-Order type, products made in advance will be waste if they do not meet customer's specifications. The company produces a wide range of products with different types, sizes and colors. As a result, the value of the total reservation creates a significant part in the framework of the company's expense. To avoid spending a considerable amount of capital only on keeping reservation, the studied company tries to apply a different strategy. For example, to fulfil order's requirements the company is willing to distribute subcontracts to other partners or to buy components from external vendors, if better economic effects will be achieved.

The objective is on-time-in-full, to achieve all tasks to be finished on time, instead of keeping expensive reservations.

Simulation by using MAS also allows the company to identify its limits, bottlenecks and robustness. Repeating experiments with different data, different controlling strategies pointed out the best strategy for controlling the enterprise in different situations.

The question about ontology creation and filling up the ontology by real data is not completely resolved. Building a complete ontology with real data requires detailed knowledge about the production processes. There is also needed to improve a method for representation so that practitioners could actively participate in the experiment, for example, feeding new data, updating existing data, editing or browsing information stored in the ontology.

## 7. Conclusion

The application of MAS to the robust modelling and controlling of an SME has been discussed. Ontology is proposed as a tool for the modelling and representation of the enterprise. It is also used as a communication language for agents.

The ontology methodology is chosen for its ability to describe a broad range of relationships. The MAS methodology is chosen for its flexibility and in modelling and controlling enterprises. The APS methodology is chosen for its robustness under uncertainty and with unexpected events.

The current phase of this research project demonstrates the performance of MAS. Future work as part of this project will involve resolving a robust scheduling problem for a CPA and the design of an ontology to be used for data mining to discover and predict new knowledge about the behaviour of customers (CAs).

## Acknowledgments

This work has been funded by the Irish Research Council for Science, Engineering and Technology (IRCSET).

## References

1. C. McLean, T. Lee, G. Shao, F. Riddick and S. Leong, "*Shop Data Model and Interface Specification*", http://www.sisostds.org/doclib/doclib.cfm?SISO_RID_1005843
2. Granville T. Wilson, M. Reale and Alex S. Morton, "*Developments in multivariate time series modeling*", Estadística, 53, pp. 353-395, 2001.

3. Young Hae Lee, Chan Seok Jeong, Chiung Moon, "*Advanced planning and scheduling with outsourcing in manufacturing supply chain*", Computers and Industrial Engineering archive, Volume 43 , Issue 1 -2, pp. 351 – 374, July 2002.

4. R. Haugen, W. E. McCarthy and A. Andersen Alumni. "*REA, a semantic model for Internet supply chain collaboration*". In the ACM Conference on Object-Oriented Programming, Systems, Languages, and Applications, *workshop Enterprise Application Integration*, Minneapolis, Minnesota USA, October 15-19, 2000.

5. http://www.w3.org/TR/owl-ref/

6. http://www.w3.org/TR/owl-guide/

7. http://protege.stanford.edu/

8. http://jena.sourceforge.net/

9. http://jade.tilab.com/

10. Frankovic B. and Budinska I., "*Advantages and disadvantages of heuristic and multi-agent approaches to the solution of scheduling problem*". In Proc. of the IFAC Conference on Control System Design, Bratislava, Elsevier, ISBN 0-08-043546 7, pp. 372-378, 2000.

11. Frankovic B. and Budinska I.: "*Single and multi machine scheduling of jobs in production sytem*". In Tzafestas, S.G. (Ed.): Advances in manufacturing, Decision, Control, and Information Technology, Springer Verlag, London, pp. 25-36, 1999.

# CHAPTER 18

# OWL-BASED DATA CUBE FOR CONCEPTUAL MULTIDIMENSIONAL DATA MODEL

DANH LE PHUOC

*Learning Resource Centre of Hue University, 20 Le Loi, Hue, Vietnam,*
*lpdanh@lrc-hueuni.edu.vn*

THANH BINH NGUYEN

*Information Technology Centre of Hue University, 2 Le Loi, Hue, Vietnam,*
*ntbinh@hueuni.edu.vn*

To encourage a new novel generation of OLAP(On Line Analytical Processing) tools that enable users interact with multidimensional data in creative, visual, flexible and interactive way, there should be a sophisticated multidimensional data model (MDM) to represent natural hierarchical relationships of data related user domain of discourse. Furthermore, the ontology integration in this data model will leverages the interoperatibility among heterogeneous data warehouses. In this context, this paper introduces ontology-based MDM as an extended data model of MetaCube[1]. This model covers most of basic concepts, relationships of former model and provides a framework and mechanism to employ ontology in modeling process. Furthermore, this paper also gives an implementable OWL representation (a markup language of many of-the-shelf ontologies on the Web) for specification and data of this model.

## 1. Introduction

The Web technology development along with the business requirement evolution of expert system bring out both opportunities and challenges to build a web-based information delivery OLAP tool operating in creative, flexible, visual and interactive way [2,3]. This positive trend promises a new novel generation of OLAP tools that not only can answer fixed and ad-hoc queries but also enable users to interact and manipulate data warehouse data as semantic data with respect to knowledge domain of individual users [3]. Thus, it encourages the researches aiming to build MDMs that help not only individual users but also computers sharing common understandings.

Moreover, ontologies will play an important role in supporting information exchange processes by revealing implicit assumptions [2]. An ontology provides a shared and common understanding of a domain that can be communicated between people and across application systems. Hence, combination of OLAP data warehouse, ontologies and knowledge management will become an active research area in the near future for providing distributed strategic decision support system for the web [2].

In this context, the MetaCube concept is proposed in [1] as a multidimensional metadata framework for cross-domain data warehousing systems. In the further development, the MetaCube concept is extended to MetaCube-X by using XML [4]. Afterwards, to solve the issues concerning semantic heterogeneities of MetaCube-X, Metacube-XTM is proposed by utilizing Topic Maps to build the bridge between the domains of knowledge representation and information management [5]. However, these models do not provide a framework and mechanism to make use available ontologies that have been building more and more out there.

The goal of this paper is improving MetaCube[1] implementable data model by integrating OWL ontologies for utilizing taxonomies of off-the-shelf ontologies . This new data model covers most of basic concepts and relationships in former model. Moreover, this model handles natural hierarchical relationships with respect to relationships among concepts related human domains of discourse. Besides, this paper also gives a demonstration of integrating ontology for modeling dimensions in OWL (Web Ontology Language) syntax.

The remainder of this paper is organized as follows. In section 2, we discuss about related works. Then in section 3, we map basic concepts of object oriented (OO) Conceptual Multidimensional Models (CMMs). Next, we model a multidimensional database (MDB) by ontologies in section 4. The paper concludes with section 5, which presents our current and future works.

## 2.  Related Works

Our work is related to researches within area of multidimensional modeling, metadata for MDBs, ontology-based modeling and ontology integration. There are many modeling approaches for multidimensional data for OLAP referred in [1]. Proper metadata is absolutely necessary for using, building, and administering data warehouse[3], thus there are series of approaches using metadata in MDBs in [2,4,5,6]. In addition, this paper also refers to some works in ontology integration in and ontology-based modeling in [7,8,9,10].

In [1] a conceptual MDM is introduced to facilitate a precise rigorous conceptualization for OLAP that provides a foundation to handle natural hierarchical relationships among data elements within dimensions with many levels of complexity in their structures. This MDM organizes data in the form of metacubes. Instead of containing a set of data cells, each metacube is associated with a set of groups each of which contains a subset of the data cell set. Furthermore, metacube operators (e.g. jumping, rollingUp and drillingDown) are defined in a very elegant manner. In addition, to provide access and search among multiple, heterogeneous, distributed and autonomous data warehouse, Metacube-X [4] is proposed as an XML instance of the MetaCube. MetaCube-X provides a "neutral" syntax for interoperability among different web warehousing systems. The described framework defines a global MetaCube-X stored in the server site and local MetaCube-X(s), each of which is stored in a local Web warehouse. The emerging issues to be handled in the global MetaCube-X are mainly issues concerning semantic heterogeneities of the local MetaCube-X, while the capability for accessing data at any level of complexity should still be provided by local Web data warehouse. Consequently, The MetaCube-XTM [5] is introduces to use topic maps to deal with these issues.

As a consequence, in this paper, we extend the MetaCube CMM to an ontological model by using OWL to represent OLAP components in explicited and formalized concepts and relationships. Hence, this approach will provide a framework of ontology employing to resolve semantic issues in MetaCube-X and MetaCube-XTM. The main contributions are: (a) the introduction of the mapping from MetaCube components model to ontological terms and concepts; (b) the providing a framework and mechanism of inheriting available ontologies in modeling process; (c) the demonstration in OWL syntax for implementation; (d) the building the bridge between user domains of knowledge representation and OLAP data.

## 3. Mapping Conceptual Multidimensional Data Model Concepts to OWL Abstract Syntax

A suitable conceptual MDM with sound concepts is the necessary and essential foundation for modeling a MDB. As mater of fact, scientific community struggles hard to deliver a common basic for such MDMs [1]([11,12,13,14,15,16,17]). However, the target of this paper is providing a implementation oriented OWL representation of MDB schema and data, we will focus in OO CMM such as [1,18,19], especially MetaCube[1]. This section will select some typical and basic components in such models to map to OWL abstract syntax for later section's task as below table 1.

Table 1. Mapping from OO conceptual MDM to OWL abstract syntax.

| Data cube Concepts | OWL abstract syntax |
|---|---|
| Dimension Hierarchical Domain | Ontology(…) |
| Dimension Member | Individual(…) |
| Dimension Level | Class(…) |
| Measure | Class(Measure) |
| Data cube | Class(OWLCube) |
| Group/View | Class(OWLGroup) |
| Relation $\prec_E$ | ObjectProperty(rollingUp) |
| Relation $\prec_L$ | SubClassOf(…) |
| … | … |

To cover most of essential concepts and components in above mapping, we just build a simple abstract class diagram for expressing typical MDB scheme as below figure 1.

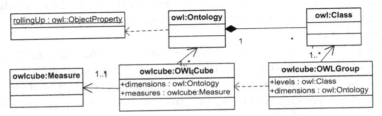

Figure 1. Abstract class diagram for Data Cube model on OWL representation.

## 4. Modeling Multidimensional Database with OWL

This section will model MDB using OWL-based schema. Such schema is constituted of dimension schemata, cube schema and aggregate view schemata. In this approach, all of these schemata are represented under OWL for following reasons. The first reason is that OWL was designed for modeling taxonomies underlying user's domain of discourse. In that sense, each dimension can be modeled as an ontology (dimension schema and dimension member data can be encoded in implementable OWL markup format), thus it is appropriate for representing natural hierarchical relationship among dimension members as above mentioned mapping table 1. Furthermore, these dimension ontologies can inherit predefined concepts of available ontologies. These lead to the consequent reason. The next reason is the easiness and simpleness for representing cube and group schemata with OWL as above abstract class diagram. The last reason is that this OWL-based schema can be encoded in markup language as user friendly and computer understandable metadata.

The input of this modeling process is a schema of a certain multidimensional database with natural taxonomies of dimensions. And the output is an OWL-based schema that covers OLAP components such as dimensions, dimensions levels, operators, cube and views/aggregates. This process will follow below steps:

*a. Modeling dimensions*: we suppose dimension members as instances of ontologies (each ontology for a dimension), and we group these instances into levels. After that, we define classes corresponding to these levels. Then we add "rollingUp" attribute to all these classes. Next, we find suitable off-the-shelf ontologies to inherit and include their predefined concepts and relationships. Afterwards, we build a class diagram to represent dimension schema by importing predefined artifacts from selected available ontologies. Consequently, we create OWL instances of such diagrams.

*b. Define measure schemata*: we define Measure class as template for measures' schemata and then define measures' schemata as instances of Measure class.

*c. Building cube and views/aggregates*: we represent following realizations to OWL syntax to create cube and view/aggregate schema.

*c.1.Cube realization*: we build Cube schema by realizing OWLCube class in abstract diagram (figure 1) and then represent Cube schema as instances corresponding to certain dimensions and measures from step *a* and *b*.

*c.2.View/aggregate realization*: we build views/aggregates' schemata by using OWLGroup class in figure 1 as template; each view/aggregate schema is represented by an instance of OWLGroup classes.

We will depict this process by a specific example of multidimensional database PizzaSale (data about Pizza sales) with three dimensions PizzaProduct, TimeCategory and StoreGeography along with three measures on these dimensions TotalSale, Price and UnitCount in figure 2. The input of this process

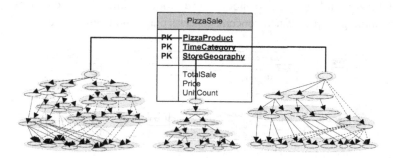

Figure 2.

is taxonomies of dimensions PizzaProduct, TimeCategory and StoreGeography (in figure 2) and measure specifications (in section 4.2). From this input, we follow above steps to realize those class diagrams and their instances to OWL-based syntax and aggregate all outputs to OWL schema of expected MDB as below.

## 4.1. *Dimensions*

### 4.1.1. *PizzaProduct dimension*

PizzaProduct dimension members together with relationships among them are given as a taxonomy in figure 3 below:

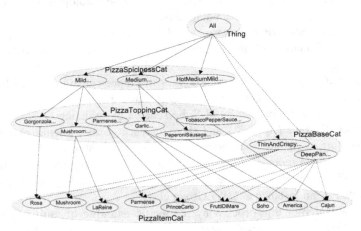

Figure 3. Taxonomy of PizzapProduct dimension.

We group dimension members as above figure 3, then we import off-the-shelf Pizza ontology [22] to model PizzaProduct dimension accompany with Pizza ontology's predefined concepts as class diagram in below figure 4.

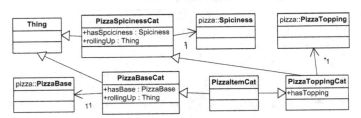

Figure 4. Class diagram of ontology representing for PizzaProduct dimension.

From this diagram we express PizzaProduct dimension specification on OWL syntax in examples 1 and 2 below.

*Example 1*: Class specification on OWL of PizzaBaseCat, PizzaItemCat

```
<?xml version="1.0"?>
<rdf:RDF
  xmlns:pizza="http://www.co-
ode.org/ontologies/pizza/2005/10/18/classified
/pizza.owl#"
  xmlns:rdf="http://www.w3.org/1999/02/22-
rdf-syntax-ns#"
  xmlns:xsd="http://www.w3.org/2001/
XMLSchema#"
  xmlns:rdfs="http://www.w3.org/2000/01/rdf-
schema#"

xmlns:owl="http://www.w3.org/2002/07/owl#"
....
<owl:Class rdf:ID="PizzaBaseCat"/>
<owl:FunctionalProperty rdf:ID="hasBase">
  <rdfs:domain
rdf:resource="#PizzaBaseCat"/>
  <rdfs:range
rdf:resource="&pizza;PizzaBase"/>
    ...
</owl:FunctionalProperty>
```

```
<owl:FunctionalProperty rdf:ID="rollingUp">
  <rdf:type
rdf:resource="&owl;ObjectProperty"/>
  <rdfs:domain>
    <owl:Class>
      <owl:unionOf
        rdf:parseType="Collection">
        <owl:Class
        rdf:about="#PizzaBaseCat"/>
        <owl:Class
        rdf:about="#PizzaSpicinessCat"/>
...
</owl:FunctionalProperty>
<owl:Class rdf:ID="PizzaItemCat">
  <rdfs:subClassOf
rdf:resource="#PizzaBaseCat"/>
  <rdfs:subClassOf
rdf:resource="#PizzaToppingCat"/>
</owl:Class>
....
```

*Example 2*: OWL syntax of dimension members All $\prec_E$ MildSpicinessCat $\prec_E$ MushroomToppingCat $\prec_I$ LaReine and MushroomToppingCat $\prec_E$ Mushroom

```
<PizzaBaseCat rdf:ID="DeepPanBaseCat">
    <rollingUp rdf:resource="#All"/>
      <hasBase
        rdf:resource="#DeepPanBase"/>
...
<PizzaSpicinessCat
rdf:ID="MildSpicinessCat">
  <hasSpiciness
    rdf:resource="#MildSpiciness"/>
  <rollingUp rdf:resource="All"/>
...
<PizzaToppingCat
  rdf:ID="MushroomToppingCat">
  <hasTopping
    rdf:resource="#MushroomTopping"/>
  <hasSpiciness
rdf:resource="#MildSpiciness"/>
  <rollingUp rdf:resource="MildSpicinessCat"/>
...
<PizzaItemCat rdf:ID="Mushroom">
  <hasTopping
  rdf:resource="#MushroomTopping">
  <hasTopping
```

```
  rdf:resource="#TomatoTopping">
  <hasTopping
  rdf:resource="#MozzarellaTopping">
  <hasBase rdf:resource="#ThinAndCrispy...
  <hasSpiciness
  rdf:resource="#MildSpiciness"/>
  <rollingUp
  rdf:resource="MushroomToppingCat"/>
...
<PizzaItemCat rdf:ID="LaReine">
  <hasSpiciness
  rdf:resource="#MildSpiciness"/>
  <hasTopping
  rdf:resource="#TomatoTopping"/>
  <hasBase
  rdf:resource="#ThinAndCrispyBase"/>
  <hasTopping rdf:resource="#"OliveTopping"
  <hasTopping
  rdf:resource="#MushroomTopping"/>
  <hasTopping rdf:resource="# HamTopping "/>
  <hasTopping
  rdf:resource="#MozzarellaTopping"/>
...
```

### 4.1.2. *TimeCategory dimension*

Similarly, we model hierarchical domain of TimeCategory dimension in figure 5 by using OWL-Time ontology [21] as class digram in figure 6. Then we show OWL version of TimeCategory ontology representing for this dimension.

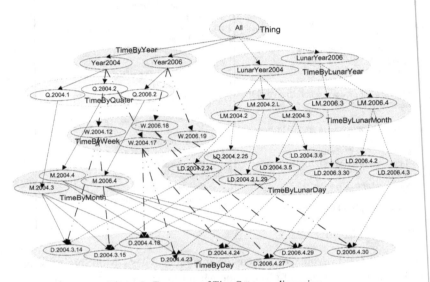

Figure 5. Taxonomy of TimeCategory dimension.

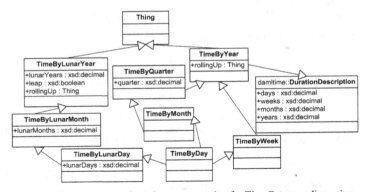

Figure 6. Class diagram of ontology representing for TimeCategory dimension.

*Example 3*: Class specification on OWL of TimebyYear, TimeByQuarter. TimeByLunarYear

```
<owl:Class rdf:about="#TimebyYear">
<rdfs:subClassOf
rdf:resource="&owl;Thing"/>
<rdfs:subClassOf
rdf:resource="&dalmtime;DurationDescription"
...
<owl:Class rdf:ID="TimeByQuarter">
<rdfs:subClassOf
  rdf:resource="#TimebyYear"/>
...
<owl:Class rdf:about="#TimeByLunarYear">
<rdfs:subClassOf
rdf:resource="&owl;Thing"/>
<rdfs:subClassOf>
<owl:Restriction>
<owl:onProperty>
```

```
<owl:DatatypeProperty
rdf:ID="lunarYears"/>
<rdfs:range rdf:resource="&xsd;decimal"/>
...
<owl:Class rdf:ID="TimeByWeek">
<rdfs:subClassOf rdf:resource=" #TimebyYear
..
...
<owl:Class rdf:ID="TimeByDay">
<rdfs:subClassOf
  rdf:resource="#TimeByMonth"/>
<rdfs:subClassOf
  rdf:resource="#TimeByWeek"/>
<rdfs:subClassOf
  rdf:resource="#TimeByLunarDay"/>
....
```

*Example 4*: OWL syntax of dimension members Year2004 $\prec_E$ Q.2004.2 $\prec_E$ M.2004.4

```
<TimebyYear rdf:ID="Year2004">
<dalmtime:years
rdf:datatype="&xsd;decimal">
  2004 </dalmtime:years>
<rollingUp rdf:resource="#All"/>
...
<TimeByLunarYear rdf:ID="LunarYear2004">
<lunarYears   rdf:datatype="&xsd;decimal">
  2004 </lunarYears>
<leap
rdf:datatype="&xsd;boolean">true</leap>
<rollingUp rdf:resource="#All"/>
...
<TimeByDay rdf:ID="D.2004.4.18">
<lunarMonths  rdf:datatype="&xsd;decimal">
  2 </lunarMonths>
<dalmtime:years
rdf:datatype="&xsd;decimal">
  2004 </dalmtime:years>
```

```
<dalmtime:days
rdf:datatype="&xsd;decimal">
  18 </dalmtime:days>
<lunarDay  rdf:datatype="&xsd;decimal">
29</lunarDay>
<leap
rdf:datatype="&xsd;boolean">true</leap>
<dalmtime:months
  rdf:datatype="&xsd;decimal">4
</dalmtime:months>
<quarters rdf:datatype="&xsd;decimal">
  2</quarters>
<dalmtime:weeks
  rdf:datatype="&xsd;decimal">17
</dalmtime:weeks>
<lunarYears  rdf:datatype="&xsd;decimal">
  2004</lunarYears>
<rollingUp rdf:resource="#LD.2004.2.L.29"/>
<rollingUp rdf:resource="#W.2004.17"/>
<rollingUp rdf:resource="#M.2004.4"/>
...
```

### 4.1.3. *StoreGeography dimension*

By the same process, we have class diagram of   ontology (refer to ISO 3166 Code List of countries [21]) for StoreGeography dimension in figure 8 from input taxonomy in figure 7 and OWL version of this ontology in example 3 and 4.

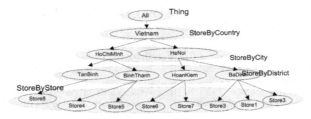

Figure 7. Taxonomy of StoreGeography dimension.

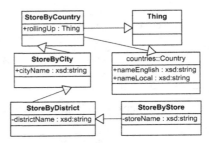

Figure 8. Class diagram of ontology representing for StoreGeography dimension.

*Example 3*: Class specification on OWL of StoreByCountry

```
<owl:Class rdf:ID="StoreByCountry">
 <rdfs:subClassOf
rdf:resource="&owl;Thing"/>
 <rdfs:subClassOf
  rdf:resource="&contries;Country"/>
</owl:Class>
<owl:ObjectProperty rdf:ID="rollingUp">
 <rdf:type
```

```
rdf:resource="&owl;TransitiveProperty"/>
 <rdfs:domain
  rdf:resource="#StoreByCountry"/>
 </owl:ObjectProperty>
<owl:Class rdf:ID="StoreByCity">
 <rdfs:subClassOf
  rdf:resource="StoreByCountry"/>
...
```

*Example 4*: OWL syntax of dimension members All $\prec_E$ Vietnam $\prec_E$ HaNoi

```
<StoreByCountry rdf:ID="Vietnam">
 <rollingUp rdf:resource="#All"/>
 <countries:nameEnglish
 rdf:datatype="&xsd;string">Vietnam
 </countries:nameEnglish>
 <countries:nameLocal
  rdf:datatype="&xsd;string">Viet Nam
</countries:nameLocal>
```

```
</StoreByCountry>
<StoreByCity rdf:ID="HaNoi">
 <rollingUp rdf:resource="#Vietnam"/>
 <cityName rdf:datatype="&xsd;string">
  Ha Noi</cityName>
 </StoreByCity>
....
```

## 4.2. *Measures*

On three above dimensions, we define three distributive measures $M_1=$ TotalSale, $M_2=$Price and $M_3=$UnitCount with functions $F_1(i,j,k)$, $F_2(i,j,k)$ and $F_3(i,j,k)$ defined by :

    ○   if $(i,j,k) \in Dom_1 \times Dom_2 \times Dom_3$ ($Dom_1$, $Dom_2$ and $Dom_3$ are sets of all instances of classes PizzaItemCat, TimeByDay and StoreByStore respectively) above functions are defined by tuples in below table 2.

Table 2

| Dom$_1$ | Dom$_2$ | Dom$_2$ | $F_1$ | $F_2$ | $F_3$ |
|---------|---------|---------|-------|-------|-------|
| ... | | | | | |
| Mushroom | D.2004.4.23 | Store1 | 500 | 50 | 10 |
| LaReine | D.2004.4.23 | Store1 | 600 | 30 | 20 |
| ... | | | | | |

    ○   Else $F_1(i,j,k)$, $F_2(i,j,k)$ and $F_3(i,j,k)$ are defined by there respectively *distributing functions* Sum, Min and Max as following :

*Example 5*

- $F_1(i,j,k)=\text{Sum}(F_1(i_r,j,k)) \ \forall \ i_r : \exists \ F_1(i_r,j,k)$ and $i \prec_E i_r$, else $F_1(i,j,k)=undefined$; and similarly with j,k
- $F_2(i,j,k)=\text{Min}(F_1(i_r,j,k)) \ \forall \ i_r : \exists \ F_2(i_r,j,k)$ and $i \prec_E i_r$, else $F_1(i,j,k)=undefined$; and similarly with j,k
- $F_3(i,j,k)=\text{Max}(F_1(i_r,j,k)) \ \forall \ i_r : \exists \ F_3(i_r,j,k)$ and $i \prec_E i_r$, else $F_3(i,j,k)=undefined$; and similarly with j,k

*Example 6*

- $S_1^1=$Mushroom, $S_1^2=$LaRiene, $S_1=$MushroomToppingCat, $S_2=$D.2004.4.23, $S_3=$Store1 and $S_1 \prec_E S_1^1$, $S_1 \prec_E S_1^2$
- $F_1(S_1,S_2,S_3)=\text{Sum}(F_1(S_1^1,S_2,S_3),F_2(S_1^2,S_2,S_3))=1100$
- $F_2(S_1,S_2,S_3)=\text{Sum}(F_1(S_1^1,S_2,S_3),F_2(S_1^2,S_2,S_3))=30$
- $F_3(S_1,S_2,S_3)=\text{Sum}(F_1(S_1^1,S_2,S_3),F_2(S_1^2,S_2,S_3))=20$

## 4.3. *Data Cube*

Data cube C constituted from 3 ontology-based dimensions $D_1=$PizzaProduct, $D_2=$TimeCategory, $D_3=$StoreGeography and 3 measures TotalSale, Price and UnitCount is defined by $Dom(C)=<Cells(C), \prec_C^*)[1]$, where:

- $Cell(S_1,S_2,S_3) = \langle S_1, S_2, S_3, F_1(S_1,S_2,S_3), F_2(S_1,S_2,S_3), F_3(S_1,S_2,S_3) \rangle$

- $Cells(C) = \{ Cell(S_1,S_2,S_3) : <S_1,S_2,S_3> \in \overset{3}{\underset{i=1}{\times}} Dom(D_i) |$

$F_i(S_1,S_2,S_3) \neq undefined, \forall i \in 1..3 \}$

*Example 4.3.1*: following example 5, we have

- $Cell(S_1^{1},S_2,S_3) = \{Mushroom, D.2004.4.23, Store1, 500,50,10\}$

- $Cell(S_1^{2},S_2,S_3) = \{LaRiene, D.2004.4.23, Store1, 600,30,20\}$

- $Cell(S_1,S_2,S_3) = \{MushroomToppingCat, D.2004.4.23, Store1,1110,30,20\}$

- $Cell(S_1,S_2,S_3) \prec_C^* Cell(S_1^{1},S_2,S_3), Cell(S_1,S_2,S_3) \prec_C^* Cell(S_1^{2},S_2,S_3)$

*Example 7*: to sum up all OWL representation examples of this paper, we give some instances of OWL representation of backbone MDB schema (base on abstract class diagram in figure 1) as below:

```
<owl:Class rdf:ID="Measure"/>
<owl:Class rdf:ID="OWLCube"/>
<owl:ObjectProperty rdf:ID="dimensions">
  <rdfs:domain rdf:resource="#OntoCube"/>
</owl:ObjectProperty>
<owl:ObjectProperty rdf:ID="measures">
  <rdfs:domain rdf:resource="#OWLCube"/>
  <rdfs:range rdf:resource="#Measure"/>
...
<OWLCube rdf:ID="cubeID">
  <dimensions rdf:resource="&pizzacat;"/>
  <dimensions rdf:resource="&timeacat;"/>
```

```
<dimensions rdf:resource="&storeacat;"/>
<measures rdf:resource="#TotalSale"/>
<measures rdf:resource="#Price"/>
<measures rdf:resource="#UnitCount"/>
...
<OWLGroup rdf:ID="groupID">
<dimensions rdf:resource="&pizzacat;"/>
<dimensions rdf:resource="&timeacat;"/>
<levels
  rdf:resource="&pizza;InterestingPizza"/>
...
```

## 5. Conclusion and Future Works

In this paper we have presented an implementable OWL representation for MDB schema that covers most of components in MetaCube[1] and some other typical OO CMM. Furthermore, the demonstration of modeling MDB gives a blue-print for a framework and mechanism for ontology-based modeling process.

In the context of future works, we are investigating two main tasks. In the first task, we concentrate in providing more expressive ontology-based representation of MDB schema for more sophisticated components. We also aim to build an infrastructure and framework for implementing this ontology-based MDB schema in the second task.

# References

1. Nguyen, T.B., Tjoa, A M., Wagner, R.R.: Conceptual Multidimensional Data Model Based on MetaCube. In Proc. of First Biennial International Conference on Advances in Informa-tion Systems (ADVIS'2000), Izmir, TURKEY, October 2000. Lecture Notes in Computer Science (LNCS), Springer, 2000.
2. Bruckner R. M, Ling T. W., Mangisengi O., Tjoa A M.. A Framework for a Multidimensional OLAP Model using Topic Maps. In Proceedings of the Second International Conference on WebInformation Systems Engineering (WISE 2001) Conference (Web Semantics Workshop), Vol.2, pp. 109-118, IEEE Computer Society Press.Kyoto, Japan, December 2001.
3. Ponniah P., *Data Warehousing Fundamentals: A Comprehensive Guide for IT Professionals.* John Wiley & Sons, Inc., 2001.
4. Nguyen T.B., Tjoa A M., Mangisengi O.. MetaCube-X: An XML Metadata Foundation for Interoperability Search among Web Warehouses. In Proceedings of the 3rd Intl. Workshop DMDW'2001, Interlaken, witzerland, June 4, 2001.
5. Nguyen T.B, Tjoa A M., Mangisengi O.. MetaCube XTM: A Multidimensional Metadata Approach for Semantic Web Warehousing Systems. DaWaK 2003: 76-88.
6. XCube. http://www.xcube-open.org.
7. Calvanese D., Giacomo G. D., and Lenzerini M. A framework for ontology integration. In Proceedings of the international semantic web working symposium, pages 303--316, Stanford, USA, 2001.
8. Pinto, H. S. and Martins, J. P. 2001. A methodology for ontology integration. In Proceedings of the 1st international Conference on Knowledge Capture (Victoria, British Columbia, Canada, October 22 - 23, 2001).
9. Calvanese, D., De Giacomo, G., Lenzerini, M.: Ontology of Integration and Integration of Ontologies. In Proceedings of the 2001 Description Logic Workshop (DL 2001).
10. Priebe, T. and Pernul, G. Ontology-based Integration of OLAP and Information Retrieval. Proc. of the DEXA 2003 Workshop on Web Semantics (WebS 2003), Prague, Czech Republic, September 2003.
11. Albrecht, J., Guenzel, H., Lehner, W.: Set-Derivability of Multidimensiona Aggregates. First International Conference on Data Warehousing and Knowledge Discovery.DaWaK'99, Florence, Italy, August 99.
12. Cabibbo, L., Torlone, R.: A Logical Approach to Multidimensional Databases. EDBT 1998.
13. Gyssens, M., Lakshmanan, L.V.S.: A foundation for multidimensional databases, Proc. VLDB'97.

14. Lehner, W.: Modeling Large Scale OLAP Scenarios. 6th International Conference on Extending Database Technology (EDBT'98), Valencia, Spain, 23-27, March 1998.
15. Li, C., Wang, X.S.: A Data Model for Supporting On-Line Analytical Processing. CIKM 1996.
16. Mangisengi, O., Tjoa, A M., Wagner, R.R.: Multidimensional Modelling Approaches for OLAP. Proceedings of the Ninth International Database Conference "Heterogeneous and Internet Databases" 1999, ISBN 962-937-046-8. Ed. J. Fong, Hong Kong, 1999.
17. Shoshani, A.: OLAP and Statistical Databases: Similarities and Differences. Tutorials of PODS 1997.
18. Nguyen T. B., A Min Tjoa, Wagner R. R.. An Object Oriented Multidimensional Data Model for OLAP. Proc. of the First International Conference on Web-Age Information Management (WAIM-00), Shanghai, China, June 2000.
19. A. Abello, J. Samos, and F. Saltor. Understanding analysis dimensions in a multidimensional objectoriented model. In Proceedings of DMDW'01, 2001.
20. OWL-Time. http://www.isi.edu/~pan/OWL-Time.html.
21. The ISO 3166 Code List of countries. http://www.bpiresearch.com/BPMO/2004/03/03/cdl/Countries
22. The ontology used in the Protege-OWL Tutorial. http://www.co-ode.org/ontologies/.